STAFFORDSHIRE
Unusual & Quirky

Andrew Beardmore

HALSGROVE

First published in Great Britain in 2016

British Library Cataloguing-in-Publication Data
A CIP record for this title is available from the British Library

ISBN 978 0 85704 295 8

HALSGROVE
Halsgrove House,
Ryelands Business Park,
Bagley Road, Wellington, Somerset TA21 9PZ
Tel: 01823 653777 Fax: 01823 216796
email: sales@halsgrove.com
website: www.halsgrove.com

Printed and bound in China by Everbest Printing Investment Ltd

Staffordshire – Unusual and Quirky

Welcome to *Staffordshire – Unusual and Quirky*. This is the fourth book in a new series that calls to mind that classic series of travel books called *The King's England*, written in the 1930s by Arthur Mee, since each volume in Mee's series was suffixed with *"There have been many books on <insert county>, but never one like this…"* Well the very same tag line could be applied to this book, as some of its elements are certainly unique. Having said that, the book still has plenty to offer in terms of conventional reference, but it delivers this in a lateral and humorous format never seen before.

Essentially, then, the book is comprised of two main sections which are called *Conventional Staffordshire* and *Quirky Staffordshire*. The *Conventional* section kicks off with some county maps along with key facts and figures relating to the county – such as county town, population, highest point, key industries and famous sons and daughters. The facts are then followed by a history of the Staffordshire *area* from the Stone Age to the 11th century – by which time Staffordshire, along with most of England's counties had been officially formed – after which the last one thousand years of county history are covered, bringing us up-to-date and into the 21st century. Nevertheless, in keeping with the title of the book, the *County History* also has a number of small, but appropriately historical "Quirk Alerts" interspersed, too; like an anecdote about Hobbits popping up in prehistoric times and how a certain Roaring Meg interceded between a divided family during the English Civil War.

The *Conventional* section then hands over to the *Quirky* section… and it is here that we really begin to earn the *"…but never one like this…"* tag line. For although the *Quirky* section delivers some "seen it before" place-name origins and historic trivia, it does so via a quirky poem known as a Shire-Ode! Told in rhyming verse, the Shire-Ode portrays imaginary inhabitants of Staffordshire but, as an extra twist, the poem contains dozens of place-names found within the historic county, each subtly woven into the tale – and it is these place-names upon which the *Quirky* section focuses. Firstly, the places have their location pin-pointed via two maps, one depicting the historic county of Staffordshire and the other the modern ceremonial county. A series of chapters then follow in (largely) alphabetical order for each place featured in the Shire-Ode – and it is here that the strangest and most interesting facts and features about each place are explored. As a result, you get a random almanac of places that would ordinarily appear together – along with place population, earliest recording, name derivation, famous sons and daughters, historic trivia, Quirk Alerts… and lots of accompanying photographs, too.

So, feel free to commence your obscure Staffordshire fact-digging; to read about some very famous people and their Staffordshire exploits, to read about ancient battles and, quite frankly, some ridiculous legends, too… but to hopefully have a little chuckle along the way. For example, find out which Staffordshire village's caves are thought to have inspired J.R.R. Tolkien's *The Hobbit*, and which Staffordshire town saw its brand-spanking new canal lock destroyed by the very cannon that was supposed to be heralding its grand opening! Or what about which Staffordshire village is home to an ancient annual dance involving one thousand year-old reindeer horns, which village has an annual parade behind a giant teapot and which village had an annual medieval custom involving a fire, a brass statue filled up with water, and a goose!

Alternatively, absorb some conventional facts from the Black Country – part of Staffordshire until 1st April 1974. Like which Black Country parish has the oldest church register in England, which Black Country area made the anchor and chains for the RMS *Titanic* and which Black Country town is immortalised on the cover of Led Zeppelin IV. Staffordshire is also famous for brewing. But do you know which Russian Empress was "immoderately fond" of Burton ale, which Walsall pub doesn't have a bar and which Staffordshire brewing company owns Britain's first ever trademark?

Historically, Staffordshire has been home to some shocking events, too, like the cataclysmic explosion at Fauld in November 1944 that was the largest non-nuclear explosion on British soil and obliterated farms, businesses and people in the immediate area, leaving a crater 100ft deep and 900ft wide. More light-heartedly, find out which Staffordshire constituency returned the oldest-ever MP (aged 93), which very famous British writer was named after a Staffordshire lake, and which 12th century Staffordshire monks were renowned for singing "disgraceful songs".

Finally, check out *The Trentham Triangle*, the quirky Shire-Ode that drives the idiosyncratic *Quirky Staffordshire* section and learn how Ladymoor's coven lies at the heart of a string of mysterious disappearances!

Anyway, that's the introduction completed. As you have probably gathered by now, this book is indeed "unusual and quirky"… so it's time to prime the quirkometer and pull up a pew at St Strangeways – oh, and did I mention Leek's noisy peace memorial, Britain's unluckiest church, the vicious Sleep Rouser of Trysull, the man who danced for a dozen days…

Contents

Introduction
Staffordshire Unusual and Quirky 3

Conventional Staffordshire
    Staffordshire Facts and Figures..6
    Staffordshire Maps..7
    Staffordshire County History 8
        Prehistory 8
        Romans, Anglo-Saxons and Vikings 10
        From the Conquest to the Dissolution..20
        From the Elizabethan Era to the Eve of the Industrial Revolution 32
        Staffordshire's Industrial Revolution..43
        From the Late Victorians to Present Day..52
        Some Quirky Staffordshire Stats...57

Quirk Alerts
    Hobbit Holes and Jealous Giants 9
    Ceadda, Headda and Bēda...17
    Dangerous Neighbours 21
    Squirrelled Away..23
    Canon Fodder...25
    The Origin of Theses..28
    Affronted from Stafford..29
    Give or Take 500 Years...30
    Take Breath, Pull Strong 32
    Jack of Hilton...32
    Roll Up 33
    Brereton vs. Brereton 37
    The Cost of War 38
    Half-Baked Duke 39
    The Village Methuselah and RHIP! 39
    The Sleep Rouser 40
    Royally Empressed 41
    By George!..41
    The Beautiful Shepherdess of Calwich 42
    Radcliffe's Stable 42
    The Man Who Danced for a Dozen Days 42
    Every Tic In The Book...43
    From Cromwell to Kaiser Bill 44
    Exceedingly Beautiful 46
    The Knotty – The Musical 47
    Not Amused 48
    The Black Country – Literally 48
    Chain Reaction 51
    Five Churches in Eighty-Three Years 52

Quintessentially Quirky – Abbots Bromley
    Abbots Bromley Quirk Alert: Getting Horny 60

Quirky Staffordshire
    Introducing the Shire-Ode 62
    Staffordshire Shire-Ode: The Trentham Triangle...62
    Staffordshire Location Maps for The Trentham Triangle......................................64
    Place-Name Table for The Trentham Triangle 64
    The Trentham Triangle – A Staffordshire Shire-Ode Almanac.............................65

Abbey Green 65
Ashley 66
Three's Up: Acton, Aston and Beech...68
Bentley 70
Three's Up: Booth, Boundary and Bromley Hall 71
Broughton...73
Burston..75
Three's Up: Cellarhead, Cotes and Coton...76
Coven 79
Three's Up: Crackley, Deadman's Green and Druids Heath 81
Dudley Port..83
Eve Hill 85
Farewell 86
Fauld 87
Three's Up: Field, Finney Green and Ford...89
Flash 91
Three's Up: Four Crosses, Hawthorns and Hayes..95
Foxt...96
Great Barr 98
Hales...100
Haunton..101
Three's Up: Hazles, High Heath and High Onn..102
Heaton..103
Hints 104
Hope (and Alstonefield)..105
Hopton..107
Three's Up: Hyde Lea, Jack Hayes and Kerry Hill...109
Keele 110
Knighton...112
Knutton...113
Three's Up: Ladymoor, Lea Heath and Little Onn 114
Leek 116
Littleworth..120
Three's Up: Loggerheads, Lynn and Olive Green..121
Maer 123
Meir 125
Three's Up: Roughley, Round Oak and Scot Hay..126
Onecote 129
Ranton 130
Rushall 132
Salt 134
Two's Up: Sideway and Stone Cross...135
Sheen 136
Standon...138
Stanley and Stanley Moor..139
Stoke..141
Stone..143
Stowe...146
Talke 148
Three's Up: The Straits, Woodmill and Yew Tree..150
Tixall..151
Trentham, Trentham Lake and Trentham Park...153
Wall..156
The Best of the Rest...158

Bibliography...160

Staffordshire Facts and Figures

County Status:	Ceremonial county and (smaller) non-metropolitan county (minus Stoke)
County Town:	Stafford
County Population:	1,098,300
County Population Rank:	15th out of 48; note, though, that the pre-1974 administrative county of Staffordshire was ranked 8th out of 39 counties
Cities:	Lichfield, Stoke-on-Trent, Wolverhampton (pre-1st April 1974; now West Midlands)
Largest City (current):	Stoke-on-Trent
Largest City Population:	249,008
Largest City Pop. Rank:	18th (English); 22nd (UK)
Largest City Status:	Unitary Authority
National Parks:	Peak District
Other Areas:	Cannock Chase (AONB), The National Forest
County Area:	1,047 miles^2 / 2,713 km^2
County Area Rank:	18th out of 48
Highest Point:	Cheeks Hill (1,706ft / 520m)
Longest River:	Trent (185 miles / 298 km)
Football Clubs:	Stoke City, West Bromwich Albion (Premier League); Burton Albion, Wolverhampton Wanderers (Championship); Port Vale, Walsall (League 1)
Rugby Union Clubs:	Longton RUFC, Lichfield (National 3 Midlands [3]); Burton RUFC, Leek RUFC, Stoke-on-Trent RUFC, Walsall (Midlands 1 West [6]), Handsworth, Stafford RUFC, Willenhall RUFC, Wolverhampton RUFC (Midlands 2 West (North) [7])
Industries (Present):	Agriculture, Brewing, Clothing, Construction, Distribution, Engineering, Finance, Food, Logistics, Manufacturing, Pottery, Retail, Services, Tyres, Tourism
Industries (Past):	Anchors, Brewing, Chains, Cheesemaking, Coal Mining, Ironmaking, Lockmaking, Pottery, Sadlery, Shoe-making, Textiles
Born in Staffordshire:	Thomas Allen, Emma Amos, George Anson, Carole Ashby, Elias Ashmole, William Astbury, Thomas Astle, Philip Astley, John Aynsley, Frances Barber, Richard Barnfield, Glenys Barton, Michael Bass, Arnold Bennett, Nigel Bennett, Philip Bond, Thomas George Bonney, Frank Bough, Steve Bould, Hugh Bourne, Havergal Brian, Mark Bright, Vera Brittain, Sian Brooke, Bruno Brookes, Robert Buchanan, William Carlos, Glenn Carter, Stan Collymore, Paddy Considine, Elijah Cope, Charles Cotton, Garth Crooks, Mark Curry, Hugh Dancy, Isabel Dean, Jakki Degg, Dud Dudley, K.K. Downing, Steve Edge, James Fleet, Sir John Floyer, Alan Gardner, Richard Garnett, Goldie, David Gorman, Nick Hancock, Thomas Harrison, George Heath, George Heming Mason, Sir Alfred Hickman, Barbara Hicks, Ian Hill, Noddy Holder, Jeffrey Holland, David Hopwood, Saul Hudson (Slash), T.E. Hulme, Joe Jackson, Robert James, Jerome K. Jerome, John Jervis, Samuel Johnson, Freddie Jones, Leanne Jones, Lemmy Kilmister, Alan Lake, John Lightfoot, Oliver Lodge, John Madejski, Miles Mander, Darren Matthews, Stanley Matthews, Shane Meadows, Neil Morrissey, Sir Henry Newbolt, Sue Nicholls, William Palmer, Adam Peaty, Robert Plant, Cyril Raymond, Reginald Pole, Bryan Pringle, Adrian Rawlins, Sian Reeves, Charlotte Salt, Henry Salt, Gilbert Sheldon, Rachel Shenton, Captain E.J. Smith, Josiah Spode, Rebekah Staton, Meera Syal, Phil Taylor, Glenn Tipton, Thomas Toft, James Trubshaw, Anthea Turner, John Wain, Izaak Walton, David Warrilow, Anna Watkins, Richard Wattis, Josiah Wedgwood, Thomas Whieldon, Jonathan Wild, Jonathan Wilkes, Robbie Williams, Sarah Willingham, A.N. Wilson, Peter de Wint, John Wyatt

Staffordshire Maps

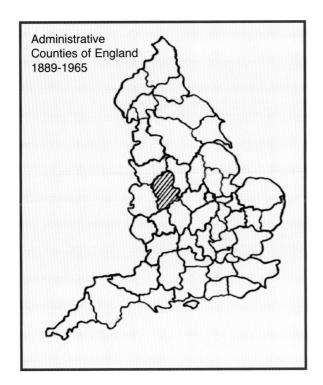

Administrative Counties of England 1889-1965

Ceremonial Counties of England 1997-2016

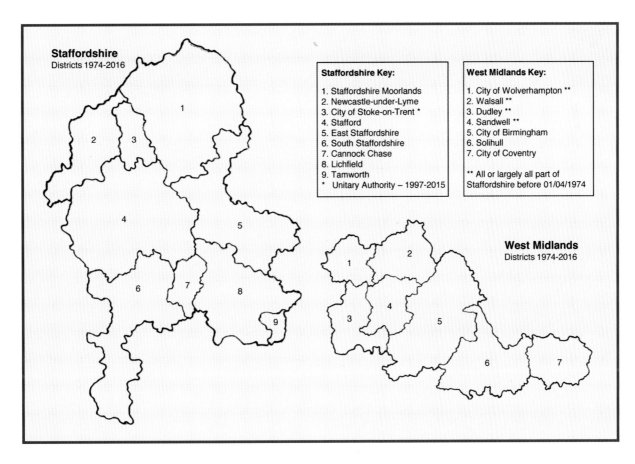

Staffordshire
Districts 1974-2016

Staffordshire Key:

1. Staffordshire Moorlands
2. Newcastle-under-Lyme
3. City of Stoke-on-Trent *
4. Stafford
5. East Staffordshire
6. South Staffordshire
7. Cannock Chase
8. Lichfield
9. Tamworth
* Unitary Authority – 1997-2015

West Midlands Key:

1. City of Wolverhampton **
2. Walsall **
3. Dudley **
4. Sandwell **
5. City of Birmingham
6. Solihull
7. City of Coventry

** All or largely all part of Staffordshire before 01/04/1974

West Midlands
Districts 1974-2016

Staffordshire County History

Prehistory

Like most other English historic counties, Staffordshire dates from the 11th century, and was formed towards the end of the two hundred year conflict on English soil between Anglo-Saxon and Viking. The name means "shire or district of the town of Stafford", and is clearly derived from the place-name *Stafford*, plus the Old English word *scīr*, meaning "shire or district". As for Stafford itself, the name appears as *Stæfford* in the mid-11th century, and then again as *Stadford* in Domesday Book (1086). The name means "ford by a landing place", and is derived from the Old English words *stæth* and *ford*, meaning "landing-place" and "ford or river-crossing", respectively. But of course, the *area* of Staffordshire goes back much further still.

Before continuing, though, it is worth pointing out that the shape of South Staffordshire changed significantly on 1st April 1974 when the metropolitan county of West Midlands was formed, absorbing Wolverhampton, Walsall, West Bromwich and Dudley in the process. There is much more on this later, but suffice to say that this book largely treats "Staffordshire" as the pre-1974 *historic* county of Staffordshire, and which survived as such for over a thousand years.

Geographically, the area of Britain that would eventually become Staffordshire is divided into three areas – and whose history has been influenced by their own differing geologies. These areas are nicely summarised by William Camden's *Britannia*, written as long ago as 1586: "*The north part is mountainous, and the less fertile; but the middle, which is watered by the Trent, is fruitful, woody and pleasant, by an equal mixture of arable and meadow grounds; so also is the south, which has much pit coal and mines of iron.*" But we will come to the industrial influences of the geology in good time. In terms of prehistory, it is thought that humans settled in the area that would eventually become Staffordshire before the last Ice Age, thanks to the discovery of two Palaeolithic axes at Shenstone and Drayton Bassett. Once the ice had retreated, humans began to live in a number of caves in the Manifold Valley such as Ossum's Cave and Thor's Cave, as evidenced by flint and bone tools found there. The Mesolithic period (c.9000 B.C to c.4500 B.C.) saw this cave occupation continue, while more flint

Thor's Cave in the Manifold Valley, one of a number of Staffordshire caves that were home to prehistoric man.

tools were discovered at Bourne Pool near to Aldridge in what is now the county of West Midlands. As for the Neolithic period (c.4500 B.C to c.2000 B.C.), contemporary stone axes have been found from all four corners of the county, but it is the burial mounds that still provide visual evidence with around 200 round barrows alone discovered within the confines of the historic county of Staffordshire. The majority are to be found in the Staffordshire Moorlands, although this doesn't mean that they weren't as prolific elsewhere; it's just that the focus of agriculture and industry in the rest of Staffordshire has destroyed a great deal of evidence.

The most striking of Staffordshire's burial mounds can be found at Long Low a mile or so south-east of Wetton where a unique configuration, in England, of two round barrows or cairns is linked by a bank. The more northerly barrow is around 75ft (23m) in diameter and survives to a height of just under 8ft (2.4 m), while the southerly barrow measures 49ft by 4ft (15m by 1.2m); the connecting bank is around 656ft (200m) long, 6.5ft (2m) high and 33ft (10m) wide. The northern barrow was excavated by Samuel Carrington in 1849 where he discovered the bones of 13 individuals along with three leaf-shaped arrowheads, while the southern barrow contained evidence of a cremation burial; further cremations were found in the connecting bank.

Long Low just south of Wetton, boasts a prehistoric burial chamber configuration that is unique in England, with two round barrows linked by a 200m long bank.

As to the age of Long Low, this isn't clear; it may have originally been created as a mid-Neolithic bank barrow, later converted into a late-Neolithic chambered barrow (the northern cairn), and later still, to a Bronze Age round barrow (the southern cairn). Other local barrows that have yielded Stone Age relics are those just to the east of Butterton and at Cauldon Low 5 miles to the south-west. Meanwhile at Mucklestone in the west of the county, there are two stones known as the Devil's Ring and Finger, and which once formed part of a

Quirk Alert: *Hobbit Holes and Jealous Giants*

On Kinver Edge, down in the south-westernmost point of Staffordshire, there are a number of sandstone caves that were occupied by prehistoric man and which are acknowledged as the last troglodyte dwellings to be occupied in England. One of the rocks is known as Holy Austin Rock, and was a hermitage until the 16th century, while later centuries saw the façades of regular homes fronting complete cave-built houses on Kinver Edge, and which were occupied until the 1960s. They are now owned by the National Trust, with one house restored to Victorian standard, while other caves demonstrate life here in the 1930s. It is thought that these caves on Kinver Edge were the inspiration for J. R. R. Tolkien's The Hobbit, *especially the home of Bilbo Baggins. The caves were a popular daytrip for Brummies in the early 20th century, and Tolkien's family would almost certainly have visited along with their impressionable son, John Ronald Reuel!*

These rock houses on Kinver Edge have probably been inhabited since Stone Age times, whereas others...

Meanwhile, local legend has it that Holy Austin Cave was once occupied by a giant and his rather comely wife, who together had created the caves by scooping out the sandstone with their fingernails. Now it also happened that the giant went to collect water each day, from a nearby spring that merely trickled – and hence the time to fill up a giant's water pitcher was considerable. This afforded enough time for a neighbouring giant to visit the comely giantess – which was apparently three strides from a neighbouring hill! However, on one occasion, he tarried for too long, and the Holy Austin giant spotted him – at which point he picked up a large rock and hurled it at the interloper. The stone apparently missed and planted itself upright, and for many generations after, it bore the name of the Bolt Stone. Alas, in 1848 the farmer in whose field it stood blew it to pieces with gunpowder!

...may have inspired a certain fantasy writer...

...and others are simply more modern!

chambered tomb for mass burial. They are so-named, because one stone is round with a hole of around 20 inches in the middle, while the other more slender stone stands at a height of around 6 feet. A number of the other barrows were originally intended for one occupant, but were later extended to take many.

Returning to the Staffordshire Moorlands, this area is also the location of many beaker finds, thus dating the objects to the Beaker people who flourished in the early Bronze Age, from around 2000 B.C. to 1300 B.C. Examples include finds at Alstonefield, Blore, Grindon and Ilam, and again at Wetton where burial sites include containers used for food as well as beakers. As the Bronze Age progressed (c.2000 B.C. to 600 B.C.), burials were gradually replaced by cremations and there are numerous barrows throughout the county that fall into this category, while also discovered all over the county are Bronze Age palstaves (bronze axes fitted into wooden handles). Also dating from the Bronze Age are two bracelets found in the north-eastern parish of Stanton, and a gold necklace found at Pattingham in the south-west of the historic county.

Moving onto the Iron Age and lasting evidence is

fort, at the northern end of Kinver Edge, was of the univallate Iron Age hillfort type, with a massive rampart and outer ditch along the south-west and south-east sides, but with natural defences forming the remaining sides. The other hillfort at the southern end of Kinver Edge was built on a promontory known as Drakelow Hill.

The Iron Age occupants of these hillforts may have belonged to one of three Celtic tribes, depending upon where they were located in the area that a thousand years later would become known as Staffordshire. To the south-east, they would likely have belonged to the *Corieltauvi* tribe whose territory swept down from Lincolnshire, through Nottinghamshire and Leicestershire and into Warwickshire, with southern Derbyshire and south-eastern Staffordshire making up the rest of the territory. To the north-east, the people would most likely be aligned to the Brigantes, whose territory covered the Staffordshire Moorlands most of Derbyshire and large tracts of land further north. However, the rest – the largest slice of Iron Age Staffordshire – belonged to the *Cornovii*, whose territory swept down from the Wirral through Cheshire

Castle Ring was the site of a vast, 9-acre Iron Age hillfort, and was located at the highest point of Cannock Chase (801ft).

The toposcope on the site of the Kinver Edge Iron Age hillfort.

best provided by a number of former hillforts. These include Berth Hill near Maer, Berry Ring near Stafford, Bishop's Wood near Eccleshall, Bunbury Hill near Alton, Bury Bank north of Stone, Castle Old Fort near Brownhills, and Castle Ring on Cannock Chase, as well as further hillforts at Kinver Edge and at Marchington. Of these, Castle Ring is the largest and most elaborate, fortified with banks and ditches. At 801ft, it is located at the highest point of Cannock Chase and covers 9 acres, although apart from the perimeter earthworks, little other visible evidence remains. Castle Ring was thought to be still occupied by the Celtic *Cornovii* tribe as late as A.D. 50, while the centre of the ring shows later evidence of farming where the ground has been ploughed – although an alternative theory suggests that these marks were made by medieval hunters, as there was a hunting lodge within Castle Ring during the medieval period. Meanwhile, the Kinver Edge hill-

and Shropshire to the tip of Herefordshire and Worcestershire, and included two thirds of Staffordshire, plus the westernmost parts of the county of West Midlands, formerly of Staffordshire.

Romans, Anglo-Saxons and Vikings

The Romans invaded Britain in A.D. 43, and by A.D. 45, the legions had defeated the *Corieltauvi*, and constructed the Fosse Way, which ran all the way from Exeter (*Isca Dumnoniorum*) in the south-west to Lincoln (*Lindum Colonia*) in the mid-east. For a few years, the Fosse Way – which ran to the south and east of Staffordshire – was thought to mark the temporary frontier of the embryonic province of *Britannia*, with all areas to the south and east of that line under Roman control.

However, the Romans certainly operated beyond that line under the second and third Roman governors of Britannia, Publius Ostorius Scapula (A.D. 47 to A.D. 52) and Didius Gallus (A.D. 52 to A.D. 57), both of whom slowly brought large areas of Staffordshire under Roman control. Interestingly, the distribution of known Roman camps has a bias towards the west of the county, suggesting that the *Cornovii* may have put up more of a struggle than the *Corieltauvi*. That said, the most startling evidence of Roman occupation can be found at Wall, just south of Lichfield. It was here that Publius Ostorius Scapula, set up a fort in around A.D. 48, thus establishing a forward base during the Roman forays westwards towards Wales, along the ancient Brythonic grassy trackway that they named as Watling Street. However, it is the town that developed beneath the fort, and which became known as *Letocetum*, that supplies the most lasting Roman legacy. Excavations in the 19th century and particularly between 1912 and 1913, uncovered the foundations of the Roman baths, alongside the foundations of a former Roman *mansio*, with other evidence suggesting a substantial settlement including, perhaps, a basilica, temples and an amphitheatre (for much more on *Letocetum*, see *Quirky Staffordshire [Wall]*).

As for Watling Street, its route passed right through what would later become Staffordshire territory, and which connected first Colchester (*Camulodunum*, the early provincial capital) and later London (*Londinium*) to Wroxeter (*Viroconium Cornoviorum*). As well as being on this road, *Letocetum* was also situated at its crossroads with Ryknield Street, another important Roman road that crossed the south-eastern quadrant of Staffordshire, running from Little Chester at Derby (*Derventio*) down through Staffordshire via Shenstone and heading out of the county towards Birmingham. Indeed, two Romano-British farmsteads have been discovered on Ryknield Street at Shenstone and Fisherwick, thus suggesting that farming was established in the valleys of the Trent and the Tame.

Twelve miles west of *Letocetum*, and also on Watling Street, the Romans established another settlement known as *Pennocrucium* and which was just south of modern-day Penkridge. Excavations have suggested that another fort was established here along with a small settlement, and which remained occupied throughout the Roman period; certainly, pottery unearthed here dates from A.D. 50 to A.D. 200. It is estimated that the main civilian site was a rectangular enclosure of 700ft by 450ft (210m by 140m), which was surrounded by three ditches. In addition, there was also a large double-ditched enclosure known as a vexillation fortress around 800 metres to the north-east, with two smaller forts also erected around 200 metres to the south-east and 60 metres to the north. *Pennocrucium* also stood at the centre of an important road junction because as well as the routes east and west on Watling Street (to *Letocetum* and *Viroconium*, respectively), the settlement was also met by roads heading south-east to

Looking down on the remains of the Roman mansio and baths at Wall (Letocetum).

A close-up of the remains of one of the Roman baths.

Metchley, south to Greensforge and south-west towards Shropshire and a possible crossing of the River Severn, as well as north-west to Whitchurch and north-east to Buxton. This makes *Pennocrucium* one of the most arterial Roman settlements in England – and yet there is no evidence of the site today. In fact, the place was only identified prior to excavations thanks to its mention in the 2nd century *Antonine Itinerary*, which pinpointed its location, and to 20th century aerial photography that, in 1946, revealed tell-tale cropmarks and a Roman enclosure. Further surveys in the 1960s and '70s revealed a whole series of additional Roman military enclosures, including a civil defensive work, the vexillation fortress, the two additional forts, and five temporary camps – all of which further indicate that occupation ran from the mid-1st century to the 4th century.

Other Roman roads crossing Staffordshire territory included a second Ryknield Street which ran from *Derventio* again, but entered Staffordshire at Rocester. From here it ran due west before turning in a north-westerly direction towards Chesterton before exiting the county and splitting in Cheshire territory, with the left-hand fork terminating at Chester (*Deva Victrix*), and the right-hand fork providing the route north into *Brigante* territory, and further conquest and annexation.

It is thought that the first fort at Rocester was built in around A.D. 69 when the natives were being pacified by Agricola, as the earliest pottery finds here date from between A.D. 60 and A.D. 100. Its positioning was perfect for defence, lying in an area of dry land a mile or so north of the confluence of the Dove and the Churnet – thus providing a natural line of defence on three sides. Despite this, the first fort was soon abandoned but was succeeded by a second fort in the first quarter of the 2nd century, and then by a third fort in around A.D. 140 which was also abandoned by the end of the 2nd century. As with *Letocetum*, the settlement at Rocester saw a civil settlement grow around it, and which itself was fortified in around A.D. 160 and again in A.D. 280 – presumably to help quell local uprisings. Excavations show that the *vicus* that developed from the early settlement extended to the north and south of the forts, with a shrine probably located to the south and the industrial quarter to the north. The southern area indicates the first phase of development from around A.D. 90 to A.D. 130, while the second appears to run from around A.D. 150 to the early 3rd century – and is thus consistent with the various fort constructions.

As for this second Ryknield Street, it was almost certainly built at around the same time as the first fort at Rocester (A.D. 69). Meanwhile, on Ryknield Street at the other side of the county, Chesterton was also home to a late 1st century fort built on top of Mount Pleasant, while around 350 metres to the south was another rectangular military enclosure. There was also a settlement or *vicus* that developed around 800 metres to the south of the fort at Holditch, and which was occupied from the 1st to the 3rd century. Given the locality, it is no surprise that the Romans and locals alike exploited the natural resources here, of coal, ironstone and clay, and a Roman kiln was discovered around 5 miles south-east of Chesterton, at today's Trent Vale. In terms of evidence today, the majority is buried underneath 20th century urbanisation, but a certain Sampson Erdeswick recorded ruined fortifications at Chesterton towards the end of the 16th century. That said, these had disappeared by the end of the 17th century, and the 20th century has now put paid to any excavations of the fort – at least for now, anyway! However, the mid-20th century saw a significant breakthrough in further understanding of the site when the Holditch area was excavated, and revealed a significant Roman settlement. The settlement or *vicus* appears to have expanded towards the end of the 1st century, and also appears to have been engaged in small-scale industry, largely to the east of the settlement; the western side appeared to be biased more towards residential accommodation and business. It was also surmised that a large stone building was located at the northern edge of the former colliery here, and which dated from the early 2nd century – so possibly a *forum-basiclica* or a *mansio*, perhaps even a Roman villa.

So far, we've mentioned four key Roman forts, at modern-day Wall, Penkridge, Rocester and Chesterton.

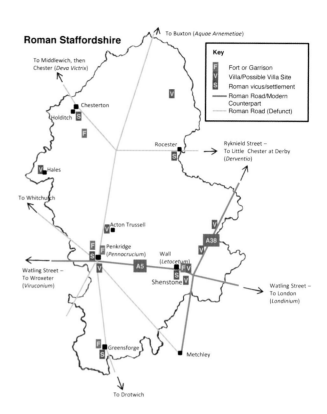

A fifth fort was also constructed at Greensforge in the south-west of the county. This fort has long-been known about due to the large rectangular earthwork there which is located on an area of raised ground to the east of Smestow Brook. However, there was another and probably older fort there approximately 100 metres to the south of the earthwork. Then in 1994, evidence was uncovered of a *vicus* to the west of Smestow Brook. This means that Greensforge, along with the other four key Roman forts in Staffordshire territory, all saw the settlements that grew up around them eventually develop into full-blown *vici* – although excavations at the site at Penkridge don't provide concrete evidence of this. With the establishment of a monetary economy, this brought in traders to the growing *vici*, along with families of the soldiers.

However, the development of each *vicus* almost certainly took place after A.D. 70 with the main bulk of the Roman army having moved north by this stage. The forts would still have been occupied, though, in order to quell any local rebellion or threats from the Welsh.

Throughout Roman Britain, a recurring arrangement was that of the villa-estate, and we are able to pinpoint Roman villa sites courtesy of archaeological finds such as fragments of building material, pottery, coinage, tiles, plaster and mosaic flooring. However, there are only three Roman villa sites in Staffordshire that we can be certain of, and which have been subject to detailed excavations. Three separate excavations have been carried out at Hales, 12 miles south-west of Chesterton, and have revealed that there was once a Roman corridor villa here that probably dates from the late first century. The villa was then complemented by a detached bath-house which was built in the early 2nd century, was altered in the 3rd century, but eventually fell into disuse by the middle of the 4th century. Another corridor villa has also been discovered close to the site of *Pennocrucium* at Engleton, with pottery finds suggesting it dates from the late 2nd century and survived well into the 4th century. It had a hypocaust at one end of the building and a bath suite at the other. The final villa of the trio was located around 6 miles north-north-east of the Engleton villa at modern-day Acton Trussell, with much of its footprint lying in St James' churchyard. This villa probably dates from the early 2nd century and comprised of a house with stone footings surrounded by a ditch. By the 3rd century the house had undergone a considerable expansion, including an east wing that was discovered in 1985 and is believed to date from the late 2nd century. Further expansion occurred during the 4th century, by which stage the villa is believed to have incorporated features such as a pantile roof, mosaic floors, painted wall plaster, a hypocaust and window glass. Interestingly, excavations have also shown that occupation of the Acton Trussell site actually dates back to at least the Neolithic period, with finds from the Bronze-Age and Iron-Age proving continuous occupation up to and including the Romano-British period.

In addition to these three villas, it is fairly certain that four other villas existed at currently unexcavated sites, thanks to the discovery of artefacts discovered nearby and the recovery of building materials of either brick or tile or both. The final area of Roman evidence is supplied by the remoter farmsteads, settlements and field systems. It is thought that there are many examples in the Staffordshire Moorlands, although to date, only a handful have been proven by excavation to be Romano-British earthworks, these being located in the Manifold Valley. It is also certain that the Manifold Valley was occupied during the Roman occupation, with Romano-British activity proven in the form of burials. Other farmsteads and field systems have been revealed close to known Roman towns, especially in the vicinity of Wall; indeed the majority of Staffordshire cropmarks of Roman or prehistoric origin can be found in the Lower Dove, Trent and Tame Valleys in the south-eastern quadrant of the county.

Throughout the Roman occupation, the native Britons of Staffordshire lived in relative harmony with their Roman masters, while their houses, enclosures and field systems remained similar to those that preceded the Roman Conquest. This suggests a country in which a foreign administration had been superimposed upon a Celtic society that largely survived the Roman occupation intact. After the Roman departure in around A.D. 410, Britain gradually became settled by the Angles and Saxons of northern Europe. The traditional view of Anglo-Saxon colonisation of England is that these particular Angles had originally settled in Lincolnshire before pushing their way up the Trent Valley into Nottinghamshire, Derbyshire and eventually Staffordshire, as is evidenced by mid-6th century heathen burial sites found from Newark to Burton upon Trent. Indeed, 19th century excavations at Stapenhill, Burton upon Trent, resulted in the discovery of a large cemetery with traces of 36 burials. Two of these were cremations, a pagan custom, which helps to date the burial site as the Anglo-Saxons didn't convert to Christianity until the mid-7th century.

Similarly, another site further up the Trent at Wychnor contains only inhumation burials, while at nearby Catholme, there was a large Anglian settlement of some 66 buildings. This latter site appears to have been populated from the 5th century to the early 10th, so it is a fair guess that its abandonment had something to do with marauding Vikings; certainly the name Catholme is part-derived from the Old Scandinavian word *holmr*, meaning "river-meadow". Back to the Anglo-Saxons, though, and having reached the confluence of the Trent and the Dove, they also began to push up the Dove Valley, too. This explains further burial sites discovered in the Staffordshire Peak District at

The River Tame (shown here at Hopwas), which along with the River Trent is where the first Anglo-Saxons settled in Staffordshire. Those who clustered around the River Tame were known as the Tamsætan.

The Anglo-Saxons also pushed up the Dove Valley and settled here too – perhaps in this very spot at the foot of Thorpe Cloud.

Alstonefield, Blore, Ramshorn and Waterhouses, while much further up the River Trent at Barlaston, yet another burial site shows features of both Anglo-Saxon and Celtic cultures.

Talking of the Peak District and Wychnor, it is interesting that both have connections with Celtic tribes that survived the Roman occupation and the early Anglo-Saxon colonisation. In the Peak District the *Pecsætan* were known as "peak dwellers", while the south-west of Staffordshire was part of the tribal kingdom of the *Hwicce*. The *Hwicce* lasted from 577 until around 780, although after 628, the *Hwicce* had become a sub-kingdom of Mercia; the connection with Wychnor is that the latter is named after the kingdom. As for the *Pecsætan*, they were also likely to have been Britons descended from the original Neolithic farmers who first settled in the Peak District. Their lands show up in the *Tribal Hidage* of the 7th century, where it is referred to as *Pecsætna lond*. The *Pecsætan* then survive for at least another 300 years, for they appear again in the *Anglo-Saxon Chronicle* of 920, and again in a charter of 963. The name derives from the Old English word, *pēac*, while the ancient name of *Pecsætna lond* means "land of the peak dwellers". There are also other place-names in Staffordshire that still derive from their original Celtic names, some of which are captured in the following table:

Of these Celtic-sourced place-names, Eccleshall implies that British Christianity may have survived in Staffordshire after the Romans departed. However, the earliest Anglo-Saxons were pagans and Staffordshire place-names also reflect this – for example, both Wednesbury and Wednesfield commemorate in their names the Saxon god of war, Wōden.

A further Anglo-Saxon incursion into Britain probably arrived via The Wash and headed westwards, eventually migrating along Watling Street into southern Staffordshire territory. Much of Staffordshire was thought to have been unreclaimed forest wilderness during these times, and the Angles were credited with founding villages and hamlets in self-created clearings. These people may have belonged to the Middle Anglian group of peoples, which included the *Bilsætan* (centred on Bilston) and the *Tamsætan*, the people who clustered around the River Tame. By the end of the 6th century, though, the Staffordshire area had become part of the Anglo-Saxon kingdom of Mercia, with the name deriving from the *Mierce*, people of the Welsh marches and occupants of the land between the Anglo-Saxons and the Celtic Britons of Wales. There is archaeological evidence which suggests that the Anglo-Saxon colonisation west stalled for a number of years at Lichfield, and that the area around

---

Staffordshire Place-Names with a Celtic/pre-Anglo-Saxon Origin

Place-name	Earliest Records	Meaning	Derivation
Cannock	*Chenet*, 1086; *Canoc*, 12th cent.	The small hill or hillock	From the Celtic word *cnoc* (hill) or the Old English equivalent, *cnocc*
Eccleshall	*Ecleshelle*, 1086; *Eccleshale*, 1227	Nook of land near a Romano-British Christian church	From the Celtic word *eglēs* (Romano British Christian church) and the Old English word *halh* (nook of land)
Kinver	*Cynibre*, 736; *Chenevare*, 1086	Hill (and possibly "royal hill")	From the Celtic word *bre3* (hill), with an obscure first element perhaps deriving from the Old English word *cyne* (royal)
Penkridge	*Pennocrucium*, 4th century; *Pancriz*, 1086	Tumulus on a headland	From the Celtic words *penn* (head, end or hill) and *crūg* (hill, mound or tumulus)
Penn	*Penne*, 1086	Place at the hill	From the Celtic word *penn* (head, end or hill)
Walsall	*Waleshale*, 1163	Nook of land belonging to either a Briton/Welshman, or a man called Walh	From either the Old English word *walh* in the genitive singular (Welshman) or the Celtic personal name, Walh, plus the Old English word *halh* (nook of land)
Walton	*Waletone*, 1086	Farmstead or village of the Britons	From the Old English words *walh* in the genitive plural (Welshmen) and *tūn* (farmstead or village)

the town marked a boundary between the Anglo-Saxons and the British; indeed, the Anglo-Saxons tasted defeat against the Welsh in 655 at the hands of Cynddylan, a prince of Powys. Allied with Morfael, a Celtic leader in the Lichfield area, they defeated the Anglo-Saxons at the Battle of Caer Luitcoet, generally thought to be close to modern-day Wall. Interestingly, a Welsh poem about the battle mentions that there were bishops and monks among the Anglo-Saxon ranks – thus adding further weight to the argument that British Christianity had indeed survived the departure of the Romans.

As for Mercia, the kingdom was centred on the Trent Valley and its territories, thus covering much of modern South Derbyshire, Leicestershire, Nottingham-shire, Staffordshire and northern Warwickshire, with the Mercian capital sited at Tamworth. The most authentic source of information at this time was from

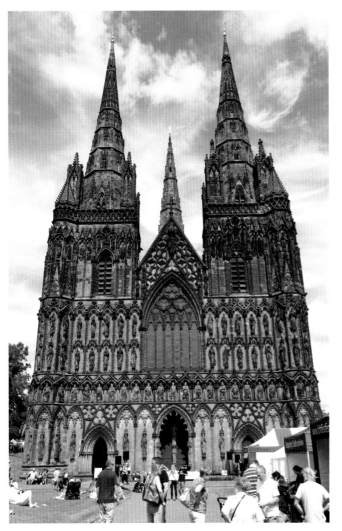

The magnificent Lichfield Cathedral. A minster or cathedral has existed here since the earliest days of Mercia, in the late 7th century. The spectacular frontage portrays dozens of saints and apostles – and there across the bottom row, above the doors, are many of the Kings of Mercia, Wessex and early and medieval England. The earliest half are shown in close-up on page 17.

the early 8th century Northumbrian monk and scholar known as the Venerable Bede, and who describes Mercia as being divided in two by the River Trent.

In 653, Peada, son of King Penda of Mercia, was converted to Christianity so that he could marry the Christian daughter of King Oswy of Northumbria. At this time, the Mercians also invited four priests to join the kingdom as missionaries, with their leader, Diuma, based at Repton in Derbyshire. A double abbey under an Abbess was built at Repton, but the Bishop of Mercia and Lindsey moved his See from Repton to Lichfield in 669. This bishop also happened to be one of Staffordshire's most famous early evangelists, Ceadda – and who later was canonised as St Chad. Originally a monk from Northumbria, Ceadda continued convert-ing locals until his death from the plague in 672. The site of the church that Ceadda occupied at Lichfield is not known; it may well have been on the site of the current Lichfield Cathedral, or it may have been further east, at Stowe, and where the current church of St Chad now stands. In 700, Bishop Headda built a new church on the current Lichfield Cathedral site, and there has been a church on this spot ever since.

Returning to Bishop Ceadda again, two of the people that he allegedly converted, were Prince Wulfad and Prince Rufin, both sons of King Wulfhere (658-674). Historians think that the commonly-told story of King Wulfhere killing his two sons for converting to Christianity is most likely to be a romanticised inven-tion of the 12th century (for the full tale with different slants, see the Burston, Stone and Stowe chapters of the *Quirky Staffordshire* section of this book). King Wulfhere is reputed, however, to have founded a monastery at Stone, but probably not in remorse for having killed his two sons! Meanwhile, his daughter, Werburga, founded a nunnery at Hanbury. She was later canonised as St Werburgh, following her death at Hanbury in 700, while 174 years later in 874, her remains – by now the relics of a saint – were removed to Chester to prevent them falling into Danish hands. Even more significant was that in the reign of King Offa (757-796), Lichfield was raised to the status of an archbishopric, thus becoming a third arm of the Church, along with Canterbury and York. After Offa's death in 796, though, the archbishopric was reduced to its former status, although King Æthelweald later established a cathedral chapter at Lichfield in 822, for 20 canons under a provost.

One other significant Anglo-Saxon monastic house was Burton Abbey, founded by St Modwen (or Modwenna), perhaps as early as the 7th century. Modwen was an Irish noblewoman who became a nun and later an abbess and she founded the community on an island in the middle of the Trent known as Andressey (Andrew's Isle), with her church there dedi-cated to St Andrew. According to the medieval *Life of St Modwenna*, Modwen spent seven years there with two other Irish nuns before they embarked upon a pilgrim-age to Rome. On their return, St Modwen is said to

Sculpture of St Modwen on Andressey Island, Burton upon Trent.

location where King Ina of Wessex ate, sheltered and held council whilst besieging King Ceolred of Mercia. Ceolred was holed up in an old hillfort on Bunbury Hill around which Alton Towers would eventually be built. An ancient Saxon chronicle states that Ceolred had constructed a fortress at Bunbury, which in some places had a double or single ditch, with accompanying embankments – some of which survived up until the late 19th century. The battle that followed was particularly bloody, and the valley in which it was fought has been known variously as the Valley of the Slain, Slain Hollow, Slain Valley and Slade Valley.

St Modwen's church, Burton upon Trent, is named after the 7th century saint who founded the first Burton Abbey. The Grade I-listed parish church of Burton, St Modwen's was built between 1719 and 1728, replacing the remains of the church that had belonged to Burton Abbey.

have had a vision which led to her building a church at Stapenhill at the foot of what was then called Mount Calvus (now Scalpcliffe Hill), with the church dedicated to St Peter and St Paul. An Anglo-Saxon cemetery was discovered here in 1881, with the recovered artefacts now housed in the town museum. As for St Modwen, she died in Scotland, allegedly aged 130. On her death, her companions are said to have seen her soul taken to heaven by silver swans. Her body was returned to Burton for burial and a shrine built to her on Andressey. Alas, this was destroyed by the Danes in 874, along with what was probably a wooden church, although Modwen's remains were rumoured to have been recovered and ended up at the successor Burton Abbey after it was established in 1002 by Wulfric Spot. During her time at Burton Abbey, though, Modwen was reported to have performed many holy miracles, and became renowned for healing blindness.

Despite this rather compelling biography, though, other historians are dubious about its veracity, and suggest that St Modwen has actually been confused with St Monenna (Moninne) of Ireland or with a Scottish saint also called Modwenna. This may account for how St Modwen has also been associated with Alfred the Great – who reigned in the 9th century some two hundred years after the "Burton Modwenna" founded her abbey!

Swapping one possible legend for another, it is also said that King Ina's Rock at Alton Towers, is the exact

The white swan in Stapenhill Gardens is the emblem of St Modwen, chosen because her companions allegedly saw silver swans take her soul to heaven following her death.

From very early on in the Anglo-Saxon period, minster or mother churches were erected around the county – these being churches which served a large area in the days before parishes were introduced. As already covered, the grandmother of them all was first erected at Lichfield in the late 7th century, and the episcopal estates around Lichfield and Eccleshall may have originally been the areas served by the minster priests. Another minster church had been founded by the 10th century at Stafford and was dedicated to St Bertelin, a legendary Anglo-Saxon saint who had lived in a hermitage at Stafford, while it is also likely that St Editha's at Tamworth served its surrounding areas, too. In addition to these, the later collegiate churches at Penkridge, Tamworth, Tettenhall and Wolverhampton, along with the semi-collegiate church at Gnosall, probably originated as minsters in the 10th and 11th centuries.

THE AMAZING EARLY KINGS OF MERCIA, WESSEX AND ENGLAND AT LICHFIELD CATHEDRAL

Below is a selection of figures from the Anglo-Saxon period of history that appear on the front of Lichfield Cathedral today. Of course, these sculptures aren't anywhere near as old as their subjects; they were carved in the late 19th century, but as an attempt to recreate the medieval splendour of the cathedral that Sampson Erdeswick describes in 1600, in the first ever written history of Staffordshire, as "exceedingly finely cut and cunningly set forth".

Here we have from second left to right, Ceadda, or St Chad (c.634-672), one of the monks who introduced Christianity to Mercia, King Peada (655-656), the first Christian Mercian king, and King Wulfhere (658-675).

From left to right, we have King Wulfhere again, King Æthelred (675-704), King Offa (757-796), and King Ecgbert of Wessex (802-839), with Mercia now a sub-kingdom of Wessex, ruled by Mercian ealdormen serving Wessex.

From left to right, we have King Ecgbert again, King Æthelwulf (839-858), King Æthelbehrt (860-865) and King Æthelred (865-871), all of Wessex.

From left to right, we have King Edgar of England (959-975) and King Canute of England (1016-1035).

Quirk Alert: *Ceadda, Headda and Bēda*

When Bishop Headda built his new church at Lichfield in 770, he had the tomb of St Chad (formerly Bishop Ceadda) transferred to a shrine in the new cathedral. That great scholar of the early 8th century, Bēda, and known later as the Venerable Bede, reported on the shrine as follows: "Ceadda's place of burial is a wooden coffin in the shape of a little house, having an aperture in its side, through which those who visit it out of devotion can insert their hands and take out a little of the dust. When it is put in water and given either to cattle or to men who are ailing, they get their wish and are at once freed from their ailments and rejoice in health restored." A later shrine was built in the early 14th century but was destroyed at the Reformation. However, the bones passed into Roman Catholic custody, and still survive today at the Roman Catholic cathedral of St Chad in Birmingham.

In terms of surviving relics, there are a number of Anglo-Saxon crosses dotted about the county, such as those at Alstonefield, Checkley, Chebsey, Ilam, Leek, Rocester, Stoke and Wolverhampton. A number of churches also retain Saxon stonework in their lower courses. However, in recent years, Staffordshire has become a focal point for Anglo-Saxon "treasure" following the discovery of the "Staffordshire Hoard" in 2009. The discovery, in a field near to the village of Hammerwich amounted to the largest hoard of Anglo-Saxon gold and silver metalwork ever found, consisting of over 3,500 items dating back to the Mercian heyday of the 7th and 8th century. Interestingly, the hoard – as well as also being of an extremely high standard of workmanship – is almost completely comprised of implements of war – typically removed ornamental parts of swords and helmets. None of the artefacts appear to have been used for female decoration, and the only exceptions to weaponry are two (perhaps three) crosses, possibly used as an altar or processional cross. But perhaps the most intriguing artefact recovered was a gold strip, inscribed in Latin on both sides with a quotation from the Old Testament: "Rise up, Lord; may Your enemies be scattered and those who hate You be driven from Your face."

The hoard was eventually valued at £3,285,000 and was purchased by Birmingham Museum and Art

been stripped from sword hilts and pommels, as well as pieces of helmet, may well have been trophies won in battle. This sort of tallies with yet another theory which suggests that the hoard may have belonged to the Mercian court armourer, who would have acquired such artefacts on the death of Anglo-Saxon nobles, or opponents in battle. This then leads on to the most interesting speculation of all, which is that the hoard may have originally belonged to King Edwin of Northumbria, famously defeated and killed by the combined forces of Mercia and Gwynedd at the Battle of Hatfield Chase, a site as yet unproven with at least three counties claiming it as their own. Whatever the reason for the hoard's burial, though, the quality of the artefacts suggests that at one time they belonged to people in the upper echelons of Saxon society. That leaves one final thing that the hoard reveals about its creators – that the Saxon goldsmiths were capable of techniques not previously credited to them.

By the end of the 9th century, Mercia had fallen into decline, losing its kingdom status completely and eventually ruled by ealdormen serving under the throne of Wessex. The kingdom's weakness therefore meant that it was ripe for plunder when the Danes invaded in the late 860s. After harrying much of England, the Danish army under Halfdan then established a base at Nottingham where he was joined by a second army led

Above from left: *Anglo-Saxon cross at Chebsey; Anglo-Saxon cross in St Peter's churchyard at Alstonefield, Anglo-Saxon cross in the churchyard of St Peter's church at Wolverhampton, which dates from around 996 when a college was founded on this site.*

Gallery and the Potteries Museum and Art Gallery. Today, items from the hoard can be found at both of these establishments, along with smaller collections at Lichfield Cathedral and Tamworth Castle. It is assumed that the hoard was buried by its owners at a time of perceived Mercian peril, and the fact that it was never recovered suggests that the perceived peril became a reality. Another theory is that the artefacts that had

by Guthrum. This left Mercia appealing to their old enemy, Wessex, but that didn't stop the Danes invading Staffordshire territory in 873. Under Ivar the Boneless they saw out the winter of 873-874 at Repton in South Derbyshire, from where they subdued the surrounding countryside and destroyed Tamworth. By 877, the Danes had begun to partition Mercia and it is at this point in time that the area of Staffordshire began to take

This stone coffin can be found in the churchyard of St Mary and St Chad's church at Brewood. Not only is it thought to be Anglo-Saxon, but it is also the sort of coffin in which Saxon chiefs were buried.

What is known as St Bertram's tomb at Holy Cross church at Ilam. The tomb over the coffin dates from the 13th century, but the legend of St Bertram dates from Mercian times. According to legend, he was a Mercian prince whose Irish wife and new baby were killed by wolves in the forest. He then lived as a hermit in the Stafford area and later in Ilam. The tomb has been and still is a place of pilgrimage – and those sheets of paper visible on top of the tomb are the prayers of modern-day pilgrims.

shape, along with the other counties of the "North Midlands", with each new "shire" named after their respective military stronghold. The west of the Mercian kingdom was given to Ceolwulf II, a puppet king to the Danes, while in the east the area became known as the Five Boroughs, the name deriving from the Old English word *burh* meaning "fortified place or stronghold". Then in the following year (878), King Alfred of Wessex and the Danish King Guthrum agreed to carve up England between them following the Treaty of Wedmore and a temporary peace was established. Maps of England in the late 9th century tend to show all of Staffordshire as being part of the reduced Kingdom of Mercia, with the border between Mercia and the Danelaw partly formed by Staffordshire's eastern boundaries.

Interestingly, Greenslade and Stuart (*A History of Staffordshire*) claim that the area of Staffordshire north of Watling Street also fell under Danish control – which

would have covered all of central and northern Staffordshire; a Roman road defining the boundary between Saxon and Dane! However, there is little evidence of Danish settlement in Staffordshire, although a few place-names are Danish in origin, such as Croxall (named after the Dane *Krókr*) and Thorpe Constantine (derived from the Old Scandinavian word *thorp* [outlying farmstead or hamlet]), both of which are in the south-east of the county. A number of islands in the Trent, such as Broadholme and Horsholme are also suffixed with "holme" – deriving from *holmr* an Old Scandinavian word for "island". Finally, a number of street names in Tamworth suffixed with "gate" were named during Danish occupation – such as Aldergate and Gungate – with both deriving the latter part of their names from the Old Scandinavian word *gata*, meaning "road or street".

Despite the Treaty of Wedmore of 878, the Danish renewed their attacks on Mercia in the late 9th century. By this stage, though, Mercian links with Wessex had been cemented further by the marriage of Earl Æthelred of Mercia to Æthelflæd, daughter of King Alfred of Wessex. Edward the Elder of Wessex helped to check the Danish advance at the Battle of Tettenhall in 910, but the following year (911), Æthelred died, leaving Æthelflæd to rule Mercia as the 'Lady of the Mercians'. Æthelflæd immediately set about fortifying Mercia's eastern borders and by 913 she had encroached deep into Danish territory, having established *burhs* (strongholds) at both Stafford and Tamworth. Along with her brother (Edward the Elder), Æthelflæd then launched her first offensive foray in July 917 and selected the fortress at Derby as her target, expelling the Danes and annexing the whole region back into English Mercia.

As for Æthelflæd, she died in 918 at which point the Mercians submitted to the rule of Edward the Elder. Edward was then succeeded by his son, Æthelstan (924-939), and it was under his rule that royal mints were established at both Stafford and Tamworth. By 943, though, the Danes had hit back, Tamworth was destroyed and many of its inhabitants were massacred. Possession of border territory ebbed and flowed over the next century or so, with recordings of Danish incursions in the late 10th century, but also of a

Statue of Æthelflæd, Lady of the Mercians, who took back Tamworth from the Danes in 913 and then built an Anglo-Saxon burh here. She stands in the western shadow of Tamworth Castle, built by the Normans over a century and a half later.

massacre of Danes in the area around Marchington in 1002. Back came the Danes with King Sweyn of Denmark in 1013, with many areas of Staffordshire ravaged by his advance…but who only survived for another five weeks after which the formerly ousted Æthelred the Unready returned to reclaim his crown…only for the Danish King Cnut to invade in 1016 and claim it back. By 1035, what was now the Earldom of Mercia was back in Anglo-Saxon hands, under Leofric, Earl of Mercia. Despite this turmoil, though, it was clearly sometime during this period that the county of Staffordshire was first created. Many believe this first happened during the reign of Edward the Elder (899-925) – although we don't actually see the name *Staffordshire* appear until the *Anglo-Saxon Chronicle* of 1016. The county was also created at this time with very similar borders to those that existed all the way up to 1974.

One other casualty of the Vikings was the aforementioned Burton Abbey, on the island known as Andressey, and thought to have been founded by St

Known as "Land and Water", this is a sculpture of a partially submerged Viking longboat on Andressey Island at Burton upon Trent. If you visit, check out the prow (behind the photographer). It represents an upturned jug with water gushing out, reflecting the importance of water to the later brewing industry, while the stern is a carving of a bunch of hops. Very clever indeed.

Also on Andressey Island is this Cherry Orchard, the sole remnant of the ancient Anglo-Saxon Burton Abbey that was destroyed by the Danes in the late 9th century.

Modwen in the 7th century. A shrine to Saint Modwen had also been built at the church on Andressey but this was destroyed by the Danes in 874. However, St Modwen's remains were reputedly recovered and ended up at Burton Abbey when it was re-established in 1002 by Wulfric Spot, a Saxon thegn, and a new shrine was created for the saint.

Throughout the 10th century, we then see evidence in various charters where distinct areas within Staffordshire are allocated to Mercian thegns and which closely resemble our modern-day parishes. A further and typically Anglo-Saxon administrative subdivision was also created in the form of five hundreds. The five were Pirehill in the north-west of the county, Totmonslow in the north-east, Cuttlestone in the mid-west, Seisdon in the south-west and Offlow in the south-east, with each name deriving from local and prominent topographical features. At the courts of each hundred, taxation was levied, the maintenance of peace and order was discussed and agreed, and some criminal and civil offences were also dealt with.

Undoubtedly, therefore, Staffordshire and its internal areas had clearly taken shape long before the Normans arrived in 1066.

From the Conquest to the Dissolution

Following the Norman Conquest of 1066, Staffordshire was soon subjected to the same ruthless overhaul of ruling class and high clergy that was to be repeated in most other English counties. In other words, out went the previous Anglo-Scandinavian incumbents, to be replaced by Norman gentry and bishops. By far the most important and extensive new landowner in Staffordshire, was William himself. He automatically inherited the royal manors which had previously belonged to Edward the Confessor, such as those at Kingswinford and Penkridge, but he also helped himself to those manors previously held by the Earls of Mercia, too, such as those at Kinver, Leek and Uttoxeter.

The rest of Staffordshire was largely carved up between four of William's closest followers and councillors. Roger de Montgomerie, the 1st Earl of Shrewsbury, was given 30 manors in Staffordshire, while Robert de Stafford (previously Robert de Toeni) was given the manor of Stafford (from which he then took his name) and numerous manors around the town, including Barlaston to the north and Bradley to the west. Of the remaining two new landowners, Henry de Ferrers was the owner of 210 manors throughout England, the majority of them in neighbouring Derbyshire and Leicestershire, but with his Staffordshire manors including Tutbury where he built the first castle and also founded a priory in 1080. De Ferrers also served William I as castellan of Stafford. The last of the inheritors, William Fitz-Ansculf, became lord of numerous manors in the south-west of Staffordshire, such as those at Wolverhampton,

Wombourne and Sedgley, and also at Dudley where he made his base at the castle of the ousted Saxon, Earl Edwin. Finally, a Norman priest called Peter succeeded Leofwine, the Anglo-Saxon bishop of Lichfield in 1072, and thus inherited the extensive episcopal estates. This followed the resignation of Leofwine two years earlier, who did not fit the model of a Norman priest, given he was married with a family!

Many of England's southern counties surrendered relatively meekly to the Conqueror, but that wasn't the case in Staffordshire. William, therefore, had to visit Staffordshire twice during the early years of his reign. The first occasion was to put down a rebellion in 1069 during which a battle was fought at Stafford, with the Normans defeating the rebels. However, resistance persisted, particularly in the north of England, and therefore William returned to Staffordshire in 1070, including the county in his brutal "Harrying of the North", where vast areas were ravaged; the aim being to lay waste to the northern shires in order to eliminate further rebellion. As well as fortified buildings, William's army also destroyed the homes, stock and crops of ordinary people, as well as the means of food production and many starved to death as a result. In Staffordshire, the destruction was so widespread, that one chronicler records "a huge crowd of old men, young men, women and children wandering as far south as Evesham Abbey in search of food."

Stafford Castle. This particular incarnation of the castle was built in the 19th century, but much of its masonry is comprised of its 14th century predecessor, built by Ralph de Stafford in the late 1340s. However, the medieval castle was built on top of the Norman earthworks and defences constructed in the 1070s by Robert de Stafford.

Chartley Castle was first built in around 1100 by the Earls of Chester. This later stone-built castle was built in 1220 by Ranulf de Blondeville, 6th Earl of Chester but was abandoned after 1485. Some of the five towers and the curtain wall survive, along with a cylindrical keep, which is very rare.

> ## Quirk Alert: *Dangerous Neighbours*
> *Mavesyn Ridware takes its name from its Norman Mavesyn owners of the late 11th century – whose name means "dangerous neighbours", derived from the French mal-voisin.*

Following the ravaging of Staffordshire, William built a wooden castle at Stafford in 1070, on a hill to the west of the county town. The idea was that the presence of a castle would deter any further uprisings. Along with the subjugation following the brutal Harrying, his plans worked so well that it became unnecessary to maintain the castle and it rapidly fell into disrepair. However, built in the classic motte and bailey style, the motte or mound is still very well defined today, as are the 10 acres-worth of earthworks and ditches used to defend the castle. Stafford Castle was later rebuilt in stone by Ralph de Stafford (1301-1372), 1st Earl of Stafford in the mid-14th century on the earthworks of the 11th century castle. The castle was eventually slighted after the English Civil War, and the current incarnation was built in the 19th century, using much of the masonry of its medieval predecessor.

A second early Norman castle was built at Stowe-by-Chartley, around half way between Stafford and Uttoxeter. Chartley Castle was possibly built in around 1100 by either the 1st or the 2nd Earl of Chester, although other sources suggest it was built by the later 4th Earl of

Chester, Ranulph de Gernon (1129-1153). The castle was then re-built in stone in around 1220 by Ranulph de Blondeville (1181-1232), 6th Earl of Chester. On his death, the castle passed to the de Ferrers family, courtesy of the marriage of William de Ferrers, 4th Earl of Derby, to Ranulph's sister, Agnes. The de Ferrers' owned the castle between 1232 and 1453, after which it passed to Walter Devereaux courtesy of his marriage to Elizabeth, the Ferrers heiress. Created the 1st Baron Ferrers in 1461, Devereaux was the last occupant of Chartley Castle, for he was killed at the Battle of Bosworth in 1485, after which the castle was abandoned and a new moated and battlemented manor house built at Stowe-by-Chartley.

Another castle initially built of wood in 1071, and with the intention of quelling local unrest, was Tutbury Castle. The first castle was built by Henry de Ferrers, who used it as his administrative centre from which he controlled his many manors. Henry de Ferrers also founded a Benedictine priory alongside the castle in 1080, as a satellite of St Pierre-sur-Dives in Normandy. However, the castle was destroyed in 1174 thanks to

Remarkably, Tutbury Castle was built and destroyed three times between 1071 and 1322, thanks to its owners' participation in rebellions against their monarch. These are the remains of the fourth build of the mid-14th century.

William de Ferrers' role in the revolt of 1173-74 against King Henry II. William de Ferrers, who was also the 3rd Earl of Derby, was then imprisoned at Caen, but somehow managed to regain the favour of Henry, while he also accompanied his successor, Richard I, on the Third Crusade and died at the Siege of Acre in 1190. The castle was then re-built in the late 12th century, and the former wooden keep was replaced by a stone one. Alas, one of the de Ferrers' successors, Robert de Ferrers (1239-1279), 6th Earl of Derby, had learned little from his family history and he, too, joined a rebellion against a King. This rebellion was known as the Second Barons' War (1263-1264), and was led by Simon de Montfort against King Henry III. Robert de Ferrers was involved in the taking of three castles in South Wales that belonged to Prince Edward, while Prince Edward's response was to attack de Ferrers at Chartley Castle, and to later destroy Tutbury Castle. De Ferrers and de Montfort eventually fell out over the ownership of Peverel Castle in Derbyshire and de Ferrers was imprisoned in the Tower of London. The death of de Montfort at the Battle of Evesham on 4th August 1265 didn't help de Ferrers, either, and he was eventually disinherited of most of his estates. After a further rebellion in 1269, Tutbury Castle, along with many other de Ferrers estates, were given to Edmund Crouchback, and have remained part of the Duchy of Lancaster ever since. It was also Edmund Crouchback who began the rebuild of the 3rd post-Norman Conquest castle at Tutbury – although that was *also* destroyed in 1322 after the rebellion of Thomas, Earl of Lancaster against Edward II. Tutbury Castle was then re-built for a 4th time in the mid-14th century and was given by Edward III to his fourth son, John of Gaunt, who was created Duke of Lancaster in 1362. Finally, since 1399, when Henry, Duke of Lancaster became Henry IV, Tutbury Castle has also belonged to the Crown as well as the Duchy of Lancaster. The castle was also extensively enhanced during the 15th century, but had fallen into disrepair by the 16th century. It is the ruin of this last castle that we see today.

Yet another important Norman castle was built at the former Mercian capital of Tamworth. Indeed, when the manor was inherited by Robert de Marmion in around 1070, it was probably still a fortress town, thanks to the original efforts of Æthelflæd, Lady of the Mercians, who had built a *burh* there in 913. There was no castle, *per se*, though, and so another timber castle was constructed here in the 1080s on typical Norman earthworks along with a motte and bailey, and was positioned in the south-western part of the *burh*. As for the de Marmion family, they originated from Fontenay-le-Marmion in Normandy, and they held Tamworth Castle for six generations from the late 11th century until 1294. In between these times, Robert Marmion, 3rd Baron Marmion of Tamworth (1185 – 1218), was appointed Head of the Itinerant by King Henry II, and he became known as "Robert the Justice". However,

Tamworth Castle was originally built of wood in the 1080s by Robert de Marmion, in the typical Norman motte and bailey style. A stone castle replaced the wooden one around a hundred years later, and the tower on the right-hand side of the photograph dates from this build.

Robert was later to turn on King John in 1215 by supporting the French King, Phillip II, a move which backfired when John ordered Robert's son Geoffrey to be imprisoned, all of Robert's lands to be confiscated and Tamworth Castle to be demolished. It would appear, though, that only part of the castle was demolished, thus enabling Robert's sons to regain their father's lands on the death of King John in 1216. The last of the Marmions to own Tamworth Castle was Philip Marmion (1241-1291), but when he died without a legitimate son, the castle and its manor passed to his daughter. She died just three years later in 1294, also without an heir, and the castle passed to her niece and thus to the de Freville family via her husband Sir Alexander. However, the de Frevilles only held the castle until 1423 before it passed to the de Ferrers family through marriage. By the 1540s, the castle was in ruins.

Throughout the medieval period, though, Tamworth Castle remained important, and was visited by Henry I (sometime between 1109 and 1115), Henry II (1158, and accompanied by Thomas á Becket), Henry III (1257), Edward II (1325), Edward III (1330), and later by James I (1619). As for today, the shell of the keep retains an original 12th century gate tower, while some of the three-storey residential accommodation is still 13th century.

Dudley Castle was also first built in wood, this time by Ansculf de Picquigny in 1070. It was succeeded by a stone castle built by the Paganel family in the 12th century, but which was demolished in 1173 after Gervase Paganel joined the failed rebellion against Henry II. The castle was rebuilt in stone by the Somery family in the late 13th and early 14th century, and it is from this build that the keep dates and which is visible from the town today, perched on top of the original 11th century earthwork.

One final medieval castle of Staffordshire was Alton Castle, built by Bertram de Verdun in the late 12th century, and some fragments of that incarnation of the castle still survive today. The castle passed to the Furnivalle family in 1316, and thence to John Talbot, who was created the 1st Earl of Shrewsbury in 1442. This would also have been around the time that the castle was re-built. The 2nd Earl of Shrewsbury was killed during the Wars of the Roses at the Battle of Northampton in 1460, fighting for the Yorkists.

Moving back to the early years after the Norman Conquest, the see of Lichfield (which covered Staffordshire, Derbyshire, Cheshire, and parts of Warwickshire, Shropshire and Lancashire) was moved from Lichfield to Chester in 1075, and then from Chester to Coventry in 1102. It wasn't until 1228 that Lichfield was formally recognised as a cathedral, and even then, the diocese was shared as Coventry and Lichfield. Despite the loss of the see in 1075, though, the rebuilding of Lichfield Cathedral was begun shortly afterwards during the tenure of Bishop Limesey (1086-1117), and was completed during the tenures of Bishop Peche (1121-1126) and Bishop Clinton (1129-1148) – although

much of the Cathedral that we see today dates from the 13th and 14th centuries, making it the only surviving medieval cathedral in the UK with three spires.

It is generally accepted that Lichfield Cathedral is Staffordshire's ecclesiastical jewel in the crown, but the county is also home to many more Norman and early medieval gems, too. High on the list are the six collegiate churches that originated from the 10th or 11th centuries at Gnosall, Penkridge, Stafford, Tamworth, Tettenhall and Wolverhampton, although Gnosall's St Lawrence church didn't develop along the same fully collegiate and independent lines that the other five did.

Of these collegiate churches, St Editha's at Tamworth originates from the 9th century when Tamworth was the capital of the kingdom of Mercia. However, the original Anglo-Saxon church was destroyed by the Danes when they ransacked Tamworth in 874. By 925, though, a successor church had been built in its place, as this was the year that Sigtrygg of Northumbria attempted to marry the sister of King Æthelstan of England, and who happened to be called Editha – after whom the church was subsequently named when she was canonised shortly after her death in 960. Alas, this church was also destroyed by a later Dane raid in 943, and was rebuilt this time by King Edgar in 963 – nephew of Editha, and who made his late aunt the patron saint of what was by this stage a collegiate church. Unsurprisingly, nothing remains of the 10th century church, but much of its

SUCCESSORS TO STAFFORDSHIRE'S ELEVENTH CENTURY COLLEGIATE CHURCHES

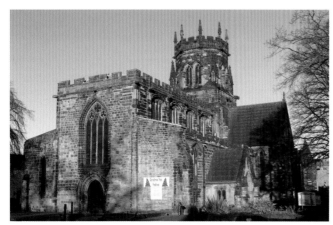

St Mary's church at Stafford dates from the early 13th century, with 14th century transepts and 15th century tower and clerestory. The octagonal tower is one of very few in the UK.

St Editha's church at Tamworth, named after the 10th century sister of King Æthelstan. Nothing remains of the Anglo-Saxon build, but much of the stone of the succeeding Norman build was included in the above 14th century build.

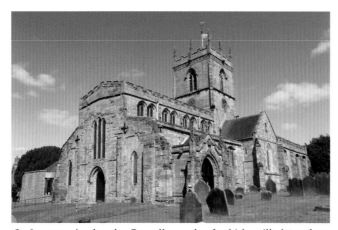

St Lawrence's church, Gnosall, much of which still dates from Norman times including the four arches of the central tower as well as the south transept.

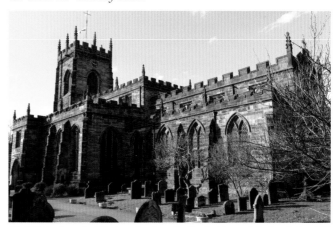

St Michael and All Angels church, Penkridge. Much of the 13th century build remains, including nave and chancel, while the tower is 14th century.

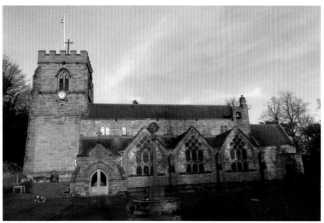

St Michael and All Angels church, Tettenhall which still retains some Norman features, including two round piers and one arch. The tower is 14th century.

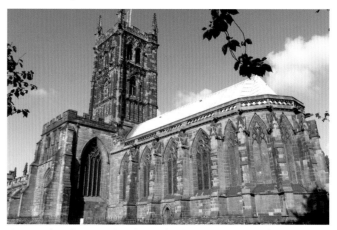

St Peter's collegiate church, Wolverhampton, much of which dates from the 15th century, although the tower rises up from 13th century arches.

Norman replacement does – including Norman stonework at the eastern and western ends that indicate a church of the same size as the current 14th century one – although the Norman church was cruciform in shape with a central tower supported by four great Norman arches, two of which still remain. The Norman church was thought to have been built by Robert de Marmion, the same Norman lord who had built the first Tamworth Castle. Alas, the Norman church was largely destroyed by a fire on the 23rd May 1345. Its replacement – much of which survives to this day – was rebuilt by Dean Baldwin de Witney between 1350 and 1369, and today, St Editha's is the largest medieval parish church in Staffordshire, with much of it dating to the mid-to-late 14th century, with some 15th and 19th century additions. As for the foundation date of the college of canons at St Editha, this is unknown, but probably dates to the 10th century. The right to appoint canons was later disputed in the 12th century, though, and all appointments became Royal. The college was eventually dissolved in 1548 under the terms of the Dissolution of Colleges Act 1547; it was at this point that the church became the parish church of Tamworth.

Quirk Alert: *Canon Fodder*

In 1191, Peter of Blois became dean of St Peter's collegiate church at Wolverhampton. Alas, he was to find standards "deplorably low". After eleven years of failing to reform the church, he resigned in 1202. He did, however, eventually persuade King John and the Archbishop of Canterbury to replace the canons with monks. He also wrote a long letter to the Pope explaining the nature of the canons' "evil ways", urging him to support their change. An extract from his letter is something of an eye-opener: "While I was piercing the meaning of the Scriptures they would be singing their disgraceful songs … They publicly and openly preach fornication like Sodom its own sin, and they took as wives each other's daughters or nieces in the very face of popular infamy … Convert this sty of pigs, this hiding-place of Satan, into a temple of God, a dwelling place of the Holy Spirit."

Meanwhile, another dark hour occurred at the collegiate church of St Mary's at Stafford in 1258, when Roger de Meuland, Bishop of Coventry and Lichfield, led an armed force to impose discipline a month after his consecration. The Stafford canons were obviously expecting him, for they barricaded themselves in, leading to a subsequent struggle in which a number of the canons were wounded

---

Regarding Staffordshire's many medieval monastic houses, the table overleaf captures their order, founding and ownership. From a purely Norman perspective, though, we will return again to the story of St

Modwen, for it is alleged that some of Modwen's remains were transferred from the chapel on Andressey Island (which had been sacked by the Danes in 874), to Burton Abbey and a new shrine built there. Given the abbey's dedication is recorded as St Benedict and All Saints in 1008, this transference must have taken place after then, but before the abbacy of Leofric (1051-1066) who is alleged to have despoiled poor Modwen's shrine. However, there is also known to have been an altar dedicated to St Modwen in Burton Abbey by the time of Abbot Geoffrey Malaterra (1085-1094). As for the Norman connection, William the Conqueror himself was known to have visited Modwen's shrine on at least one occasion, one of which was likely to have coincided with an undated grant to the abbey. Perhaps he even visited in his final years, when he is reputed to have become repentant for what he had done to England as a result of his invasion and subsequent brutal suppression, particularly of the North.

From its re-founding in 1002 by Wulfric Spot, Burton Abbey also became Staffordshire's most important religious house, and it was certainly to become the richest. Its position at an important crossing of the River Trent brought it many important visitors throughout England's medieval centuries, and its Annals therefore provide an important commentary on life during these times. From William I onwards, many other kings visited, too, earning one particular room at the abbey the moniker of "The King's Chamber".

Burton Abbey also played its part in medieval politics, no more so than in 1322 when, during the rebellion of Thomas, 2nd Earl of Lancaster, against Edward II, the earl occupied and fortified the bridge over the Trent at Burton in an attempt to prevent the crossing of royal troops. In the meantime, he was said to have stored his "treasure" at Burton Abbey. However, on 10th March 1322, Edward's main force crossed the river at Walton-on-Trent and proceeded to the south side of Burton. The ruthless Lancaster moved his men outside the town, setting fire to it as he went. His intention was to face the king in open battle, but he withdrew northwards when he saw that he was heavily outnumbered. Lancaster was pursued by the king's men to Tutbury and eventually captured at the Battle of Boroughbridge in Yorkshire, after which he was executed on the king's orders. As for Lancaster's treasure, the Abbot of Burton Abbey was later accused of having retained it for himself – although nothing was ever proven! The abbot certainly claimed that all he had found was a single silver cup which he subsequently gave to the king. Interestingly, in 1831, a large quantity of silver coins that date to the 14th century were found in the River Dove, near Tutbury – thus suggesting that the abbot may have been telling the truth and that Lancaster had managed to get his treasure at least that far. Despite the accusation, though, Edward awarded Burton Abbey the advowsons of Tatenhill and Hanbury the following year, which had previously belonged to the Earl of Lancaster.

STAFFORDSHIRE'S MEDIEVAL MONASTIC HOUSES

Establishment	Order	Founding and Ownership
Baswich Priory	Augustinian	Founded c.1174 by Gerard Fitz Brian and dedicated to St Thomas the Martyr.
Blithbury Priory	Benedictine	Founded mid-12th century by Hugh de Ridware.
Brewood Priory	Benedictine	Founded as Black Ladies Priory in the mid-12th century.
Burton Abbey	Benedictine	Founded by Wulfric Spott in 1003 on the site of the former 7th century abbey founded by St Modwen.
Calwich Priory	Augustinian	Founded 1130 as a satellite cell of Kenilworth Priory. Dedicated to St Margaret.
Canwell Priory	Benedictine	Founded in 1149 by Geva (illegitimate daughter of Hugh, Earl of Chester) and dedicated to St Giles.
Croxden Abbey	Cistercian	Founded in 1176 by Bertram de Verdun, lord of Alton, and dedicated to the Virgin Mary.
Dieulacres Abbey	Cistercian	Founded by Ranulf de Blondeville, Earl of Chester, at Poulton, Cheshire, but moved to Abbey Green in 1214.
Dudley Priory	Cluniac	Founded in 1160 by Gervase Paganel as a dependency of Much Wenlock Priory, and dedicated to St James.
Farewell Priory	Benedictine	Founded in the 1140s by Roger de Clinton as a foundation for monks or hermits, but soon became a nunnery.
Hulton Abbey	Cistercian	Founded 1223 by Henry de Audley as a daughter house of Combermere Abbey.
Keele Preceptory	Knights Templar	Granted to the Knights Templar by Henry II in c.1168. Became a preceptory in the 13th century.
Lapley Priory	Benedictine	Founded in 1061 as an alien priory and a satellite house of St Remigius at Rheims.
Lichfield Greyfriars	Franciscan	Founded in 1237, possibly by Alexander Stavensby, Bishop of Coventry and Lichfield.
Newcastle-under-Lyme Blackfriars	Dominican	Founded before 1277.
Radmore Abbey	Cistercian	Originally a hermitage endowed by King Stephen in the late 1130s. The hermits dedicated their abbey to St Mary in the 1140s, while the Empress Matilda (Stephen's rival for the throne) persuaded the hermits to adopt the Cistercian order in around 1145.
Ranton Abbey	Augustinian	Founded in c.1150 by Robert fitz Noel as a cell of Haughmond Abbey in Shropshire.
Rocester Abbey	Augustinian	Founded between 1141 and 1146 by Richard Bacon, and dedicated to St Mary. Annexed to the Crown in 1237.
Stafford Greyfriars	Franciscan	Established by 1274, possibly by Edmund de Stafford, 1st Baron Stafford.
Stafford St Thomas	Augustinian	Priory founded in 1174 by Gerard fitz Brian and dedicated to St Thomas Becket, murdered at Canterbury Cathedral four years earlier.
Stone Priory	Augustinian	Founded in c.1135 in an existing church dedicated to St Wulfad.
Trentham Priory	Augustinian	Founded c.1100 by Hugh d'Avranches, 1st Earl of Chester, and became an Augustinian house in the 1150s under Ranulph, 4th Earl of Chester.
Tutbury Priory	Benedictine	Founded in 1080 by Henry de Ferrers as an alien priory and satellite of St Pierresur-Dives in Normandy.

Alas, when it came to the Dissolution in the 1530s, the nobility and gentry – who had once been the patrons of these religious institutions – suddenly partook in a mad scramble to acquire the then-redundant buildings from the Crown. And some weren't averse to laying it on, either. For example, Ranton Abbey was subject to at least three claims; from George Blount, from Simon Harcourt,

and best of all, from Lord Stafford, who had the nerve to plead his 12 children and his poverty. Meanwhile, the Bishop of Coventry and Lichfield requested St Thomas's Priory on behalf of "the poor boys, my nephews". As for the buildings, those that survived best became parish churches; many of the rest became derelict within decades, which is why, today, almost five hundred years on, only a few ruins remain.

One of the most important facets of Norman nobility life was hunting, and it was the Normans who created the majority of the hunting forests and royal forests in the late 11th century. Staffordshire had two royal forests. The largest was Cannock Forest, which stretched from Stafford in the north to Wolverhampton and Walsall in the south, and from the River Penk in the west to the River Tame in the east. A number of kings were known to have hunted there, including William II and Henry I, while Henry II replaced the hunting lodge at Cannock with a new one at Radmore in the 1150s. Later, in 1290, Roger de Meuland, the Bishop of Coventry and Lichfield, was granted a large area to the north of the forest around his own manors of Rugeley and Cannock, and it is this area that survives today as Cannock Chase. Staffordshire's other royal forest was Kinver Forest, down in the south-west of the county, and once again, it hosted William II and Henry II as well as King John. Similarly, a hunting lodge initially close to Kinver village was replaced by another in around 1190, a couple of miles to the north-east and which was built above the River Stour at Stourton. The lodge was home to the forest officials, and gradually increased in size over the years; it was then fortified in the 1220s and eventually became known as Stourton Castle.

Staffordshire was also home to the Forest of Needwood, which largely covered the territory in the east of the county between the Rivers Blithe, Dove and Trent. However, it wasn't classed as a royal forest as it was held by a subject and not a monarch – this initially being Henry de Ferrers who was granted the forest following the Norman Conquest. Following the demise of Robert de Ferrers in 1266, the forest changed ownership to the Earls of Lancaster, and therefore later became part of the Duchy of Lancaster in 1351 when the earls were elevated to dukes. There were also two smaller medieval hunting forests in Staffordshire. These were New Forest, which stretched from Tixall to Tunstall, and Brewood Forest which was located to the west of both the River Penk and Cannock Forest. However, both had been disafforested by 1204.

STAFFORDSHIRE'S "SURVIVING" MEDIEVAL RELIGIOUS HOUSES

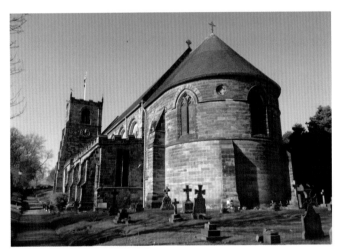

St Mary's church at Tutbury is the only surviving part of Tutbury Abbey, which was founded in 1080 by Henry de Ferrers.

Croxden Abbey founded in 1176 by Bertram de Verdun as a daughter house to its Cistercian mother house of Aunay-sur-Odon in Normandy.

The remains of Dudley Priory, founded in 1160 by Gervase Paganel as a dependency of Much Wenlock Priory. The priory was dedicated to St James.

Lapley All Saints' church is all that remains of Lapley Priory, originally founded in 1061 as an alien priory and a satellite house of St Remy, Reims.

Quirk Alert: *The Origin of Theses*

According to records, William I made an Englishman and former Saxon thegn, called Richard Chenvin, his keeper of Cannock Forest – an extremely important post and highly unusual that it didn't go to one of his Norman followers or councillors. Then again, those of a particularly suspicious mind might well question the origins of Richard Chenvin's forename and surname! It's just a theory, mind!

As was the case in most English counties, Staffordshire was dominated throughout the medieval period by a number of pre-eminent families who were extensive landowners and feudal lords. The most notable Staffordshire family were the de Staffords, who owned vast tracts of land around the county town from which they took their name. We've already discussed the Norman de Staffords, but in 1299, Edmund de Stafford (of the seventh generation) was summoned to parliament as a baron. His son, Ralph, was elevated to the 1st Earl of Stafford in 1351 for his military and diplo-

matic role in the Hundred Years' War. It was also Ralph who vastly extended the de Stafford estates through marriage and inheritance, adding the Audley estates which stretched from Norfolk to the Welsh border and then the Corbet estates in Shropshire. Further estates in the Midlands and the Welsh Marches were added by Edmund, 5th Earl of Stafford in the late 14th century, while his son, Humphrey, 6th Earl of Stafford became one of the wealthiest men in England and was created Duke of Buckingham in 1444.

By this stage, English nobility were inextricably tangled up in the Wars of the Roses, and Humphrey de Stafford was killed at the Battle of Northampton in 1460 while fighting for the Yorkists. His grandson, Henry, became the 2nd Duke of Buckingham, and he stuck with the Yorkists, supporting Richard of Gloucester's successful bid for the throne in 1483, and all of the dark shenanigans that went with it. It didn't do him much good, though, for he rebelled against Richard III and was executed without trial. A similar fate befell Edward, the third duke, too – executed by Henry VIII in 1521 on a fairly baseless charge of treason – at which point, the dukedom and all other titles were forfeited.

NORMAN FEATURES IN STAFFORDSHIRE

Above left to right: *St Mary's, Tutbury (south doorway); St Chad's, Stafford (west doorway); some of the fine capitals and mouldings at St Chad's, Stafford; this Norman font at Holy Cross church, Ilam, dates from 1120-1130.*

St Mary's, Tutbury (west doorway). It contains the earliest-known use of alabaster in England.

The Bagots also date back to the Conquest, and originally owned the manor at Bramshall, but then acquired Blithfield in 1362 through marriage, and here they still reside today. During medieval times, Sir John Bagot (1358-1437) was privy councillor to Henry IV and fought with Henry V at Agincourt in 1415. Sir John's son, Sir William Bagot, was a favourite of Richard II, while his grandson, Richard, was killed during the Battle of Bosworth whilst fighting for Henry Tudor.

Another family that date back to the Conquest are the Giffards, who held the manor of Chillington in Brewood from around 1178. Later Giffards were either knighted or held high positions of state in medieval England, such as Sir John Giffard who held various offices in the household of Henry VIII as well as being a leading political figure in Staffordshire. This probably accounted for why the Giffards inherited both Brewood Priory (known as Blackladies) and White Ladies Priory after the Dissolution.

Quirk Alert: *Affronted from Stafford*

The Bagots of Blithfield date back to the early Norman period with a Bagod recorded in Domesday Book (1086) as holding land at Bramshall, just west of Uttoxeter. Of course, there was also much inter-marrying between these powerful Staffordshire families, and one such example occurred in 1194 when Hervey Bagot married the sister and heiress of his feudal lord, Robert de Stafford. Hervey Bagot thus inherited the Stafford lands, and also changed his name to Stafford. However, this union was vehemently denied by Edward, Lord Stafford some four hundred years later in 1590. It having been suggested by Richard Bagot that he, Lord Stafford, was in fact also a Bagot, Lord Stafford wrote a long and affronted letter to Richard Bagot, accusing him of "untrue speeches you have said unto divers others although some drunken igno-rant herald by you corrupted therein hath soothed your lying" (basically, you've been telling lies to various drunkards). He then clarifies his position, as understood by himself as follows (take a deep breath…) "I do therefore answer you, that I do better know the descents and matches of my own lineage than any creature can inform me, for in all my records, pedigrees and arms from the first Lord Stafford that was possessed of this castle afore the Conquest bearing the very same coat I now do – the field gold a chevron gules – I cannot find that any Stafford hath married with a Bagot or they with him … we have been nine descents barons and earls of Stafford before any Bagot was known in this shire, for Busshe, Bagot and Green were but raised by King Richard the Second … No, surely I will not exchange my name of Stafford for the name of a bag of oats, for that is your name, 'Bag Ote'".

Other later families who rose to the top of the British nobility ladder included the Levesons of Wolver-hampton. Having made their fortune from the wool trade, the 16th century saw the family purchase landed estates through appropriate marriages, culminating in the acquisition of the Trentham estate, including the priory and all of its monastic lands shortly after the Dissolution. Meanwhile, acquiring the lands of Burton Abbey were the Pagets. William Paget had entered the service of Henry VIII in 1529, was knighted in 1537, became principal secretary of state in 1543… all of which helped him to acquire Burton Abbey and its monastic lands in 1546, as well as property on Cannock Chase that had previously belonged to the Bishop of Coventry and Lichfield.

By contrast, one important Staffordshire family who went untitled were the Sneyds of Keele. By the early 15th century, they owned a number of estates in north-west Staffordshire and over the border in Cheshire. Originally, their chief seat was at Bradwell near Newcastle-under-Lyme, and it wasn't until 1544 that William Sneyd bought the manor of Keele. Before that, the manor had belonged first to the Knights Templar until that organisation's persecution in the early 14th century, and then to the Knights Hospitaller until the Reformation of the early 16th century.

From the Norman Conquest to the beginning of the 14th century, Staffordshire's population gradually increased, while the county saw the agricultural indus-try continue to grow as more land was progressively brought under cultivation. Towns and villages increased in size, and many markets were established. Meanwhile, out in the wilds of the Staffordshire Moorlands, the local religious orders saw that the more remote areas were developed, too, and sheep farming, in particular, became hugely successful. By the 13th century, Croxden Abbey had around 7,200 sheep and Dieulacres around 4,800, while at Burton Abbey, the Benedictine monks there became the second largest producer of wool, thanks to their c.6,000 sheep. Many

of these religious houses exported their wool, including the Augustinians at Rocester and Trentham; even the Knights Templar at Keele had 260 sheep. In addition,

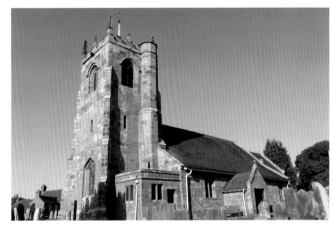

Chebsey All Saints' church is Grade I listed and dates mostly from the 12th and 13th centuries, although the tower is 15th century. Note the unusual external staircase turret, which is fairly common in southern England but rare in the Midlands.

Holy Trinity church at Eccleshall still retains some of its 11th century stones at the base of its tower, while the pillars and arches of its nave date from the late 12th century. Most of the rest dates from the 13th century with its striking clerestory added in the 15th century.

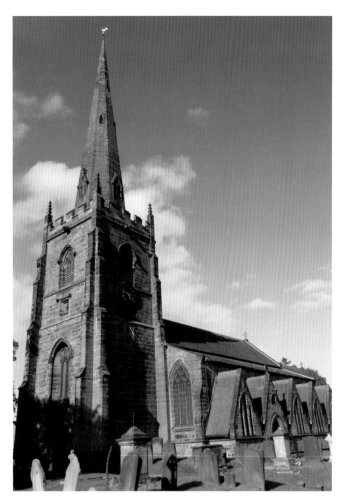

Parts of the Grade I-listed St Mary and St Chad's church at Brewood date back to the early 13th century, and most of the rest is medieval.

many of these orders had begun to breed cows, too, with Burton Abbey having large herds as early as the 12th century.

Alas, the steady growth of the 13th and early 14th centuries came to an abrupt end during the crisis years of 1315 to 1322 when a number of disasters occurred including cattle plague, sheep murrain and harvest failure followed by famine. As a result, the national population declined by at least 15 per cent. The chronicle of Croxden Abbey records that the year 1316 was "memorable for dearness, famine, disease and death", while a 1319 entry states that it was the year of "a plague or murrain of animals unseen and unheard of hitherto". At Keele in the 1320s, land was lying unused as tenants had departed due to poverty and famine. But then, as if that wasn't enough, in 1348 the Black Death began to wreak devastation throughout Western Europe and eventually reached Staffordshire in 1349. At Alrewas, the court rolls record nearly 60 deaths in May, 70 deaths in June and another 50 deaths in July. It was a similarly bleak outlook in most other Staffordshire villages and towns, too. Thus it was that by the 1350s many Staffordshire mines lay unworked, fields lay uncultivated and villages began to shrink, sometimes to extinction, thus explaining why modern maps some-

times pinpoint a "shrunken medieval village", or a "deserted medieval village". Overall, the population of England almost returned to its Domesday Book level of just over 2 million. As a result, concessions were made to tenants to encourage building repairs and improvements, as evidenced by those at Pattingham in the 1360s. As time went by, the difficulties of the lords of the manor enabled peasants to claim greater freedom, such as a refusal to accept their monopoly of milling on the Burton Abbey estates, while by the 1370s, it was acknowledged that the nuns of Farewell Priory had not received tenant services since 1349. Similarly, at Kinver, the tenants refused to perform their labour services of ploughing, mowing, haymaking and carrying. As a result, landlords were forced to lease out land that they had once cultivated for profit in order to cut their losses; those who continued to farm had to pay higher wages. Towards the end of the medieval period, the agricultural industry began to recover, and by the 15th century, cattle markets at Birmingham and Stafford demonstrated that stock farming had begun to flourish again.

Quirk Alert: *Give or Take 500 Years*
The earliest-dated gravestone in Bradley-in-the-Moors' churchyard is the tombstone dedicated to Anne Snape who was laid to rest in 1307. Or was she? For it turns out that the gravestone is actually 500 years younger, for the sculptor unwittingly dated the stone as 1307 instead of 1807!

In terms of other medieval industry, it is thought that mining was already in progress in the Biddulph area by the end of the 11th century, while there was definitely ironstone mining and ironworking in the Cheadle area by the late 12th century. There were also forges in the Cannock and Rugeley areas by 1273, and probably at Sedgley, too – and the latter was probably also home to coal mining before the end of the 13th century. By 1298, coal mining was also occurring side-by-side with ironstone mining at Tunstall and on Cannock Chase, as it was in the Wednesbury and West Bromwich areas by the early 14th century – although the pits were shallow and only near-surface mining took place. As for Staffordshire's famous pottery industry, kilns dating from around 1300 have been discovered at Sneyd Green near Burslem – and which no doubt took advantage of the local clay and the quick-burning coal. It is also thought that tiles were being made by the monks of nearby Hulton Abbey in the 14th century. Also being mined from the late 12th century in the Tutbury area was alabaster. We know this for sure because its employment on the west doorway of the priory church at Tutbury dates from 1160 to 1170 and is the earliest-known alabaster usage in England. Similarly, the effigy of Sir John de Hanbury in Hanbury church, dates from his death in 1303, making it the oldest usage of alabaster for an effigy in England, too.

LATE MEDIEVAL STAFFORDSHIRE

Lichfield House (nearside) in Bore Street, Lichfield, was built in 1510. There are four styles of timber framing on the façade which was a status symbol in Tudor times.

Also in Bore Street, Lichfield is Five Gables which dates from the late 16th century, and is a classic herringbone timber-framed house of the period.

Old Hall Country House at Madeley dates from the 16th century. Henry VIII's sister, Queen Margaret of Scotland stayed here, while a century later during the English Civil War, Charles II is believed to have hidden here from Parliamentarian soldiers.

Ancient High House at Stafford was built in 1594 by the Dorrington family. It is the largest timber-framed town house in England.

This Grade I-listed packhorse bridge at Great Haywood is known as Essex Bridge. It was built over the River Trent in 1550 by the Earl of Essex and is the longest surviving packhorse bridge in England, with 14 arches. That said, back in 1550, it actually had 42 arches, having been built over both river and meadow.

This is the gatehouse to what is known as the Manor House at West Bromwich, and which is thought to be the most complete example of a medieval timber-framed hall in Britain. The oldest part of the building is the Great Hall which is built with timbers that have been dendrochronologically dated to 1275, meaning that the Great Hall was probably built in the late 13th century. Additions were made to the hall in the 15th century, including a chapel, while further improvements were made by the Stanley family in the late 16th century, including a kitchen block and a gatehouse.

Other medieval industries included cloth-making, and glass-making. The earliest fulling mill in the county was recorded at Betley in the 1270s, while by the mid-14th century, Staffordshire had a glass industry of some repute and which was located in the area between Abbots Bromley and Rugeley. Indeed, Edward III ordered glass from Staffordshire for St Stephen's chapel in Westminster Palace in 1349.

Quirk Alert: *Take Breath, Pull Strong*

In 1513, Sir John Giffard of Chillington Hall had captive a leopard, apparently given to the Giffards as a gift. However, one day it escaped. Tracked by Sir John and his son, they found it poised to strike down a woman holding her baby in her arms. Armed with his crossbow, Sir John fitted an arrow, but before he released it, his son whispered, "take breath, pull strong". The arrow pierced the leopard in mid-strike. As the news travelled, Henry VIII got wind, and promptly granted Sir John a coat of arms that included leopard, hunter, cross-bow…and the words "take breath, pull strong". The arms survive thus to this day.

Quirk Alert: *Jack of Hilton*

In medieval times, Shareshill was home to an extraordinary feudal charter, whereby the lord of the neighbouring manor of Essington held his lands on the condition that each New Year's Day, he brought to Shareshill a live goose, and drove it three times around the central fire of Shareshill Hall. However, proceedings could not commence, until Jack of Hilton – a brass figure of a man leaning on his knee, and with his other hand on his breast – was placed into the fire, filled up with water, and had begun to issue steam from the hole in his mouth. Once the goose had been driven three times around the steaming Jack, the lord of Essington would present the bird to the lord of Shareshill, at which point the former would receive his title deed for another year's tenancy!

From the Elizabethan Era to the Eve of the Industrial Revolution

One of Staffordshire's lasting legacies of the period from the late 16th century to the 18th century is the number of stately homes that were built, usually by the resident members of the aristocracy. These people were generally members of the same families who had dominated medieval times. That said, the fortunes of the most prominent medieval family – the Staffords – were definitely in decline when Elizabeth I first sat on the throne in 1558. The Staffords had been created Dukes of Buckingham in 1444, but the 3rd Duke of Buckingham

was executed by Henry VIII in 1521 on a trumped-up charge, and the title became forfeit. Despite the barony of Stafford being restored in 1547, the family fortunes never reached their former level, and by 1640, the heir to the title surrendered it to Charles I in return for a measly £800. The barony and viscountcy were then given to Sir William Howard, who had married the sister and heiress of the 5th Baron Stafford, and who thus became the 1st Viscount Stafford. However, he became a victim of the Popish Plot of Titus Oates, and was executed for treason in 1680. The earldom later became extinct in 1762, although the barony was later revived in 1824 and survives to this day, with the title having passed to the Fitzherbert family in 1913. The current incumbent is the 15th Baron Stafford, and lives at Swynnerton Hall, a Grade I-listed house that was built in the late 1720s at Swynnerton, around 10 miles north of Stafford. This impressive Georgian mansion replaced the former hall which had been badly damaged during the English Civil War, when the staunchly Royalist Fitzherberts found their home irreparably damaged by Parliamentary forces.

Also effectively destroyed during the English Civil War in similar circumstances was the medieval Stafford Castle. Still held by the Stafford family in the mid-17th century, Lady Isabel Stafford, widow of Edward, Lord Stafford, conducted a staunch defence of her seat against attacking Parliamentary forces. However, it was so badly damaged that it was eventually abandoned and the Parliamentary committee at Stafford ordered its destruction. The castle that stands on the same motte today was largely rebuilt in 1813 in the Gothic Revival Style by Sir George Jerningham, the then-claimant to the Stafford barony.

By the Elizabethan era, Tutbury Castle had passed from the de Ferrers family to the Earls of Lancaster, although it had fallen into disrepair – a fact constantly bemoaned by Mary Queen of Scots, who was held captive there on four occasions between 1569 and 1585. Among other complaints about dampness and general conditions, she was particularly upset by her room being directly above the privy! The castle was later garrisoned for Charles I during the English Civil War, but like so many others was slighted after the war. However on this occasion, not all was destroyed, and after the Restoration, some of the rooms were repaired.

By the Elizabethan era, Chartley Castle was also in ruins, and the Devereuxs had built a moated and battlemented timber mansion nearby that became known as Chartley Hall. Robert Devereaux, 2nd Earl of Essex, became a favourite of Queen Elizabeth and also held an increasing influence over the House of Commons. However, he was placed under house arrest following a poor campaign in Ireland during the Nine Years' War in 1599, while in 1601, he led a failed coup d'état against the government and was subsequently executed for treason. The earldom was also forfeited, although his son, Robert, was restored as the 3rd earl on the accession of James I in 1603. He later became a Parliamentary commander-in-chief during the English Civil War, but died childless in 1646 and Chartley eventually passed to the Shirley family. Sir Robert Shirley was created Lord Chartley and later Baron Ferrers in 1677 and Earl Ferrers in 1711.

It was also at Chartley that Mary Queen of Scots' fate was sealed, when she was held there over Christmas 1585. She had the misfortune to trust the duplicitous Gilbert Giffard, latest in a long line of Catholic Giffards of Chillington Hall. Allegedly the intermediary between Mary and the conspirators of the Babington Plot, he was secretly passing on all letters to Queen Elizabeth's master of spies, Francis Walsingham, while also keeping Philip of Spain in the loop for his support and subsequent invasion, should they succeed in murdering Elizabeth and crowning Mary. Of course, Mary's reward for trusting Giffard was the exposure of the Babington Plot and her execution at Fotheringhay the following year. As for Chartley Hall, it was eventually destroyed by fire in 1781; the present house

dates from 1847, when it was rebuilt in an Elizabethan style.

Bucking the trend of Royalist stronghold and Parliamentarian siege was Alton Castle, although this Parliamentary stronghold suffered much damage during the war, too. Normal service is resumed with the Bagots of Blithfield, who were staunch Royalists – and which meant confiscation of their estates after the war. By this stage, the south range of Blithfield Hall existed, having been built in the late 16th century by

STUNNING SHUGBOROUGH

Shugborough Hall. This Grade I-listed house was initially built in the late 17th century by William Anson. The two flanking pavilions were added in the 1740s by Thomas Anson.

Shugborough Hall from the rear.

The gardens behind the hall include what is known as "The Ruin", shown here in the background, and which dates from c.1750. Originally much larger, with a pigeon house and a classical colonnade, much of it was washed away in floods during the late 18th century.

The Chinese House in the background was built in 1747 on an island in an artificial canal reached by a pair of bridges. Both the Chinese House and the Garden Bridge (shown here) are Grade I listed.

Richard Bagot. It was built in typical Elizabethan style with tall clustered chimneys and steep-pitched gables – although a Gothic façade was added in the 1820s.

Arguably the finest of Staffordshire's stately homes is Shugborough Hall, built in the late 17th century by William Anson. The predecessor manor house had been owned by the Bishops of Lichfield until the Dissolution of the Monasteries in the late 1530s. It then passed through several owners before it was purchased in 1624 by William Anson, a lawyer from Dunston. It was his grandson, William, who built the three-storey building which still forms the central part of the hall today, and his eldest son, Thomas Anson, further extended the house in the 1740s, adding two pavilions either side of the central block. Meanwhile, his younger brother, George, went on to become Admiral George Anson, was created Lord Anson in 1747, and then First Lord of the Admiralty in 1751. Several generations further on, in 1806, Thomas Anson was created 1st Viscount Anson, while the 2nd Viscount was also created Earl of Lichfield in the coronation honours of William IV.

Next up is Ilam Hall in the Staffordshire Moorlands. The Ilam estate was acquired by the Port family in the 16th century and they owned it for more than 250 years. The first Ilam Hall was built in the 16th century but was sold to David Pike Watts in 1809. On his death in 1816,

the estate was inherited by his daughter and her husband Jesse Watts-Russell. High Sheriff of Staffordshire in 1819 and Conservative MP for the rotten borough of Gatton, Watts-Russell demolished the old hall and then commissioned James Trubshaw to build a new hall to designs by John Shaw between 1821 and 1826. Alas, much of this hall was demolished in the 1920s before Sir Robert McDougall bought the estate and donated it to the National Trust in 1934. Since then, the main remaining part of the hall has been used as a Youth Hostel and the grounds have been open to the public.

Next, the Ingestre estate passed to the Chetwynd family in the 14th century, although it was nearly 300 years later before Sir Walter Chetwynd (another High Sheriff of Staffordshire [1607]) built the red brick manor house there. The house was renovated in the early 19th century but was badly damaged by fire and largely rebuilt in 1882 – while thirteen years later in 1895, Charles Chetwynd-Talbot, 20th Earl of Shrewsbury, founded the Staffordshire Polo Club at Ingestre Hall. The estate was eventually sold in 1960 and today is a Residential Arts Centre.

Finally, other privately owned Grade I-listed houses from this period, many of which have been altered or added to at a later date, are as follows:

Grade I Stately Home	Location	Build	Founding Family
Barlaston Hall	Barlaston	1756-1758	Mills
Broughton Hall	Broughton	1637	Broughton
Caverswall Castle	Caverswall	1615	Caverswall
Chillington Hall	Brewood	1724	Giffard
Hilton Hall	Hilton	1720-1730	Vernon
Patshull Hall	Pattingham	1730s	Astley/Pigot
Swynnerton Hall	Swynnerton	c.1725	Fitzherbert
Whitmore Hall	Whitmore	1676	Mainwaring
Weston Park	Weston-under-Lizard	1670s	Wilbraham
Wootton Lodge	Ellastone	c.1600	Fleetwood

Part of Ilam Hall, gardens and its stunning Peak District setting. The original 16th century hall was rebuilt in the 1820s by Jesse Watts-Russell, but much of it was demolished in the 1920s. What remains is now home to the Youth Hostel Association.

The 16th and 17th centuries were renowned first for religious intolerance in the 16th century, and then for a later softening towards non-conformism which saw a whole range of diverse denominations blossom in the late 17th century and which accelerated throughout the 18th and 19th centuries. Prior to Elizabeth I acceding to the throne in 1558, a certain Ralph Baynes, Bishop of Coventry and Lichfield from 1554 to 1559, and zealous anti-Protestant, had burnt at the stake several alleged heretics in his diocese, three of them at Lichfield. However, with the death of the Catholic Mary I in 1558, the tables were gradually turned, starting with the Elizabethan Settlement of 1559 which re-established the Church of England's independence from Rome and declared Elizabeth the Supreme Governor of the Church of England, while the Act of Uniformity outlined what form the English Church should take, including the re-establishment of the Book of Common

MASTER ALABASTER

Above left: The alabaster tomb of Sir John Giffard (d.1556) and his two wives who lie on either side of him in the church of St Mary and St Chad at Brewood. Around the base of the tomb are effigies of all of his children, many represented in swaddling clothes, indicating that they died as infants. Above centre: The alabaster tomb of Sir Thomas Giffard (d.1660), also with his two wives on either side, and his children around the base. In fact, along with other Giffard tombs at the church, there are 49 infants alone carved into the respective bases. Above right: The 17th century alabaster tomb of Robert Meverell and his wife Elizabeth of Throwley Hall in the church of the Holy Cross at Ilam.

Prayer. At this time, Staffordshire – which had a strong bias towards Catholicism, particularly amongst its gentry – was declared "recalcitrant". Many of the gentry continued to provide their own chaplains who would say Mass within their homes, and this non-conformity continued throughout Elizabeth I's reign despite increasingly heavy penalties ranging from fines, to imprisonment, to death. One Staffordshire martyr was Robert Sutton, the son of a Burton carpenter, and who had initially been ordained in the Anglican Church. However, he resigned from his post and went to study in the Low Countries, became ordained as a Catholic priest in 1578, and then returned to England, one of many who were part of a new wave of priests who had been trained abroad before returning to minister to their Catholic followers in flagrant abuse of the law. Sutton was also one of many who were caught; in his particular case it was during Mass at the home of Erasmus Wolseley of Stafford one day in 1588, and both he and his congregation were originally condemned to death. Due to a public outcry, the members of the congregation were reprieved, but Sutton was executed in a horrendous way, with reports stating that "the villainous butcher" known as Moseley, instead of completing the execution by cutting Sutton's head off at the neck, drove his axe through the still-conscious priest's mouth.

Despite this terrible persecution, many of the nobility of Staffordshire remained staunchly Catholic, none more so than the Giffards of Chillington Hall in Brewood parish. Nevertheless, the wily Giffards survived and many of the Elizabethan and Jacobean Giffards were commemorated by a series of stunning alabaster tombs in the chancel of the church of St Mary the Virgin and St Chad at Brewood. The Giffards also maintained Catholic chapels on their estate and when, in 1668, the first Catholic bishop for the Midlands (a post also known as vicar apostolic) was appointed, the post went to Bonaventure Giffard, a member of the Wolverhampton branch of the family. It was also the status of the Giffards that helped make Wolverhampton the focal point of Catholics in Staffordshire, and which

came to be known as "Little Rome" in the mid-17th century, while also prompting the local Puritan preacher to state in 1624 that here "Rome's snaky brood roosted and rested themselves more warmer and safer and with greater countenance... than in any other part of the kingdom." By 1688, six Jesuits were living at Wolverhampton's Deanery House, maintaining a very popular chapel and a school attended by around 50 local boys. Alas, that particular year was also marked by the Glorious Revolution, and the overthrowing of Catholic King James II in favour of Protestant William and Mary. This saw the aforementioned Deanery House ransacked by a mob and most of its library books symbolically burnt in the market place. It was another forty years before a replacement house and chapel were built, and somewhat inevitably this was largely funded by the next generation of Giffards – a handsome Georgian building which survives today and is known as Giffard House.

Another prominent Catholic family of the 16th and 17th centuries were the Fowlers who had acquired the former Augustinian Priory of St Thomas's at Stafford in 1543, following its Dissolution in 1538. They soon established a chapel there which lasted for nearly 200 years. It was here that the first Elizabethan Bishop of Coventry and Lichfield, Thomas Bentham, complained in 1564 that Brian Fowler was harbouring the Catholic ex-bishop of Peterborough, claiming that "divers lewd priests have resort thither". Antipathy had softened somewhat by the time that Dr George Witham, Catholic bishop for the Midlands stayed there from 1703 to 1716, while the house was also home to numerous chaplains who served the family over the decades.

As for the common people of Staffordshire, one particular report from 1562 found that "large numbers of people are generally evil-inclined towards religion and forbear coming to church and participating of the sacraments, using also very broad speeches in alehouses and elsewhere". By 1780, it was recorded that there were 3,000 Catholics living in the Staffordshire portion of the diocese of Coventry and Lichfield, and it is thought that by this stage, Catholics made up around a quarter of the population of Wolverhampton; other centres were to be found at Brewood, Draycott in the Moors, Sedgley, Stone and Swynnerton.

By the early 17th century, Protestant dissent was spreading throughout the county, too, with a strong following located at Burton upon Trent. It was also a man from Burton, Edward Wightman, who became the last heretic to be burned at the stake in England. This occurred at Lichfield on 11th April, 1612, and was justified based on some of Wightman's unorthodox views. Also gaining strength in the 17th century amongst the Staffordshire clergy was Presbyterianism, and in 1648, 36 ministers and two schoolmasters signed the Testimony, a Presbyterian declaration against the principle of religious toleration. By 1644, a number of Baptists were also active, particularly in the north-east of the county, and by the 1650s, Stafford, too, had developed a large congregation, including the military governor, Colonel Henry Danvers. It was also in 1651 that the founder of Quakerism, George Fox, preached in both Burton and Lichfield, and also in Cauldon in the Staffordshire Moorlands, an area where the movement became particularly strong. However, by 1660, a new wave of persecution of dissenters had begun with the eviction of clergy from the Anglican Church who held Puritan views, and it is thought that nearly half of the parish clergy of Staffordshire were evicted at this time. Indeed, during

The summit of Mow Cop saw the birth of Primitive Methodism in 1807 when open-air meetings were held here.

These three timber-framed houses on High Street, Kinver, date from the 17th century.

The Manor House at Harlaston dates from c.1600, with later 17th century extensions.

one visitation by Bishop Hackett in 1668, 111 of 199 alleged offenders were excommunicated. However, despite the fact that the Toleration Act wasn't passed until 1689, an ecclesiastical census of 1676 identified 155 nonconformists in Stafford, 73 in Ipstones and 43 in Grindon. Sadly, though, the 1689 Toleration Act excluded both Unitarians and Roman Catholics, while leaning favourably towards Protestant dissenters – authorising their meetings so long as they registered their meeting houses. Within days of the Act, four houses in Newcastle-under-Lyme were registered; indeed, between 1689 and 1750, there were 95 Staffordshire registrations of meeting houses, 97 from 1750 to 1800, and 874 from 1800 to 1900. This didn't leave these dissenting meeting houses immune to abuse, though, and many were wrecked by mobs in the decades after the Act, while leading dissenters themselves were often targeted by mobs. One classic example of this was when the great John Wesley preached in Wednesbury in 1743, and the mob threatened to "knock his brains out!"

Despite Wesley's early challenges, Methodism soon flourished, particularly in Staffordshire's industrial areas, and it was at Tipton in 1755 that the first Methodist chapel in the county was built, while the very area that had threatened Wesley's brains in 1743, Wednesbury, had 840 registered members by 1818 and 14 meeting centres. Similarly, the first Methodist chapel in the Potteries was built at Burslem in 1766; by 1801 there were five while by 1851 there were 46!

The success of Methodism saw further denominations appear and flourish. For example, there were 19 Congregational chapels in Staffordshire by 1800 and 46 by 1850, while various factions of Methodism also appeared. This included the Methodist New Connexion, formed in 1797 and one of its leading figures was Job Ridgway, a pottery manufacturer from Hanley who helped open a New Connexion chapel in the town in 1798, while Primitive Methodism was thought to have been born shortly after on Mow Cop, near Biddulph, following a series of open-air meetings organised by local carpenter Hugh Bourne and potter William Clowes.

Times finally improved for Catholics at around this time, too, following the Act of 1791 which legalised

Catholic chapels. Thirteen were promptly registered in Staffordshire. In 1850, Catholic dioceses were first established while by 1884, there were 51 Catholic churches and chapels and the Staffordshire Catholic population was estimated at around 33,500.

When the English Civil War broke out on 22nd August 1642, Staffordshire was not in the immediate line of fire and there was very little mobilisation of troops; indeed, as late as November the Sheriff of Staffordshire was still striving to keep the county out of the war, declaring that any riots or unlawful assemblies would be dealt with by special forces, whose officers included both future Royalists and Parliamentarians. When people eventually did start to take sides, many were influenced or coerced by their local gentry who, in turn, were largely influenced by religion; for example, Edward Leigh of Rushall was a strong Presbyterian and hence took the side of Parliament while most Catholics chose to support the king – so somewhat inevitably this included the Giffards of Chillington as well as the Lanes of Bentley. Meanwhile, Lord Paget of Beaudesert had already switched sides, having originally supported Parliament, but then changing his loyalty "out of conscience". He subsequently raised a regiment that fought at the Battle of Edgehill in 1642. In contrast to their Catholic counterparts, only 12 of the Protestant Staffordshire gentry supported the king, with the other 40 or so backing Parliament, while their number also included Robert Deveraux, Earl of Essex and appointed a Parliamentary commander-in-chief. An interesting pocket of Parliamentary support came from the Staffordshire Moorlands, led by a person known as "the Grand Juryman", and who led his troops, armed with birding guns, pitchforks, clubs and scythes, in an unsurprisingly unsuccessful attempt to displace the royal garrison at Stafford.

As happened in most other counties, both Royalists and Parliamentarians took advantage of Staffordshire villages, demanding free quarter and eating and drink- ing the locals out of house and home, while other villages – such as Hatherton near Cannock – were forced to pay levies to the Royalist forces there. Indeed, it wasn't unusual for villages to end up paying for both sides when areas changed hands. For example, the constable's 1643-44 accounts for Mavesyn Ridware, records payments to the Royalists at Lichfield of £109 18s 0d, and to the Parliamentarians of Stafford of £141 3s 10d. In terms of "free quarter", though, the best insight probably comes from a quote by Queen Henrietta Maria as she brought up reinforcements through Walsall: "I shall stay here tomorrow because our soldiers are very weary and also because they have got so much plunder they cannot well march with their bundles". Similarly, a certain Dame Joyce Blundell was later to complain after the Restoration, that as she was travelling through Lichfield during the war, the royalist governor of the garrison there, Colonel Richard Bagot, seized all her plate, to the value of £2,000, claiming that his garrison would mutiny if they were not paid!

> **Quirk Alert:** *Brereton vs. Brereton*
>
> *At the start of the English Civil War, Lord Brereton of Brereton Hall in Cheshire deemed Biddulph Hall to be more defensible against attacking Parliamentary forces. As it turned out, the force sent against him to Biddulph was commanded by none other than his uncle, Sir William Brereton. Anyone in any doubt about Sir William's resolve then thought again when he ordered Roaring Meg up from Stafford – as did Brereton the nephew, who promptly surrendered before the most infamous cannon of the English Civil War could be used against him.*

Towards the end of 1642, Charles marched twice through Staffordshire. In mid-September, he spent a night at Tutbury Castle before proceeding to Stafford via Uttoxeter, all the time looking to recruit new troops to his army – and those who refused to join at Uttoxeter were rewarded by having their houses burned down. Whether word had travelled on ahead, he received a better welcome and recruitment hit-rate in Stafford, before the Royalist army marched to Shrewsbury. Here, his forces were further bolstered by recruits from Wales, and thereafter they marched on London, this time passing through South Staffordshire en-route. Typically, Wolverhampton was plundered as they passed through, despite the inhabitants having already given generously to the Royalist cause.

It was also during the autumn of 1642 that Dudley Castle, Tamworth, Lichfield Close and Stafford were seized by the Royalists. Tutbury Castle was already in their hands, while Chillington Hall was fortified and garrisoned by the Giffards, as was Keele Hall by the Sneyds – although the latter fell to the Parliamentarians in February 1643. As for Burton upon Trent, the town assumed a similar strategic importance to the one it had held during the Wars of the Roses – as the bridge over the Trent there was still the only one for miles around – and it actually changed hands a number of times during the war.

Site of the Battle of Hopton Heath which took place in 1643 during the first phase of the English Civil War.

The church of St Mary the Virgin at Ingestre dates from 1676, and was built for Sir Walter Chetwynd of Ingestre Hall. It is thought to be the only church outside of London to have been designed by Sir Christopher Wren.

By the spring of 1643, Lichfield Close had been captured by Parliamentarians, but they only held it for a month, with Prince Rupert re-securing the Close for the king on 20th April, after which the Royalists retained it until the end of the war. On the original capture of the Close, the Royalists were allowed to march out of Lichfield to Stafford where they were joined by the Earl of Northampton who had arrived too late to help prevent Lichfield's surrender. However, the Parliamentarians were also eyeing Stafford, given its status of county town and its strategic importance, and thus Sir John Gell and Sir William Brereton, respective commanders of the Parliamentary forces in Derbyshire and Cheshire, laid their plans. What resulted on 19th March, 1643, was the Battle of Hopton Heath, around 3 miles to the north-east of Stafford (the battle is covered in detail in the *Quirky Staffordshire [Hopton]* chapter of this book). The result of the battle was inconclusive, but having retreated back to Stafford, the Royalists didn't hold the county town for long; on the night of 16th May 1643, the town was captured whilst most of them slept, and many prisoners were taken. Lady Stafford of Stafford Castle held out for considerably longer, largely thanks to her medieval defensive works – but like so many strongholds used by the Royalists during the English Civil War, the castle was captured and slighted after the war.

Also captured by the Parliamentarians during the summer of 1643 were both Tamworth Castle and Eccleshall Castle, the latter being a seat of the bishop of Coventry and Lichfield, and yet another Royalist garrison – although it did hold out for eight weeks before surrendering. By contrast, Leek fell to the Royalists on 28th November 1643 and Lapley House on 21st December, while by the spring of 1644, Burton upon Trent had been taken by the Parliamentarians, briefly lost again, and then re-taken and garrisoned for Parliament for the remainder of the war. Although they were unable to oust the Royalists from Dudley Castle, the Parliamentarians were now gaining the upper hand

in the war countrywide. By 1645, Charles I was aware that he was losing, and he attempted to re-take the North, starting with Chester. This saw his army march through Staffordshire via Himley and Bushbury and then up the county's western border towards Market Drayton. However, events elsewhere forced him to re-direct his forces towards Leicester, where two brutal sieges took place within two weeks of each other, whilst in between, the king suffered a crushing defeat on 14th June 1645 at the Battle of Naseby in Northamptonshire. The king then led his battered and beaten forces west again, passing through Lichfield and Wolverhampton en-route to Hereford. By early 1646, there was very little Royalist defiance left in Staffordshire, and the last remnants fell when Tutbury Castle surrendered in April 1646 and Dudley Castle followed suit on 13th May. Lichfield Close held out for a little longer, despite the king's instructions to surrender, and that disobedience saw the destruction of Lichfield Cathedral's central spire before the besieged finally threw in the towel on 10th July 1646.

Quirk Alert: *The Cost of War*
When the Parliamentarians gave the order to destroy Stafford Castle on 22nd December 1643, the order was carried out "with the loss of one crowbar"!

The second phase of the English Civil War took place between 1648 and 1649, following the escape of Charles I. However, this time around, he was captured by Oliver Cromwell's New Model Army. He was tried, convicted and executed for high treason on 30th January 1649. The monarchy was subsequently abolished and the Commonwealth of England established in its place. However, there was still further English Civil War activity in Staffordshire during the third phase of the war (1649-1651) when Charles II attempted to re-gain the throne. Defeated at the Battle of Worcester on 3rd September 1651, Charles fled north into south-western Staffordshire. After several close calls, including hiding in an oak tree at Boscobel on 6th September, he managed to get himself to Bentley Hall, where the Royalist Lane family helped him to escape while disguised as a servant (see *Quirky Staffordshire [Bentley]* for more on that story). Thus ended the English Civil War, after which, staunch Royalists weren't treated as badly as you might think. For sure, their properties were sequestered and they had to pay to win them back… and the cost went up depending upon how great the offender's degree of delinquency was deemed to be! So Sir Richard Leveson of Trentham, the governor of Dudley Castle, was fined the most at £9,846 – but, of course, the majority were extremely wealthy and therefore things didn't really change that much for those Royalist landowners, irrespective of their degree of delinquency!

Quirk Alert: *Half-Baked Duke*

Following the Battle of Worcester in 1651, it was not only Charles II who had to hide in bizarre places, but his senior officers too. One of them was George Villiers, the 2nd Duke of Buckingham, who having fallen from his horse and broken his arm, was taken in by a woman at Armsdale. When the Parliamentary soldiers searched the house, the woman hid Villiers in her oven where she assured the soldiers her bread was baking!

However, once Charles II was restored to the throne in 1660, woe-betide any Parliamentary commander-in-chief if they were still alive. As for those few who signed the death warrant of Charles' father, a special death lay in wait for them. Staffordshire had two signatories, both found guilty of regicide. John Bradshaw, M.P. for Stafford and Cheshire in 1654 and steward of Newcastle-under-Lyme from 1641 to his death in 1659, was the president of the court which tried Charles I and sentenced him to death. His own natural death was rather timely. Thomas Harrison was not so fortunate. Four times mayor of Newcastle-under-Lyme, and a major-general in the Parliamentary army of 1648, he was among the first to sign the death warrant of Charles I. His reward was to be hanged, drawn and quartered at Charing Cross.

Towards the end of the medieval period, lords of the manor had begun to enclose common and arable pasture for personal use, perhaps turning it over for grazing sheep. This obviously removed such land from the communal system and often provoked violent opposition. A government inquiry of 1517 showed that only 488 acres of land had been enclosed since 1489, mostly for pasture, and also evidenced minimal eviction of tenants. However, starting in the 16th century,

Quirk Alert:
The Village Methuselah and RHIP!

Arthur Mee's King's England talks of William Wakeley, who appears on a wooden tablet at Adbaston's church having died in 1714 at the age of 125. Especially for the scripture buffs amongst you, Mee wryly names him as the "village Methuselah"! He also doubts Horton's Mary Brooks, aged 119. Meanwhile, Mee's chapter on Baswich describes the chancel of Holy Trinity church as being home to a pair of huge double-decker pews raised on pillars. Apparently, one set was for the squire and came equipped with a fireplace, while the other, for the servants, was fireplace-less! Better still, the squire had a staircase from his pew to his servants, cut through the 16th century tomb of John Fowler and his wife!

The River Dove was the favourite haunt of Izaak Walton and Charles Cotton in the 17th century and inspired Walton's classic book, The Compleat Angler *in 1653. It was Cotton who completed the second volume of the book in which he writes of Viator's Bridge, shown above. The dialogue takes place between Piscator (a fisherman) and Viator (a traveller) as they descend to the bridge, with Viator saying: "What's here, a bridge? Do you travel in wheelbarrows in this country?"*

increasingly large tracts of forest land were being enclosed thus denying those enjoying common rights there. So while in 1511, John Giffard enclosed a mere 5 acres on his Chillington estate to make a park, his descendant Thomas Giffard, wiped out the whole village of Chillington in 1760, just to extend that very same park! Similarly brutal was John Whorwood of Stourton Castle. When he enclosed part of Iverley Common in Kinver Forest in order to establish a sheepcot there, he refused to allow the commoners to do the same – and when they did, he simply set his dogs upon them. Similar attempts to enclose Needwood Forest in the mid-17th century led to fierce opposition and rioting.

Not all land enclosure was controversial though. For example, at Tunstall in 1613, an agreement was made between nine freeholders to divide the six open fields there between them. However, by 1700, many of Staffordshire's fields had been enclosed in this way, and much of the rest were about to get eaten up by a number of Acts of Parliament. The first was in 1766 at Elford, when the four open fields there along with several meadows were enclosed courtesy of an Act passed in 1765. By 1800, there were very few open fields left, although the two biggest operations were still to happen, these being the enclosure of 9,400 acres of Needwood Forest in 1811 under an Act of 1801, and the enclosure of 3,000 acres of Cannock Forest during the 1860s. Finally, one of the last areas to be enclosed by an Enclosure Act was at Warslow and Lower Elkstone in 1839.

There were, of course, always losers as a result of Enclosure Acts. For example, when Needwood was enclosed in 1811, John Alcock a small proprietor from Marchington, lost all his common rights in the forest, but was offered a meagre 2.5 acre plot for which he had to pay £11 up front, and then on top of that he also had to fence the enclosure at his own expense! Some of the justification offered also makes ironic reading. At Ipstones, it was announced that the enclosure there would "put a stop to many encroachments… and will keep many bad people out of the neighbourhood", while at Needwood it was justified because "an extensive forest… affords temptations to idleness and dishonesty".

Quirk Alert: *The Sleep Rouser*

In 1725, a certain John Rudge of Trysull (and who didn't go on to become Port Vale manager), left one pound a year to be paid to somebody who would chase dogs out of the church, and would also rouse worshippers who were nodding off. The Sleep Rouser was thus armed with a staff that had a fox's tail at one end – for tickling the faces of sleeping ladies – and a knob at the other end – for whacking men on the head!

Conversely, there were success stories. For example, thirty years after the enclosure at Elford, it was claimed that about 500 out of the 1,900 acres had been given over to tillage, and that this was bringing in as much grain to market as the whole parish had previously, while the quantity of cheese made was three times its previous amount and the quantity of beef and mutton ten times more. Talking of cheese, by the 18th century, the lower Dove Valley had become a hotbed for dairy farming, and as a result of production levels, the London cheesemongers set up an agency at Uttoxeter, spending as much as £500 a day. Meanwhile, their butter was sold in long cylindrical pots which were allegedly ripe for subterfuge. These "moorlandish cheats" as the late 17th century author Robert Plot describes them, were apparently prone to putting the good butter on top and the bad at the bottom – or of sometimes only filling the top and leaving the rest empty!

The eventual success of Burton's brewery industry was dependent on its ability to export beer, so it was therefore very significant when William Lord Paget obtained an Act of Parliament to extend navigation on

Statue of a cooper in Cooper's Square shopping centre, Burton upon Trent, acknowledging the importance of brewing to the town.

the River Trent from Nottingham to Burton in 1699. He eventually leased his rights to George Hayne in 1711, and Hayne opened the River Trent Navigation the following year, constructing a wharf and other buildings close to the site of the former abbey. This opened up the world to Burton's beer, as the product could now be shipped down the Trent to Hull, from where it was exported to London and other ports all over the North Sea and Baltic Sea, including those of Russia and Prussia. By the second half of the 18th century a number of breweries were flourishing, by which stage Burton was also on the Trent and Mersey Canal and had a more direct outlet to the Atlantic via Liverpool and, in particular, to the gradually expanding British Empire. Prime amongst the town's products was Burton India Pale Ale, specially brewed to keep during the long sea voyage to India. In terms of what makes the ale so special, it is down to the quality of the local water, as the surrounding hills contain minerals that greatly assist the brewing process and also helps to preserve the beer for longer, thus enabling export around the world. Elsewhere, the glass industry was still thriving during these times, although by the 1580s, it had moved to the Eccleshall area, and then moved again to the Staffordshire/Worcestershire border near Stourbridge in the early 17th century – perhaps attracted there by the local coal and fireclay. Of course, the three Staffordshire industries that were destined to become world-famous – iron, coal and pottery – were also progressing nicely throughout these times, too. Ironmaking was revolutionised by the introduction of the blast furnace, with the first one introduced in the early 1560s by William, 1st Baron Paget, at his ironworks on Cannock Chase. The industry also benefitted from the first slitting mills, which mechanised the process of cutting rod iron into lengths for the nailers – particularly useful in Staffordshire as nailmaking had become a key industry in the south of the county by the 1580s, and at one point employed 2,000 men and boys in Sedgley alone while it has also been quoted that by the 1620s there were 20,000 smiths of all sorts within a 10 mile radius of Dudley Castle. Twenty years later during the English Civil War, it was these smiths who supplied the Royalists with cannon, swords, pikes, guns and shot. As for the earliest recorded slitting mill in the Midlands, this was the one being worked by Thomas Chetwynd in 1623 at Rugeley – and where today, as a result, there is actually a small village of around 300 people called Slitting Mill. Also established in the 1620s was a slitting mill at Kinver. It was built by Richard Foley who went on to manufacture iron, and his family became important ironmasters throughout Staffordshire until the 18th century.

Quirk Alert: *Royally Empressed*

Brewing at Burton upon Trent first came to national attention when it was discovered that the secret letters being passed between Mary Queen of Scots and the conspirators of the Babington Plot at Chartley, were secreted away in barrels of Burton ale! Meanwhile, by the late 18th century, Burton's ale had become widely exported around the world. Indeed, Russian Empress, Catherine the Great, who reigned from 1762 to 1796, is reported to have been "immoderately fond" of Burton ale, while the inhabitants of Danzig celebrated Napoleon's departure with pints of Burton beer!

The iron industry also began to flourish in the south of the county, thanks to the local supplies of iron ore as raw material, coal as fuel, limestone as flux and fireclay for the furnaces – although the coking of coal didn't come into play until Abraham Darby's breakthrough of 1709 in neighbouring Shropshire. In Staffordshire, though, it was another man, John Wilkinson (1728-1808), who pioneered the manufacture of cast iron. He was also the inventor of a precision boring machine that could bore cast iron cylinders, and which thus became known as the first machine tool, while he also developed a blowing device for blast furnaces that allowed higher temperatures thus increasing their efficiency. Wilkinson also built the first of his Black Country furnaces at Bradley near Bilston between 1757 and 1758, using coke smelting.

By 1796, there were 14 blast furnaces in the Black Country, producing 13,210 tons of pig iron; by 1810,

those numbers had risen to 55 furnaces and 115,000 tons. However, ironmaking wasn't confined to the Black Country in Staffordshire, as it also flourished on a smaller scale in the north of the county, too. The first furnace was erected in 1768 at Apedale, to the west of Newcastle-under-Lyme, while the later focal point for the industry was 4 miles to the east at Etruria. Also in the vicinity, Keele was home to one of only two frying pan manufacturers, while Walsall became famous for ironworking associated with horsemanship, such as the production of spurs, bridles and stirrups, as well as for production of copper and brass artefacts, particularly buckles.

Quirk Alert: *By George!*

In 1786, a Sunday school was opened in West Bromwich by the Presbyterian minister George Osborne, a philanthropist and pioneer of the Sunday school movement. Fast-forward to 2014, and leaders from the Presbyterian Church of Scotland challenged Chancellor of the Exchequer, George Osborne, to travel to Glasgow and talk to the poor people who live there…

Of course, Staffordshire minus the Black Country is most famous industry-wise for pottery. As early as 1680, pottery was being produced in both the north and the south of the county, but the epicentre remained at Burslem, where what were termed "farmer-potters" were renowned for churning out butter pots for the Uttoxeter market. However, the real turning point came in 1720, thanks to Shelton potter, John Astbury. He discovered that by adding heated and ground flint powder to the local reddish clay, it was possible to create a more tasteful product known as creamware – but whereas clay, salt, lead and coal were sourced locally, the flint had to be imported from either the south coast or from France. It wasn't, therefore, until the Trent and Mersey Canal was built between 1766 and 1777 that flint became more easily accessible. Before then, the transportation to the flint grinding mills in the Churnet Valley and Moddershall Valley was by pack horse. Here, the product was sorted to remove the flint with reddish-hues, and then heated to 1,200 °C (2,190 °F) to create an easily ground product. Also imported more easily thanks to the Trent and Mersey Canal was Cornish china clay which helped accelerate the production of creamware and bone china

Other industries during this period include the making of clay pipes at Newcastle-under-Lyme, with clay becoming a key material for the brick and tile industry, while limestone was quarried at Cauldon and copper mined at Ecton; indeed it is said that the Duke of Devonshire built his famous Crescent at Buxton with the profits from Ecton's copper. The brick and tile industry also flourished in the south as well as the north, with the county noted for its trademark "Staffordshire Blue" bricks. Meanwhile at Leek, the silk industry took off in the late 18th century, while cotton spinning became prevalent along the banks of the Dove, Tean and Trent. In Stafford, it was the boot and shoe manufacturing industry that established itself, thus giving rise to the saying: "May the manufacturers of Stafford be trodden underfoot by all the world".

Quirk Alert:
The Beautiful Shepherdess of Calwich

In the 18th century Bernard Granville of the converted Calwich Abbey was often visited by George Handel, who regularly played on the resident organ, while he also gifted Granville a manuscript copy of his works in 38 volumes! Then in 1766, Granville befriended Jean-Jacques Rousseau when he was staying at nearby Wootton Lodge, during which time the great Frenchman developed a liking for Granville's niece, Mary Dewes, who he described as "the beautiful shepherdess of Calwich".

Prior to the 18th century, the responsibility for maintaining roads had rested with local parishes. This was both unfair and inefficient, and so as a result, the Staffordshire road network was in a poor state of health by the 18th century, especially those roads in the Black Country where heavy wagons of coal had worn great ruts into the surface, while snowfalls rendered most parts impassable. The solution was the introduction of turnpike trusts – bodies set up by Acts of Parliament with powers to collect tolls in order to maintain principal highways, and which were generally run by groups of local trustees. The first turnpike road in Staffordshire followed an Act of 1714 to cover the stretch from Darlaston to the county boundary above Talke, and which was part of the overall route from London to Carlisle. However, it was another thirteen years before the next Staffordshire turnpike trust appeared in 1727, this one covering the Birmingham to Wednesbury road. Two years later in 1729, the whole Staffordshire stretch of the Lichfield to Chester road was turnpiked, as well as the Lichfield to Burton road, too. In 1749, three roads coming out of Walsall were turnpiked, while 1760 saw both the turnpiking of the other Staffordshire route to Chester via Brownhills and, finally, of the county's oldest road, Watling Street.

Crucial to the burgeoning industry of the Black Country was the 1766 turnpiking of the roads around Bilston – and it was one of these roads that would later become part of the historic mail-coach route from London to

Milestone on the A513 between Rugeley and Kings Bromley. This road was turnpiked in 1824 over a hundred years after Darlaston to Talke became Staffordshire's first turnpike trust in 1714.

Holyhead in the early 19th century, running through West Bromwich, Wednesbury, Bilston, Wolverhampton and Tettenhall. Similarly crucial was the turnpike road from Uttoxeter to Newcastle-under-Lyme, which greatly assisted the development of the Potteries and which was turnpiked in 1759. Over the following years, Josiah Wedgwood and his associates saw that the road system throughout the Potteries was turnpiked, thus hugely complementing the growth of their industry. The final area to be turnpiked was the high and treacherous countryside of the Staffordshire Moorlands. Probably the most important was the turnpiking in 1762 of the route between Ashbourne and Macclesfield, which passed largely through Staffordshire and, crucially, through Leek. One would presume that this particular route was in a significantly worse condition when it was used by Bonnie Prince Charlie in late 1745 on his march towards Derby, while the 1762 turnpiking also enabled a shorter established route from London to Manchester. Meanwhile, one of the last roads to be turnpiked as late as the 1840s was the route from Stoke to Leek via Abbey Hulton and Endon.

Quirk Alert: *Radcliffe's Stable*

There is a small cave in the Manifold Valley, below Thor's Cave, that is known as Radcliffe's Stable. It is so-called because Farmer Radcliffe hid his horse there to prevent it from being seized by Bonnie Prince Charlie's forces as they marched south in late 1745!

It was the arrival of a higher standard of road surface that helped to usher in the coaching era. By the late 18th century, Staffordshire folk could catch a coach to London and Bristol to the south and to Chester, Holyhead, Liverpool and Manchester to the north and the west. By 1830, Newcastle-under-Lyme alone saw 29 coaches pass through on a daily basis. Alongside these coaching routes, many coaching inns sprung up to feed, water and offer beds to the travellers – and many of these inns survive to this day.

Quirk Alert:
The Man Who Danced for a Dozen Days

In September 1752, Will Willett of Endon was lauded about as the man who danced continuously for 12 days and 12 nights. However, anyone who knows their calendar history will have clocked the year and guessed what's coming next. For in 1752, England, Wales, Ireland and the British colonies switched from the Julian calendar to the Gregorian calendar – and which meant that 11 days were dropped from early September in that year. So although Will Willett began his dance on the evening of 2nd September 1752, he actually ended his dance the following morning – on September 14th 1752!

The final word for this period of the 16th to the 18th century, will rest with Dr Samuel Johnson – for words were most certainly his trade. Born in Lichfield in 1709, Johnson went on to become a poet, essayist, moralist, literary critic, biographer, editor and, most famously, a lexicographer. He has therefore been described as "the most distinguished man of letters in English history". His early works include the biography *Life of Mr Richard Savage*, the poems *London* and *The Vanity of Human Wishes*, and the play *Irene*. However, it was for *A Dictionary of the English Language* that he is most remembered, published in 1775 after taking nine years to compile, and which continued to be the defining English dictionary for a further 150 years until the Oxford English Dictionary was completed. Towards the end of his life, he produced another magnificent tome called *Lives of the Most Eminent English Poets*, a collection of biographies and evaluations of 17th and 18th century poets. Alas, although his dictionary had probably the most indelible impact upon Modern English and has been described as "one of the greatest single achievements of scholarship", modern philistines like myself will always associate the great man with Robbie Coltrane – courtesy of his hilarious depiction of Dr Johnson in *Blackadder III* – for which I must offer my "most enthusiastic contrafibularities"!

Statue of Dr Samuel Johnson in the market place at Lichfield. The statue was erected in 1838 opposite the house where he was born (below).

Today, the birthplace of Samuel Johnson is a museum dedicated to the 18th century founder of the English dictionary.

Quirk Alert: *Every Tic in the Book*

As well as being one of the greatest ever British writers, Dr Samuel Johnson was also afflicted by odd gestures and tics. Thanks to the intricately documented Life of Samuel Johnson *by James Boswell, it has been theorised that these mannerisms approximate to the as-then undiagnosed condition known today as Tourette's syndrome.*

Staffordshire's Industrial Revolution

The Industrial Revolution is generally held to have started in the mid-to-late 18th century. One of the key catalysts to the explosion of industry was the introduction of canals, and the first of these was the Bridgewater Canal, designed and built by James Brindley between 1759 and 1761. Shortly afterwards, it was to Staffordshire that Brindley turned his attention, as part of the hugely ambitious Trent and Mersey Canal (T&M), a 93.5 mile waterway which linked the Mersey on the west coast to the Humber on the east coast via the River Trent. The first sod was cut at Middleport near Burslem in 1766 by Josiah Wedgwood, keen to develop the infrastructure around his pottery industry as he had already done by turnpiking local roads, but also offering a smoother method of transport for his potentially breakable wares. Indeed, if it hadn't been for Wedgwood's influence, the waterway might not even have passed through the Potteries. Once the project was under way, Wedgwood built his new factory at Etruria in 1771 alongside the Trent and Mersey Canal and many more soon sprang up along the canal's banks. However, it took eleven years to complete the canal, and Brindley, never saw its completion as he died in 1772. One of the lengthiest parts of the project was the construction of the 1.75-mile long Harecastle Tunnel through the hilly area to the north of the Potteries. Indeed, up until 1777, pots had to be carried on the short journey from Etruria, over the top of Kidsgrove Hill, and to the other side, where the canal headed northwards towards the Mersey. The tunnel was initially constructed without a towpath, so the bargemen had to leg through the lengthy tunnel – a physically demanding process which also created long delays. It was with this in mind in the mid-1820s, that leading civil engineer Thomas Telford was commissioned to provide a second, wider, parallel tunnel along with a towpath. This tunnel was slightly longer and was opened in 1827. The Brindley tunnel was closed in the 1900s due to severe subsidence, but the Telford tunnel remains in use, and is the fourth-longest navigable canal tunnel in the UK today.

STAFFORDSHIRE: THE CANAL CAPITAL OF BRITAIN

The Shropshire Union Canal at High Onn.

Below left: *The Trent and Mersey Canal at Stone.*

Below right: *The Shropshire Union Canal at Gnosall.*

Great Haywood Junction, the junction between the Trent and Mersey Canal (to the right) and the Staffordshire and Worcestershire Canal (to the left, under the bridge). Both canals were designed by James Brindley, the former a 93.5 mile canal built between 1766 and 1777 and the latter a 46-mile canal built between 1766 and 1772.

What is now called the Waterfront at Round Oak, and was formerly the Dudley No 1 Canal.

The Rushall Canal.

Another notable feature of the T&M Canal in Staffordshire is the flyover junction where the Hall Green Branch leaves the T&M mainline close to the county border with Cheshire, but then doubles back over the mainline before travelling a short distance north to join the Macclesfield Canal at Hall Green. As for the T&M company headquarters, they were also in Staffordshire, at Stone.

Despite its land-locked status, Staffordshire was soon linked to most major ports in England; to Liverpool and Hull via the Trent and Mersey Canal, and to Bristol and London by the burgeoning canal network throughout, and to the south of, Staffordshire. The link to Bristol came courtesy of another James Brindley project, the Staffordshire and Worcestershire Canal (S&W), built between 1766 and 1772. Forty six miles long, it linked to the North via Great Haywood Junction on the Trent and Mersey Canal, 5 miles east of Stafford, and to the South and the River Severn via a set of staircase locks at Stourport in Worcestershire. It also provided a huge boost to Staffordshire industry, enabling trade from the Potteries to the South West and trade from the Black Country to the Potteries via the S&W junction with the Birmingham Canal at Aldersley, just north-west of Wolverhampton. The Birmingham Canal was built at more-or-less the same time between 1768 and 1772, and was actually the first branch canal to be built in England – again by James Brindley – thus linking the Black Country powerhouses of Birmingham, Smethwick, Tipton, Coseley, Bilston and Wolverhampton to the national network via its junction to the S&W Canal at Aldersley.

However, the success of the S&W Canal was compromised in 1815 when the Worcester and Birmingham Canal provided a more direct route between Birmingham and Bristol. To remain competitive, the S&W Company increased the hours when locks could be used, and eventually by 1830 they were available 24 hours a day. However, usage of the S&W Canal declined further following the opening of the Birmingham and Liverpool Junction Canal (B&LJ), which ran from Autherley Junction on the S&W Canal, 4 miles north-west of Wolverhampton, up to Nantwich on the Chester Canal, thereafter providing access to Chester and Merseyside. With its link to the Birmingham Canal half a mile south of Autherley Junction at Aldersley, this subsequently took much of the traffic away from the S&W Canal section from Autherley Junction to Great Haywood, as previous traffic destined for the North West was now using the new B&LJ Canal. So the S&W company hit back by levying exorbitant tolls on the short half-mile shared stretch of canal between Aldersley and Autherley Junctions. The response of the Birmingham Canal Company and the Birmingham and Liverpool Junction Company was to jointly promote an Act of Parliament to authorise a short canal that would have left the Birmingham Canal at a higher level than the junction, crossed the Staffordshire and Worcestershire Canal by

an aqueduct, and then dropped down by a series of locks to join the Birmingham and Liverpool Junction Canal north of Autherley Junction. Unsurprisingly, the S&W Canal company decided to reduce its tolls rather than lose the trade altogether – and despite this and later competition from the railways, the S&W Company actually paid dividends to its shareholders until the end of the 19th century.

As he had done for the T&M Canal, Thomas Telford also made later improvements in the 1820s to the Birmingham Canal, cutting out 7 miles of its length and reducing the number of locks from 30 to 24. He also constructed the Galton Bridge in 1829, carrying the road between West Bromwich and Smethwick over a 70ft cutting. At that time, it was the longest canal bridge in the world at 154ft and was, naturally, made at the nearby Horseley ironworks in Tipton. As for the B&LJ Canal – which was also built by Telford between 1825 and 1835 – it is today part of the Shropshire Union Canal.

Moving on to Staffordshire's link to London now, and that came courtesy of the 38 mile-long Coventry Canal (1768-1789), yet another James Brindley build which linked the Trent and Mersey Canal at Fradley Junction, with the Oxford Canal at Coventry which, in turn, linked to the River Thames and hence London. Also tapping into the Coventry Canal were two more waterways, the Birmingham and Fazeley Canal (B&F) and the Wyrley and Essington Canal (W&E). The B&F Canal was completed in 1789 and also linked Birmingham to London via the Coventry and Oxford Canals. Meanwhile, the W&E Canal was completed in 1797 and linked the Coventry Canal just east of Lichfield at Huddlesford Junction, with Wolverhampton. The W&E Canal also included important branch lines throughout southern Staffordshire and the Black Country, including the Lichfield Canal, the Rushall Canal, the Walsall Canal and the Bentley Canal.

There are still two more important Staffordshire canals to mention. The first completes the extraordinary patchwork of canals in south Staffordshire and the

Lock (left) and cast-iron mile marker (right) at Froghall Wharf on the Caldon Canal. The 17-mile stretch from Etruria to Froghall opened in 1779; the 13-mile extension to Uttoxeter was opened in 1811.

Black Country, this being the Tame Valley Canal, constructed much later in 1844 and which connected the B&F Canal to the Walsall Canal. The second, the Caldon Canal, is back up in the north of the county again. This canal was another of the first wave, built in 1779, and which ran for 17 miles from the Trent and Mersey Canal at Etruria to Froghall Wharf, thus supplying the limestone quarries in the Froghall area with access to the national canal network. The Caldon Canal has 17 locks and also includes the 69 metre-long Froghall Tunnel. A thirteen mile extension to Uttoxeter was opened later in 1811.

Thus it was that most of Staffordshire's canal network was already in place by the start of the 19th century. A few stragglers were added though, including the Netherton Tunnel, opened in 1858 linking the Birmingham Canal to the Dudley Canal. The last canal tunnel to be built in England, it was lit by gas and had two towpaths. And then, finally, the Cannock Extension Canal was opened in the early 1860s to link the growing industry on Cannock Chase. It first linked Churchbridge in 1860 to the Hatherton Canal, a branch of the Staffordshire and Worcestershire Canal (thus supplying links to the Potteries and the North West), and then linked Hednesford in 1863 to the Wyrley and Essington Canal at Pelsall Junction (thus supplying links to the Black Country and the South of England).

Most of the canals just discussed, along with the turnpike roads discussed in the previous chapter, all went into decline from the middle of the 19th century thanks to a faster form of transport – the railways. Ironically, railways or rail-roads/tramways had initially been used to help transport goods to and from mines and quarries to canal wharves, with wagons pulled by horses. For example, in 1777, the Caldon Low limestone quarries, 3 miles east of Froghall, were linked

to Froghall Old Wharf on the Caldon Canal by a tramway. This was actually an engineering intention from the get-go, and formed part of the original Act of parliament for a canal plus a tramway – as building a canal to the high-ground location of the quarries was obviously impractical. This particular tramway used wooden rails topped with iron which were fixed to wooden sleepers, while the wagons had flanged wheels – therefore effectively making it a railway in the modern sense. Another 1.5 mile tramway was opened in 1805 from Radford Wharf on a stretch of the Staffordshire and Worcestershire Canal south-east of Stafford, to a terminus by Green Bridge in Stafford, while a 3.5 mile stretch of tramway was opened in 1829, also linking the Staffordshire and Worcestershire Canal to Dudley's coal mines at Shut End in Kingswinford.

Staffordshire was also a significant location for the first proper railway of national importance. This was the Grand Junction Railway (GJR), linking Birmingham with Liverpool, and which went via Wolverhampton and Stafford. It was built under an Act of Parliament of 1834, was designed by the great George Stephenson and Joseph Locke, and was opened in 1837, while it was extended south in 1838 to link with the Birmingham to London line. The GJR was very profitable, always paying dividends of at least 10% and by 1846 had a capital value of more than £5.75m, having merged with the Liverpool and Manchester Railway a year earlier. The company then merged with the London and Birmingham Railway and Manchester and Birmingham Railway companies to become the London and North Western Railway in 1846; later, in 1923, it became the London Midland and Scottish Railway.

In 1842, the line from Birmingham to Derby was opened, passing through Tamworth and Burton and thus bringing Burton's brewers into play with regard to

Quirk Alert: *Exceedingly Beautiful*

Rudyard Lake was constructed in 1797-98 as a feeder reservoir for the Caldon Canal. Later acquired by the North Staffordshire Railway who routed their Churnet Valley Line down one side of the lake, the place thus became a popular destination for day-trippers. Amongst them was Burslem couple John Lockwood Kipling and Alice Macdonald, and it was here that John proposed to Alice. Their love for the place also moved them to name their son, Rudyard, who went on to become one of Britain's most renowned writers and poets. As for the village of Rudyard, that was named after Ralph Rudyard, a local man who allegedly killed Richard III at Bosworth Field.

Rudyard Reservoir, originally constructed 1797-98 to feed the Caldon Canal.

the new national railway network. Then in 1847, a more direct route to the North West from London was provided by the Trent Valley Railway, which linked Stafford to Rugby, thus avoiding Birmingham, while also passing through or close to the Staffordshire towns of Rugeley, Lichfield and Tamworth. Unsurprisingly, a railway network in the Black Country also sprung up, mirroring the canal network that had exploded half a century-or-so earlier. This led to the inevitable battles between rival railway companies as they sought to monopolise key industrial areas. In the 1850s, this actually led to two companies – the Great Western Railway and the London and North Western Railway – creating two completely separate, but parallel railway lines linking Birmingham and Wolverhampton!

Also mirroring the creation of canal branch lines were the local railway branch lines. Typical of these was the network of branch lines created by the North Staffordshire Railway (NSR), formed in 1845. Nicknamed "The Knotty", in acknowledgement of its intricacy, plus a nod to Staffordshire's county emblem, its rail network linked up the many towns of the Potteries as well as linking into key surrounding areas in Cheshire, Derbyshire and Shropshire. The main routes were constructed between 1846 and 1852, including one which ran through the Potteries from Macclesfield to Colwich, and another which ran from Crewe to Egginton Junction, 6 miles south-west of Derby. Somewhat significantly, the first sod for the NSR was cut at Etruria in 1846, as had occurred eighty years earlier in 1766 for the Trent and Mersey Canal when Josiah Wedgwood had obliged. The NSR also managed to remain an independent company until 1923 when it became part of the London, Midland and Scottish Railway Company.

Lagging slightly behind, as it had with the canals, was Cannock Chase, and it was the late 1850s before its coalfields were serviced by a branch of the South Staffordshire Railway (SSR). The SSR was also responsible for the South Staffordshire Line from Lichfield Trent Valley to Dudley via Walsall and which was built in 1849. Like the NSR, the SSR eventually became part of the London, Midland and Scottish Railway in 1923. Two years later, another new railway line was opened in the south-west of the county, linking Wolverhampton and Kingswinford.

Of course, it wasn't just the canals that suffered at the hands of the faster and cheaper railways, but the coaching services, too, and the turnpike roads upon which they ran. For example, between 1830 and 1839, the number of coaching services offered in Newcastle-under-Lyme dropped from 29 to 3. That said, a new and more local form of road transport began to appear, transporting passengers from the pubs to the railway stations, first in the form of the omnibus and later via trams, with the first of the latter appearing in the Potteries in 1862.

Clearly, one of the prime functions of the railways was the transportation of freight, particularly coal, iron-stone and limestone which were produced in copious qualities throughout the county during the 19th century. Many coal mines were opened in the 19th century in two distinct coalfields. The South Staffordshire coalfield stretched for 25 miles from the Lickey Hills in the south of the county, to Rugeley, and was around 10 miles wide from east to west. Meanwhile, the North Staffordshire Coalfield covers an area of around 100 square miles around Stoke-on-Trent and the district of Newcastle-under-Lyme. However, as well as being a boom industry in the 19th century, there were always disasters – a number of which are covered in detail in the *Quirky Staffordshire* section in the chapters on Crackley, Finney Green, Scot Hay and Talke. As for coal mining, the industry was eventually nationalised in 1947, and what became the National Coal Board owned 59 Staffordshire collieries. Alas, all of the North Staffordshire collieries closed between the 1960s and the end of the 20th century, with Silverdale Colliery the last to close in 1998. The last Cannock Chase coalfield at Littleton Colliery had closed five years earlier, while the last Black Country pit to be closed – Baggeridge Colliery near Sedgley – closed much earlier in 1968.

This is the second of two sets of lime kilns at Froghall Wharf. The first set was built in c.1785; the above set was built in c.1850, around the same time that the wharf was connected to the North Staffordshire Railway. The limestone was transported down a tramway from the limestone works at Cauldon Low and a railway siding ran along the top of the kilns so that limestone and coal could be tipped straight in to them. From c.1850, a standard gauge siding ran along the bottom, to take the lime away via the North Staffordshire Railway.

Quirk Alert: *Not Amused*

It was in the 1840s that the Black Country received its name, thanks to it having become one of the most intensely indus-trialised areas in the world and hence much of the area was covered in black soot. However, some historians suggest that the name possibly existed even before the Industrial Revolution, courtesy of the black coal which lay close to the surface of the heath and rendered the local soil very black. What is without doubt, though, is that collectively in the 19th century, the South Staffordshire coal mines, the coal coking operations, and the iron foundries and steel mills that used the local coal to fire their furnaces, produced one of the worst levels of air pollution found anywhere in the world. In fact, it was so bad, that it is claimed that Queen Victoria had the blinds lowered on her carriage as the royal train passed through!

Quirk Alert: *The Black Country – Literally*

The Black Country also has numerous connections with classic British literature. Charles Dickens's novel The Old Curiosity Shop, *written in 1841 when the Industrial Revolution was in full swing, describes how the multitude of chimneys in the area "Poured out their plague of smoke, obscured the light, and made foul the melancholy air".*

Moving into 20th century classic literature, it has already been remarked upon that many of the places described in J. R. R. Tolkien's Lord of the Rings *draw upon the author's experiences in the area in which he grew up. It is therefore a fair bet, that these belching chimneys and fiery furnaces may well have influenced his depiction of the dreaded Mordor in his books, while there are also claims that Bilbo Baggins may well have been based on the 19th century mayor of Bilston, Ben Bilboe!*

However, perhaps the most famous quote describing the Black Country comes not from a book, but from Elihu Burritt, the American Consul in Birmingham, who in 1862 described the area as "black by day and red by night", thus depict-ing the belching daytime chimneys and the glowing nocturnal furnaces. And it is this very phrase that was adopted by the area in 2012 when the folk of the Black Country designed their very own flag, with both black and red prominent and overlayed by one of the region's famous chains.

We're now going to rewind a century again, to the explosion of canals in the second half of the 18th century, for they were to provide a huge boost to the Staffordshire pottery industry. We've already mentioned how integral Josiah Wedgwood was in terms of getting the Trent and Mersey Canal to pass through the Potteries, and of how he built his new factory at Etruria in 1771 alongside the Trent and Mersey Canal. Soon after, many more sprang up along the canal's banks. However, Wedgwood is such an important Staffordshire son, and the industry so key to the county that we must dig a little deeper.

Josiah Wedgwood was born in Burslem in 1730 and had actually become a skilled potter by the age of nine. However, a bout of smallpox weakened a knee making him unable to work the foot pedal of a potter's wheel, and so he concentrated more on pottery design. In his early twenties, Wedgwood began working with the most renowned English pottery-maker of his day, Thomas Whieldon, who eventually became his busi-ness partner in 1754. The pair leased the Ivy Works in Burslem and Wedgwood began experimenting with a wide variety of techniques, turning the works into the first ever pottery factory. Wedgwood's unique glazes soon began to distinguish his products from the compe-tition and by the 1760s he was attracting the attention of the British nobility. However, when Queen Charlotte (wife of King George III) began to place orders, Wedgwood was given permission to name that particu-lar line as Queen's Ware. By the 1770s, even Catherine

the Great was ordering Wedgwood pottery!

It was also during the 1770s that Wedgwood moved his expanding business from the Ivy works at Burslem to the newly built Etruria Works on the banks of the Trent and Mersey Canal. The new works were named after the Etruria district of Italy, where black porcelain dating to Etruscan times was being excavated, and later led Wedgwood to develop a facsimile product which he called Black Basalt. Etruria soon became more than just a factory as the philanthropic Wedgwood built houses and shops there for his workers and the *village* of Etruria was born. The factory continued to prosper for another 180 years, while the "village" still survives today. As for Wedgwood, he eventually lost his right leg due to the smallpox that had struck him down as a child, but he still managed to perfect the duplication of the Portland Vase in 1789, a blue and white glass vase dating to the first century BC. When Wedgwood died in 1795, he had already passed the business on to his sons, and it has continued to thrive all the way up to today, with Wedgwood china a renowned name that means quality.

Of course, Wedgwood wasn't the only pottery manufacturer in the Potteries. Many others followed, and by the time the railways arrived in the 1840s, busi-ness was booming, with other key pottery companies including Aynsley, Burleigh, Doulton, Dudson, Minton, Moorcroft and Twyford. There is one footnote to the burgeoning pottery industry though, for the Chartist's General Strike in 1842 was actually ignited by striking

Etruria Hall was built for Josiah Wedgwood by Joseph Pickford between 1768 and 1771. It stayed in the Wedgwood family until they sold it in the 1840s.

Brick statue of Josiah Wedgwood outside Etruria Hall, and who appears to have been completely assimilated!

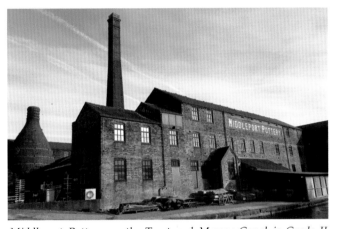

Middleport Pottery on the Trent and Mersey Canal is Grade II listed and dates from 1889. It claims to be the only working Victorian pottery in Stoke-on-Trent.

Bottle kilns at the Gladstone Pottery Museum in Longton, and typical of those that were built in the late 18th century, and flourished for another 200 years.

collieries in the Potteries and subsequently led to what became known as the 1842 Pottery Riots. It all kicked off in June 1842 thanks to a decision by a Longton coal mine owner, W.H.Sparrow, to ignore the law and impose a large pay reduction on his miners of almost a shilling a day, without giving the statutory fortnight's notice. The workers went on strike and were soon supported by other local colliery workers, while the strike was escalated by the Chartists, who called for a General Strike across the Potteries. The movement then spread across north Staffordshire and into south-east Lancashire. Then, on 15th August, the Chartist orator Thomas Cooper delivered a speech at Crown Bank in Hanley, decreeing: "that all labour cease until the People's Charter becomes the law of the land". Alas, matters then escalated into a full-scale riot, with many properties in the Hanley and Burslem areas smashed or burned down. In addition to the widespread vandalism, mine owners, clergy and magistrates were singled out for special acts of retribution. Eventually, the rioters were rounded up by troops and one of them was shot dead. A total of 274 people were tried, with 146 sent to prison and 54 transported to Australia, while the riots probably hastened the

creation of the Staffordshire Police Force, which was established before the end of 1842, and the first Chief Constable appointed.

Throughout the 19th century, Burton continued to be Staffordshire's focal point for brewing and at its height one quarter of all beer sold in Britain was produced in the town. The second half of the 19th century saw the growth of a number of local breweries, while other breweries moved from their previous locations to Burton. The net result was that by 1880, the town was home to over 30 breweries. One of the largest Burton brewers of the 19th century was Samuel Allsopp and Sons, who were founded in 1807. It was this company that was the first to export Burton Pale Ale to India in 1822. By 1890 they employed 1,750 workers and their output had reached 460,000 barrels. Nevertheless, Allsopp's brewing business was never the largest brewer in 19th century Burton; that honour went to Bass Brewery. Founded in 1777 by William Bass, Bass Brewery actually became the largest brewery in the world by 1877, shipping a million barrels of beer a year. Their main brand was Bass Pale Ale and it became the highest selling beer in the UK as well as being exported throughout the British Empire. Meanwhile, another 19th

Left: The remainder of Clarence Street maltings, built between 1882 and 1883. Much of the site was demolished in the 1970s, but this octagonal kiln survives and is topped by a goat-shaped weather vane. Right: Statue of Michael Arthur Bass, 1ˢᵗ Baron Burton, outside Burton Town Hall built in 1894. Not only did Bass continue the work originally started by his great-grandfather, William Bass, but he also gave the town its great bridge, the Town Hall (seen in-part above), St Paul's church, St Margaret's church, the drill hall and other clubs and social centres.

century Burton brewer was the Clarence Street Brewery. It was built in 1882-83 for Peter Walker and Son, which also had breweries in Liverpool and Warrington and it was Peter Walker who patented the Burton Union system of brewing. Walker was succeeded by his eldest son, Sir Andrew Barclay Walker, who expanded the Clarence Street Brewery, pioneering a number of brewing innovations relating to production, distribution and pub management.

Ironmaking continued its success story in the 19th century, with the industry in the north centred on Etruria. The furnaces here were originally owned by Lord Granville, but in time became known as Shelton Iron and Steel Ltd. The ironmaking industry probably hit its peak in around 1870. Thereafter, it was in a losing battle with steel and the industry went into decline.

It was a similar story for the cottage nail-making industry, which had previously flourished in the south of the county, but which went into decline following the introduction of factory-based machine-made nails in the 1820s. Instead, the chain and anchor-making industry took its place, with Noel Hingley opening a chain-works near to Dudley in 1838. Nearby Wednesbury began to specialise in gun barrels towards the end of the 18th century, but after the end of the Napoleonic Wars in 1815, demand wasn't quite so high! Instead, the town began to produce gas and water pipes, thus earning Wednesbury the moniker of Tube Town. By 1830, the industry had spread another 4 miles to the north-east to Walsall.

South Staffordshire also took advantage of James Watt's steam engine breakthrough in the late 18th century, with a metal works in Handsworth producing its first steam engines in 1776, one for the Bloomfield Colliery in Tipton and another for a furnace at Broseley

in Shropshire. A later steam engine was created in the late 1770s for the Birmingham Canal Navigations to pump water from one canal level to another at Smethwick, while the first iron steamship was manufactured at Tipton in 1822. As for Stafford, the town developed a significant salt industry towards the end of the 19th century, while the town also became well-known for electrical engineering in the early 20th century. In addition, Tipton became famous for anchors and pumps, Cradley for chains, Wednesfield for traps and keys, Willenhall for locks, Wolverhampton and Bilston for tinplates, West Bromwich for stoves, and Smethwick for lamps, lighthouses and their equipment.

The Industrial Revolution had a huge influence on Staffordshire's population demography. People had historically been more spread out and large proportions had lived in rural locations thanks to their involvement in agriculture. That all changed with the Industrial Revolution, as people gravitated towards the new industry in the cities and towns of Britain, and nowhere was that more acutely felt than in the Black Country. Between the censuses of 1801 and 1901, Wolverhampton's population climbed from 12,565 to 94,187, while Walsall's went from 10,399 to 87,464. West Bromwich climbed from 5,687 to 65,114, but was eclipsed, percentage-wise by Smethwick, which increased from a lowly 1,097 to 54,539. Also heavily influenced by intensive industry was Cannock (1,359 to 23,974) and Burslem (6,578 to 40,234), but in those towns where industry wasn't so intensive, only gentler population increases were encountered, such as Stafford (3,898 to 14,060) and Newcastle-under-Lyme (4,604 to 19,147). As for the Stoke-on-Trent area, this grew in just forty years from 101,200 in 1861 to a remarkable 214,700 by 1901.

Of course, one of the effects of these huge population changes was that people lived in squalor, and disease, with epidemics rife. The towns of the Black Country and the Potteries were particularly unhygienic, and even Stafford was described by an assize judge in 1870 as "the most stinking town I was ever in in my life"! He went on to explain that raw sewage ran down the streets of the town in open channels, a situation that wasn't helped by the fact that Stafford was the county's focal point for cattle markets and fairs. These conditions were almost certainly to blame for the cholera outbreaks of 1832, in which 743 people died in Bilston alone in just six weeks, and in 1848-49 when 2,683 people died, county-wide.

Conditions at work were little better, where children often worked 72-hour weeks from as young as five. Two particular dangers facing those working in the pottery industry were lead poisoning and what was known as "potter's rot", a disease caused by breathing in flint-dust. Reform and progress did take place, though. As early as 1777, a Board of Improvement Commissioners had been set up to improve facilities in Wolverhampton – such as pavements, lighting and general cleanliness. Burton upon Trent followed in 1779, Lichfield in 1806,

ILAM'S STUNNING 19TH CENTURY MONUMENTS

The Pike Watts monument in the mausoleum chapel of Holy Cross church at Ilam. The chapel was built in 1831 and the statue is by the famous sculptor, Francis Chantrey. It portrays David Pike Watts (d.1816) on his death bed.

Ilam Cross, also known as The Mary Watts-Russell Memorial. It was built in 1841 for Jesse Watts-Russell in memory of his wife who had died in 1840. Modelled on Edward I's Eleanor Crosses, the memorial was designed by John Macduff Derick and sculpted by Richard Westmacott. Mary is also the daughter at her father's deathbed in the above Chantrey sculpture.

Newcastle-under-Lyme in 1819, Walsall in 1824, Burslem and Leek in 1825 and Stafford in 1830. The Municipal Corporations Act of 1835 then created 178 municipal boroughs in England that were to be governed by town councils and elected by ratepayers, and the powers of the former commissioners were passed to these new bodies. However, the 1835 Act only created four Staffordshire municipal boroughs, at Lichfield, Newcastle-under-Lyme, Tamworth and Walsall and it wasn't until 1875, for example, that these powers were transferred to a municipal borough at Stafford.

Throughout the same period, hospitals were established, such as the Staffordshire General Infirmary, built at Stafford in 1766, and the North Staffordshire Infirmary opened near to Etruria in 1819. Meanwhile, a dispensary was opened at Wolverhampton in 1825 and which eventually became the South Staffordshire General Hospital in 1848. In addition to the hospitals, pure water was supplied by a waterworks at Hanley, opened in 1820 by John Smith, and available to the inhabitants of Hanley, Shelton and Burslem. By 1847, Wolverhampton was supplied by the Wolverhampton

Waterworks Co. at Tettenhall, and Leek was home to the Potteries Waterworks Co. A further waterworks was opened at Lichfield in 1858, using the two pools located alongside the cathedral as reservoirs. This waterworks was run by the South Staffordshire Waterworks Co., who almost a century later built the reservoir at Blithfield in 1953, this one covering 790 acres and crossed by a viaduct half a mile long – upon which you will annually spot some local horn dancers on Wakes Monday!

> ## Quirk Alert: *Chain Reaction*
> *The anchors and chains for the RMS* Titanic *were manufactured in the Black Country in the Netherton area. This included three anchors and accompanying chains, weighing in at 100 tons. The centre anchor alone weighed 12 tons and was pulled through Netherton on the start of its journey to the ship by 20 shire horses!*

Assistance also came from the industrial philanthropists of the age, too. As early as the 1760s, Josiah Wedgwood had provided housing accommodation for his pottery workers at Etruria, terraces of four-roomed cottages with a well and a pump for every few houses as well as communal bakehouses. The great Richard Arkwright also built brick terraces for his cotton workers at Rocester, following the build of Tutbury Mill in 1782 – Arkwright being the very man who was said to have triggered the Industrial Revolution when he built the first water-powered cotton mill at Cromford (Derbyshire) in 1771. Similarly, Robert Peel built houses for those working for him at the cotton mill he opened in 1790 at Fazeley. Moving forward to the 1850s, and Earl Granville built a large estate at Cobridge for his workers, equipping each with a wash-house, water closet and front garden; some even had entrance halls and a third bedroom! He also opened a school on the estate in 1854. Meanwhile, some of the first detached houses for middle-class home owners appeared at The Villas, near Boothen in Stoke in the 1850s, while Rowley Park in Stafford was laid out in the 1860s in part of the grounds of Rowley Hall, and was described as "suburban residences of a superior class".

Finally for this chapter we mustn't forget the great Sir Robert Peel, British Prime Minister 1834-1835 and 1841-1846, great reformer and founder of the modern police force – or the Peelers as they were known in the 19th century. His home for most of his life, when not at Downing Street, was at Drayton Bassett, and he lies at rest in St Peter's church in the village, while the church is also home to a stone monument to him. There is also a statue of Sir Robert standing outside Tamworth Town Hall – for it was from here that he delivered his famous Tamworth Manifesto in 1834, where he laid down the principles upon which the modern British Conservative Party is based. His second term as Prime Minister

Left to right: Wolverhampton Town Hall, built in 1871; Stoke Town Hall, built in stages between 1834 and 1850; the Town Hall in Tamworth was built in 1701 by Thomas Guy, M.P. for Tamworth. In the foreground of the latter is the statue of Sir Robert Peel, and which dates from 1852. Also a former Tamworth M.P. and twice Prime Minister, Sir Robert delivered his famous 'Tamworth Manifesto' from the window of the Town Hall in 1834.

was marked by the Mines and Collieries Act 1842, the Income Tax Act 1842, the Factories Act 1844 and the Railway Regulation Act 1844. However, as well as the founding of the police force, it is for the repeal of the Corn Laws that Sir Robert is most remembered – for following the Great Irish Potato Famine, he joined with both Whigs and Radicals to repeal the Corn Laws (which kept the price of grain artificially high), and thus openly "betrayed" his own party, bringing about his resignation as Prime Minister in 1846.

From the Late Victorians to Present Day

The 19th century had seen a number of slight changes made to Staffordshire's county boundaries. For starters, in 1844, a couple of parishes in the south-west – Broome and Clent – went to Worcestershire, while the county inherited part of the township of Foston and Scropton (in the parish of Scropton) from Derbyshire. Following the Local Government Act 1888, Staffordshire was formalised as an *administrative* county, which was based very closely on its *historic* county boundaries. Staffordshire County Council controlled the entirety of the administrative county area with the exception of Hanley, Walsall, West Bromwich and Wolverhampton, which were all declared as county boroughs in 1889. The Act also saw the towns of Tamworth (partly in Warwickshire) and Burton upon Trent (partly in Derbyshire) united entirely in Staffordshire. The early 20th century then saw Handsworth and Perry Barr lost to Warwickshire when they became part of the county borough of Birmingham. In 1901, Burton also became a county borough, and was followed by Smethwick in 1907, giving the county six county boroughs – an unusually large number that reflected the impact the Industrial Revolution had had on the county. For example, of Staffordshire's neighbouring counties, Warwickshire and Worcestershire only had two county boroughs apiece, Derbyshire only had one and Shropshire had none.

By 1910 the county had another county borough – Stoke-on-Trent – which was formed by the unprecedented grouping of six former towns of the Potteries: Burslem, Fenton, Hanley, Longton, Stoke and Tunstall. Interestingly, the borough proposed a further expansion in 1919 of annexing the neighbouring borough of Newcastle-under-Lyme and the Wolstanton United Urban District, but the Newcastle Corporation rejected the proposal. A further attempt was made in 1930, but in 1932, Wolstanton allied itself to Newcastle-under-Lyme and that was that. Stoke-on-Trent, however, was created a city in 1925.

Now, that *would* have been it for most counties until 1974, but Staffordshire underwent *another* major reorganisation in the Black Country in 1966. This resulted from the recommendation of the Local Government Commission for England, which led to the creation of an area of contiguous county boroughs. To achieve this, the County Borough of Warley was formed by the merger of the County Borough of Smethwick and the Municipal Borough of Rowley Regis, with the Worcestershire borough of Oldbury. As a result, Staffordshire lost Smethwick to Worcestershire, but at the same time, the Worcestershire county borough of Dudley (and also historically a detached exclave of Worcestershire) became part of Staffordshire. This reorganisation also led to the administrative county of Staffordshire having a thin protrusion passing between the county boroughs (to the east) and Shropshire, to the west, to form a short border with Worcestershire – in pretty much the same way that it does today, albeit with the county of West Midlands to its east, now. And that is how things remained right up to 1st April 1974 when the Local Government Act 1972 was implemented – but more on that a little later.

Quirk Alert:
Five Churches in Eighty-Three Years

Rowley Regis must be the location of the unluckiest church in England. Its Norman original stood for around 600 years, but was rebuilt in 1840. However, that building became structurally unsound and was therefore demolished and a new church built in its place in 1904. Incredibly, that church was then burnt down in 1913 during the Suffragette riots, and the current building was built in 1923!

In 1913, 40,000 Black Country steel workers went on strike in what proved to be a pivotal moment in the development of British trade unions. Their demand was for a 23 shilling minimum weekly wage for unskilled workers, thus matching the wages of their counterparts in neighbouring Birmingham. The strike badly affected the government's armaments programme, especially the procurement of naval equipment and other industrial essentials manufactured in the Black Country, such as steel tubing, nuts and bolts. Eventually, and following a ballot of the union membership, a settlement was reached on 11th July after arbitration by government officials from the Board of Trade.

The late 19th century had also seen the founding of a number of iconic football and cricket clubs. Alas, Staffordshire has never been part of the first class county cricket circuit, and still today plays in the Minor Counties Championship. However, they have won it the most times (11), first claiming the title in 1906 and most recently in 2014. In terms of football, though, Staffordshire has some of the country's most prominent teams, including Stoke City, Wolverhampton Wanderers and West Bromwich Albion, founded in 1863, 1877 and 1878, respectively. Wolves have won the old First Division Championship three times (all in the 1950s), the FA Cup four times, the Football League Cup twice, while they also won the UEFA Cup in 1972. West Bromwich Albion won the First Division title in 1919-20, the FA Cup five times and the Football League Cup once, while Stoke City, despite regularly being a top-flight club, can only boast one League Cup, won during the 1971-72 season. Less glamorous, but also hailing from Staffordshire is Port Vale (founded 1876), and winners of the Football Trophy in 1993 and 2001, Walsall (founded 1888) and Burton Albion (founded in 1950).

Twentieth century transport was, of course, revolutionised by the car. By the 1970s, Staffordshire was home to sections of the M5 and the M6, with the latter running through the county from the south-east to Audley in the north. The Stafford to Preston section was completed in 1965 and the Walsall to Stafford section in 1968, while the final section, from the A38 3 miles north-east of Birmingham to the junction with the M1 at J19, was completed in 1971. Later, the M54 from Essington to Telford was constructed, while the late 1990s saw the opening of the M6 Toll Road, as a payable but quieter alternative to the hugely congested M6. As for redundant canals and railways, many of them made a strong comeback in the late 20th century. Today, much of the previously industrial canal network throughout Staffordshire is still navigable by private barge, offering a popular holiday and general lifestyle experience to boot. As for the railways, a number have been converted into immensely popular heritage railways, some still running original steam trains. One of these is the Churnet Valley Railway which runs for 5.5 miles between Kingsley and Froghall station to the south and Leekbrook station to the north, calling at stations at

STAFFORDSHIRE'S FOOTBALL GREATS

Arguably the greatest of them all, this is a memorial to Sir Stanley Matthews (1915-2000) outside Stoke City's Britannia Stadium. Born in Hanley, Matthews made 259 appearances for Stoke City between 1932 and 1947, scoring 51 goals, before returning for a further 59 appearances between 1961 and 1965, only retiring at the age of 50. A brilliant outside right, Matthews also made 54 appearances for England between 1934 and 1957, scoring 11 goals and earning his last cap at the age of 42, making him the oldest player to represent his country. As a player, he was nicknamed "The Wizard of the Dribble" and "The Magician". He was also the first ever European Footballer of the Year (in 1956), and is the only player to date to have been knighted whilst still playing the game.

Above left: *Statue of Gordon Banks outside Stoke City's Britannia Stadium. Here he is shown holding aloft the World Cup which he won with England in 1966. Banks played for Stoke City 194 times between 1967 and 1972 and won 73 England caps during his career.*

Above right: *Statue of Billy Wright (1924-1994) outside Molineux Stadium, Wolverhampton. Wright spent his entire career at Wolverhampton Wanderers where he made 490 appearances. He captained Wolves throughout their most successful period when they won the old First Division title three times. He also won 105 England caps, 90 of them as captain.*

Consall and Cheddleton. A branch line takes you a further 4.5 miles in a loop around to Ipstones, all passing through beautiful countryside christened as Staffordshire's "Little Switzerland". Another preserved standard gauge line is the Foxfield Light Railway which runs on the original branch line built in 1893 to serve the

Steam train (known as the Polish Tank) at Kingsley & Froghall station on the Churnet Valley Railway.

colliery at Dilhorne, and this railway was featured in the BBC Television series *Cranford*. Finally, there is also the Chasewater Railway, another former colliery railway which is only 2 miles long and is contained completely within Chasewater Country Park.

Meanwhile, many of the old industrial sites have been converted into museums or visitor centres. At

Dudley, the Black Country Living Museum offers one of the largest open-air museums in the UK where a 19th century town has been beautifully re-created in order to tell the story of the Black Country, complete with working trams to travel around on. Opened in 1978 on former industrial land partly reclaimed from a former railway goods yard, disused lime kilns and former coal pits, the 26 acre site is also home to original and important buildings from the former Staffordshire County Boroughs of Dudley, Walsall, West Bromwich and Wolverhampton, which were relocated to the museum from their original sites. Then in North Staffordshire, the Apedale Heritage Centre offers insights into the coal mining and pottery industries, including underground tours, while it also runs alongside yet another heritage railway, the Apedale Valley Light Railway.

As we come towards the end of Staffordshire's history, it is important to clarify the local government and county border changes implemented towards the end of the 20th century, and which still remain in place today (2016). The first and third of the following maps show the dramatic change in the shape of South Staffordshire following the Local Government

ISAAK WALTON COUNTRY

Earlier we mentioned the fact that the River Dove was the favourite haunt of Izaak Walton and Charles Cotton in the 17th century. The above montage covers the friends' favourite stretch heading down from where Beresford Dale joins Wolfscote Dale (top left), to where Wolfscote Dale joins Dovedale at Milldale (top right), through Dovedale (bottom left) to the stepping stones at the bottom of Thorpe Cloud (bottom right). Today, the entire stretch is a magnet for thousands of tourists and daytrippers, and for which Charles Cotton's verse remains every bit as relevant: "Oh, my beloved nymph, fair Dove, Princess of rivers, how I love, Upon thy flowery banks to lie, And view thy silvery stream, When gilded by a summer's beam."

Act 1972, and which came into effect on the 1ˢᵗ April 1974. It is likely that many folk under the age of 40 who were born in Dudley, Walsall, West Bromwich, Wolverhampton, and dozens of places in between, don't know that their birthplace was in Staffordshire a mere 42 years ago. This is because one of the most radical changes brought about by the 1972 Act was to introduce six brand new metropolitan counties into the English county fold; a fold which had remained virtually unchanged for a thousand years before that. The six new counties were formed to introduce efficiencies in local government to the six most urbanised areas of England outside of London – and hence the formation of the metropolitan county of West Midlands, carved from parts of Staffordshire, Warwickshire and Worcestershire, and centred largely on Birmingham. Staffordshire ceded the most ground to West Midlands, which is evidenced by the fact that four of its seven new metropolitan boroughs created in 1974 – Wolverhampton, Walsall, Dudley and Sandwell – had previously formed the majority of South Staffordshire. The former County Borough of Dudley is worthy of a special mention, though, since it only became part of Staffordshire in 1966, having previously been an exclave of Worcestershire – bar Dudley Castle which had always been in Staffordshire. The rest of Dudley, though, had therefore only been part of Staffordshire for meagre eight years!

District Councils are responsible for local planning, environmental health, and so on. Of course, the eight districts *plus* the City of Stoke-on-Trent still collectively form the ceremonial county of Staffordshire and have one Lord Lieutenant – but he/she now presides over a smaller area than their medieval predecessors did.

There is one final element of boundary change to cover, though, and that is by referring to the middle of the three maps and which covers the highly controversial proposals for Staffordshire issued by the infamous Redcliffe-Maud Report of 1969. This report marked the culmination of the Royal Commission on Local Government in England, which had run from 1966 to 1969 under the chairmanship of Lord Redcliffe-Maud, and had been looking at restructuring local government in England. Typically, the Report's proposals for the county of West Midlands were that it would have been much larger than the one that eventually appeared in 1974. As well as stretching much further south into Worcestershire to include Bromsgrove and Redditch, it also stretched as far north and north-east as Cannock Chase, Lichfield and Tamworth, whilst falling just south of Stafford – which by definition, had to remain part of Staffordshire. Of course, this would effectively have left just the northern half of Staffordshire intact, but the Redcliffe-Maud Report had other even more radical plans, again as demonstrated by the middle of the three maps. Here we can see that a new county of "Stoke and

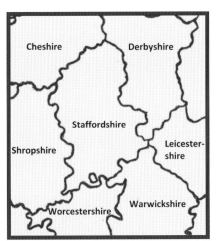

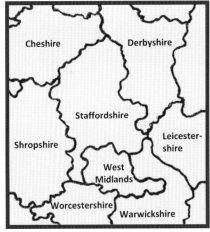

Historic Counties   *Redcliffe-Maud Proposals – 1969*   *Ceremonial Counties – 1997-2016*

The 1972 Act meant that the two other Staffordshire county boroughs of Stoke-on-Trent and Burton upon Trent were also abolished. Stoke became a non-metropolitan *district* in Staffordshire, whilst Burton formed an unparished area in the district of East Staffordshire. Mercifully, nothing much has changed for Staffordshire since 1974, with the only real local government event being the formation of Stoke-on-Trent as a unitary authority in 1997. The city now has its own City Council which runs its own affairs, while the other eight non-metropolitan districts of Staffordshire remain administrered via the standard two-tier "shire county" system – tier 1 being Staffordshire County Council run from its head offices in Stafford, while eight other

North Staffordshire" was proposed, but which as well as including all of its northern territory, would also have eaten up much of south and south-eastern Cheshire, including Congleton, Crewe and Nantwich. Poor Cheshire, meanwhile, would have disappeared altogether, with the rest of it having been swallowed up by the two new metropolitan counties of Merseyside and SELNEC (SE Lancashire/NE Cheshire). Note also, that the south-western part of Derbyshire would have taken the Staffordshire town of Burton upon Trent, too. As it happened, though, the incoming Conservatives of 1970 rejected the Redcliffe-Maud Report and its subsequent Labour-issued White Paper, and created their own White Paper instead. The subsequent Local Government Act

Uttoxeter Racecourse was built in 1907 and today hosts National Hunt racing. Back on June 15th, 1967, it was here that champion jockey Josh Gifford equalled Fred Winter's then-record of 121 winners in a season.

1972 was then based upon the Conservatives' 1971 White Paper proposals, which were considerably less incursive than its Labour predecessor, and this is largely what came to pass in 1974.

The turn of the 20th century had seen a slump in beer sales, partly due to the Liberal government's stance on drinking. This meant that many of the c.30 breweries in Burton were forced to either close or merge, with numbers dropping to 20 by 1900 and to only 8 by 1928. This trend continued all the way into the 1980s, by which time only three main breweries remained – although they were all big companies, these being Bass, Ind Coope and Marston's. Burton's largest brewer in the 19th century, Bass continued to expand in the early 20th century, taking control of a number of other large breweries, while in the 1960s, Bass merged with Charrington United Breweries to once again become the UK's largest brewing company as Bass Charrington. However, in 2000, the brewing operations side of Bass Charrington was bought by Interbrew. Concerned about the monopoly implications of this, the Competition Commission instructed Interbrew to dispose of the brewery and certain brands to the American company Coors, although Interbrew was allowed to retain the rights to the Bass Pale Ale brand. In 2005, Interbrew (now Anheuser-Busch InBev) allowed Marston's to brew draught Bass and hence the red triangle trademark lives on – but not in Burton, for it is now bottled and kegged at Anheuser-Busch InBev's own brewery in Samlesbury, Lancashire. Nevertheless, several well-known brands continue to be brewed in Burton, including Coors, Carling, Worthington, Marston, Burton Bridge and Black Hole.

The 21st century has seen the continued appearance of new attractions in Staffordshire, none more deserving than the National Memorial Arboretum which opened in 2001. Equipped with a fine visitor centre and more than 300 memorials, the 150 acre site is also home to over 30,000 trees and a vast collection of flora, fauna and wildlife habitats. The focal point of this "Centre of

Remembrance" is the Armed Forces Memorial, an immense and elevated circular wall surrounded by dozens of tall and beautifully kept trees. Ascending the steps and passing through one of the two entrances, you will find numerous memorials inside, as well as the

CARRY ON BREWING

Brewing still continues to be one of Burton upon Trent's largest employers, and here we see both large and small-scale breweries. Top is the American giant Coors, who indirectly took over Bass Breweries in 2005. Bottom is a converted water tower on Wharf Road which was built in the 1870s by Thomas Salt & Co Ltd. It was later used by Bass Breweries before falling into disuse until 2001, when the building was purchased by Tower Brewery, whose restoration went on to win a Civic Award.

WONDERFUL TRIBUTE TO OUR HEROES

View towards the Armed Forces Memorial at the National Memorial Arboretum near Alrewas, the largest of over 300 memorials on this 150 acre site.

One of many military reunions that occur at the National Memorial Arboretum on a weekly basis; this is the Royal Pioneer Corps.

This memorial is to those members of the armed forces who fought and who lost their lives in the Falklands War of 1982.

inscribed names of over 16,000 service personnel who have lost their lives in conflict or as a result of terrorism since World War II. However, the space is dominated by a towering obelisk and two stunning sculptures of our forces' personnel caring for the fallen. The whole structure has been superbly aligned so that at 11 am on 11th November, the sun shines through two slits in the outer and inner walls of the memorial, casting a shaft of light across a wreath in the centre.

All of which brings us back to 5th July 2009 – for that was the date that Terry Herbert discovered the Staffordshire Hoard with his metal detector, in a field close to Hammerwich. Over the next five days, Herbert retrieved enough golden objects to fill 244 bags, after which he called in the specialists. Subsequent excavation work was carried out by English Heritage using Birmingham Archaeology (formerly Birmingham University Field Archaeology Unit), and by the time it was complete, over 3,500 artefacts had been recovered. Once the discovery was announced to the world on 24th September 2009, the official website set up to showcase some of the artefacts received over ten million worldwide hits in just the first week! Shortly afterwards, some of the artefacts were showcased at Birmingham Museum and Art Gallery, attracting around 40,000 visitors in just over two weeks! Interestingly, the coroner

for South Staffordshire declared the hoard to be "treasure" and therefore the property of the Crown! Further excavations took place in 2010, aimed at providing a date for the hoard, while December 2012 excavations discovered another 91 pieces of gold and silver metalwork – deemed to be part of the original hoard.

Some Quirky Staffordshire Stats

To complete the Conventional Staffordshire section, here are some unique and quirky statistics. For starters, Bass Breweries' distinctive red triangle became the UK's first registered trademark, while Shugborough's Titanic Brewery is the only log-fired brewery in England that produces beer commercially.

Blithfield's church contains the only altar that used to be a farm bedstead, while Caverswall St Peter's contains the only flag riddled with 17 bullets – this being the flag of the heroic steamship *Clarissa Radcliffe*, torpedoed and battered by the Germans during World War I. Meanwhile, Betley's church includes an unusually wooden-dominated interior, including a wooden roof, clerestory, and pointed arches of the nave arcades while they are supported by eight hexagonal oak pillars. Next, Fazeley's church has clerestory windows

This yew tree in the grounds of Shugborough Hall has the largest crown spread of any evergreen tree found in Britain and Ireland.

This is the Doric Temple, also in the gardens of Shugborough Hall. Built in around 1760, and a copy of the Temple of Hephaistos in Athens, it is believed to be the first accurate revived Greek Doric Temple in Europe.

shaped like clover leaves, while Lapley All Saints' has a mysterious Dutch font. Madeley's church has an unusual outer stair turret while Tamworth's St Editha's church has the only double staircase tower in England, with both rising in double-helix style inside the north-west corner of the tower. Meanwhile, Milwich is home to the oldest dated bell in Staffordshire (1409), while Wednesbury's early 17th century church lectern, fashioned as a gilded fighting cock made of plaster on an oak pedestal, is believed to be unique in England. Sticking with churches, the alabaster monument to Sir John Hanbury at Hanbury church, dates from 1303 and is thought to be the oldest alabaster figure in England, while usage of alabaster in the innermost arch of Tutbury's west doorway is thought to be the earliest use of alabaster for a church arch in England. Weston-under-Lizard's church contains two rare oak monuments of two knights, while Whitmore's St Mary and All Saints' church is another rare part-timber built church. Finally, Wombourne's St Benedict Biscop is the only church in England dedicated to the 7th century saint, while Tipton's parish register is thought to be the oldest in the country, dating back to 24th December 1513.

Other county curiosities include Dudley's High Street – where water on one side flows eastwards towards the North Sea and from the other side flows westwards towards the Bristol Channel, while the

Caldon Canal at Endon is the highest point for a canal in England. Thomas Wedgwood of Etruria was thought to be the first photographer after his discovery of the use of light for making pictures, while Wolverhampton MP, Charles Pelham Villiers was the longest-ever serving MP (from 1835 to 1898), and also the oldest-ever candidate to win a parliamentary seat (aged 93).

Next, the 15th century St John's Hospital at Lichfield was one of the first English houses built after chimneys were introduced into domestic architecture, while the Oakamoor copper factory was where the core of the first Trans-Atlantic cable was made. Moreover James Watt's first engine was set up at Smethwick.

Finally, in 1885, 34 ladies from Leek began making a stunning copy of the Bayeux Tapestry, which took them twelve months to complete. The tapestry includes all of the detail of the original. This means that there are 1,512 embroidered objects, including 623 people, 202 horses and mules, 55 dogs, 505 other creatures, 37 buildings, 41 boats and 49 trees. The tapestry copy was bought in 1895 by Alderman Hill for £500 after which it was given to Reading Museum where it still resides today.

THE QUIRKIEST OF THEM ALL...

The Crooked House at Himley dates from 1785 and was originally perfectly upright. However, as a result of 19th century mining subsidence, the left-hand side of the building is now around four feet lower than the right-hand side!

Inside, The Crooked House is even quirkier. I walked across the bar (above) twice, and it completely confuses your senses, making you stagger!

Quintessentially Quirky – Abbots Bromley

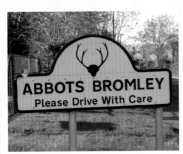

NAME (STATUS):	**ABBOTS BROMLEY** (Village)
POPULATION:	1,179
DISTRICT:	East Staffordshire
EARLIEST RECORD:	*Bromleage*, 942; *Brvnlege*, 1086 (DB); *Bromleia Abbatis*, 1203
MEANING:	Woodland clearing where broom grows.
DERIVATION:	Originally just Bromley, the name is derived from the Old English words *brōm* (broom) and *lēah* (woodland clearing). The "Abbots" affix was applied in the 12th century when the village was given to Burton Abbey.

For *Staffordshire: Unusual & Quirky*, we are introducing a new *Quintessentially Quirky* section – a three-page photo-fest that focuses on one place in the county that encapsulates everything that makes the English so... well... quintessentially quirky! And so with that kind of a brief in mind, there was really only one place to start – so take a bow you Horn Dancers of Abbots Bromley...

The horn dancers are led here up Goose Lane by their accordion players...

... before visiting the first of the farms in the parish...

... where they dance in the farmyard, after which they are given refreshments – that looked rather like tots of the fine stuff to me!

They then dance some more – seen here with the village and St Nicholas's church in the background.

Then it's "Form Up" (left) and off they go up Yeatsall Lane to the next farm... (right)

... and the next dance... and the next set of tots! Then it's off to Admaston, followed by Blithfield Hall where no doubt Lady Bagot also tot-obliges! (right).

Abbots Bromley Quirk Alert: *Getting Horny*

The Abbots Bromley Horn Dance is an English folk dance that is held annually on Wakes Monday. The origin of the custom is thought to date back to pagan times, and therefore to pre-653 which was when the Mercian royal family first converted to Christianity. If this is true, then the dance was probably a pagan fertility rite to usher in a bumper harvest. Another theory is that the Mercian dynasty based at nearby Tamworth, organised magic rituals to ensure a plentiful catch from each year's hunt in Needwood Forest and Cannock Forest; a tradition that then passed through into Christian times and gradually came to be seen as affirming the villagers' hunting rights. Special hunting rights would explain why the custom survived the harsh medieval forest laws, and so perhaps the people of Abbot's Bromley were somehow exempt from them – or perhaps the dancers came to become medieval forest officials themselves, and hence the exemption. This latter theory is supported by some evidence, because the forester positions were generally hereditary, and when Burton Abbey was dissolved in the 1530s, the position was referred to as the "Forester of Bentylee" – therefore we can assume that the Bentley family held official forester positions at that time. And indeed from the Dissolution until the early 20th century, the dance remained the traditional prerogative of the Bentley family, before eventually passing to the Fowell family in 1914 through marriage.

The dance itself is an English folk dance involving six sets of reindeer antlers, three black and three white. The dance is performed by twelve dancers, traditionally all male, and traditionally all originally from the Bentley family and now the Fowell family. Six dancers carry the horns and are accompanied by Maid Marion, the Hobby Horse, a boy with a bow and arrow, the Fool, a Musician and a boy with a triangle. The dance lasts all day. It starts at 08:00 a.m. in St Nicholas's church, where the horns are mounted on the wall. A service of blessing follows, after which the dance begins on the village green. The dancers and the crowd then move around the parish, visiting a number of local farms, before crossing Blithfield Reservoir to Admaston and then on to Blithfield Hall, still home to Lady Bagot, the direct descendant of the medieval Bagot family. The dancers then return to Abbot's Bromley in the early afternoon, making their way around the village, and taking in each of the five village pubs (The Bagot Arms, The Royal Oak (now the Royal Rushi), The Goats Head, The Crown and The Coach & Horses), before eventually returning to the church again at 20:00 where the horns are hung up for another year. A service of Compline then concludes the annual tradition – although a return to the pubs is no doubt also considered traditional!

Interestingly, the first written reference of the horn dance appeared as recently as 1686. However, the antlers have been carbon dated to around 1065, and it is thought that the 11th century set replaced an even earlier set – which could quite easily have been pre-653, the year of the Mercian royal family's conversion to Christianity. Alas, all of this theory linking the custom to pagan times is potentially spoiled by another. For it would appear that while the reindeer antlers date to the 11th century, reindeer had long-since been extinct in Britain by then. So unless domestic reindeer were kept, the antlers must have been imported from Scandinavia – presumably by the Vikings, who therefore could quite easily have owned the previous set, too!

Whatever the origins, though, it is a beautifully quirky and quintessentially English custom that will no doubt survive for many more centuries to come.

The Butter Cross on Abbots Bromley's village green is thought to be the oldest building in the village – and that's no mean feat – although date estimates range from the 13th or 14th century to the 17th.

Nearside is one of many timber-framed buildings in Abbots Bromley, while further down High Street is Abbots Bromley School for Girls, founded in 1874. The school chapel is the building on the left.

Ironically, St Nicholas's church at Abbots Bromley is largely newer than many of the houses in the village – although Arthur Mee quotes the arcades as being 14th century.

The chancel of St Nicholas's church. If you look inside the left-hand arches you will see one of the six mountings for the horns – on the one day out of 365 that they stand vacant!

Church House has a date of 1618 engraved in the door lintel.

The Bagot Arms – and first of the five pubs visited during the afternoon of Wakes Monday by the Abbots Bromley Horn Dancers. Third up is…

… what surely must be the very essence of a quintessentially English pub, The Goat's Head, which overlooks the village green and the Butter Cross.

The last of the five pubs visited by the Horn Dancers is the attractive Coach & Horses.

Quirky Staffordshire

Introducing the Shire-Ode

A Shire-Ode tells the story – in rhyming verse – of fictitious, eccentric inhabitants of the county in question. However, in so doing, it also incorporates into the flow of the verse, many place-names that can be found within that county – places which then go on to form a county almanac, of sorts. Each place appears in roughly alphabetical order, although some of the smaller places are batched up into trios known as a "Three's Up" or appear in the "Best of the Rest" section. The location of all of the places is also pinpointed in the maps on the pages following the Shire-Ode.

As for the *Staffordshire* Shire-Ode, this tells the tale of *The Trentham Triangle*, with the fictitious Bromley Hall lying at its core, the abode of the eccentric Ladymoor, and also the location of a rumoured Coven…

Staffordshire Shire-Ode: The Trentham Triangle

When **Wain Lee** vanished in **Trentham Park**
The police were not **Overley** concerned
There weren't any **Hints**, or fingerprints
Nor the trace of foul play from one spurned.
*(Or so said his girlfriend, **Kerry Hill**, anyway.)*

"Done a runner," they said, "a **Meir** tiff; he's not dead,"
But then **Olive Green** disappeared
They found her false tooth, in a telephone **Booth**
Nothing else – so a link they now feared.
*(Her husband, **Finney Green**, was inconsolable, poor chap.)*

Things soon became worse, in this **Stoke** universe
When **Lynn** and **Jack Hayes** disappeared
In their **Trentham Lake** boats, they'd left only **Cotes**
Now a full-scale mystery reared.
*(Aye, they'd left **Onecote** on the front seat and the other **Coton** the back.)*

But the force were more vexed, by what happened next
In a cell in which **Scot Hay** was locked
At five he'd been booked, but when they next looked
He'd gone – leaving coppers quite **Foxt**.
*(So by now, they had this map with **Four Crosses** marked on it.)*

Then folks were aghast, as they went thick and fast -
Ashley Dale, **Abbey Green**, **Stanley Moor**,
Miles Green, **Roseville**, **Dudley Port**, **Robin Hill**
Yes, **The Straits** were quite dire for the law.
*(Indeed, it seemed that everyone had **Hopton** to the disappearance bandwagon, and the police were all at **Loggerheads** with each other.)*

So D.I. **Hales** took over the case
He vowed to leave no **Stone** unturned
Though he first had to seal, a secure even **Keele**
Plus allay public fears and concerns.
*(Basically, the man saw himself as the proverbial **Knighton** horseback.)*

Then they mapped out the scenes, and thus saw by these means
Over **Trentham**, a **Triangle** formed
And with **Stowe** at its core, **Bromley Hall** they all saw
Where times-past, **Coven** tales had been spawned.
*(Aye, the place seemed to have a bit of a **Haunton** it.)*

In a **Flash**, **Ladymoor** was eyed by the law
A drunkard who "saved" waifs and strays
Could it be she'd **Broughton**, wicked times from long gone
A night-**Maer** spawned through a **Hayes**?
*(As D.I. Hales said: "She certainly **Tixall** the boxes!")*

So with new **Hope** in place, to Stowe they did race
And descended on **Bromley** in force
But the waifs seemed to baulk; appeared too scared to **Talke**
Whilst the lady just stuck to the sauce.
*(And apparently, she was very partial to **Red Bull**, as well!)*

Once the last waif had gone, they had so **Little Onn**
That they watched Bromley Hall from **High Heath**
But all they could see, was the lady's **Yew Tree**
And her **Aston** and **Bentley** beneath.
*(And not forgetting her old **Ford Fiesta**, either.)*

There were **Hawthorns** and **Hazles** in Ladymoor's drive
But nothing suspicious to note
Till PC **Eve Hill**, fell suddenly ill
Then vanished – left only her coat.
*(Alas, whilst DI Hales was taking a **Leek**, too…)*

Aghast they now knew, that a mystic force grew
And the Hall was still **High Onn** their list
So they waited till night, for that crypt candlelight
Where the waifs seemed to gather in tryst.
*(All huddled together in their secret little **Fauld**.)*

Then they crept down **Oak Hill**, via **Field** and **Woodmill**
'Cross **The Heath** and then into **The Woods**
Past **Beech** and **Round Oak**, to the crypt by twelfth stroke
Where lurked shapes, clad in shadowy hoods.
*(So they feared this was no time to **Standon** ceremony!)*

By the **Boundary** fence, they all hid, tight and tense
As they watched the shapes vanish from view
Then by **Wall** they were led, to the crypt **Cellarhead**
Where the sounds of chanting came through.
*(Which all added to a very **Crackley** atmosphere indeed.)*

Then **Ashley Heath**, and his brother **Lea Heath**
Were sent to explore by their boss
But on breaching the crypt, they were seized, gagged and stripped
And **Roughley** lashed down to **Stone Cross**.
*(Not exactly how they'd planned to **Burston** the scene.)*

Ladymoor tied their bounds, then rubbed **Salt** in their wounds
As she gloatingly showed them two wreaths
"There's nowhere to **Hyde Lea**; you're history **Ashley**
"None escape from beneath **Druid's Heath**."
*(A **Sideways** look passed between the two brothers.)*

"Oh, did you not know? Here's not just called Stowe,"
"It was also once called **Deadman's Green**."
As she turned the **Heaton**, their frightened eyes shone
Whilst their foreheads broke out in a **Sheen**.
*(It appeared that this particular cloud had no **Silver End**.)*

"So it's time for **Farewell**," she cruelly did tell
As she tested the edge of her knife
And with Coven chant on, Ladymoor did **Ranton**
Intent to take more human life.
*(Indeed, human life held **Littleworth** for this mad-woman.)*

But Ashley was ready, his **Stanley** quite steady
As he secretly severed their ropes
He then tipped Lea the wink, who did **Acton** instinct
And their breakout went just as they'd hoped.
*(Yep, they managed to **Rushall** those waifs, and brush 'em aside.)*

With a shriek, Ladymoor, threw herself at the door
But then fell on her knife with a cry
How she so craved a drink, as she slipped to the brink –
Then she joined that **Great Barr** in the sky.
*(And thus leaving one less **Knutton** this planet!)*

View to the south-west from The Roaches.

STAFFORDSHIRE LOCATION MAPS FOR THE TRENTHAM TRIANGLE

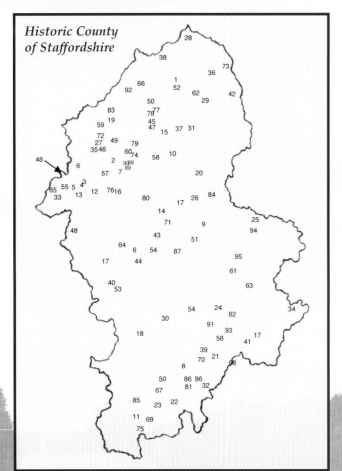

Historic County of Staffordshire

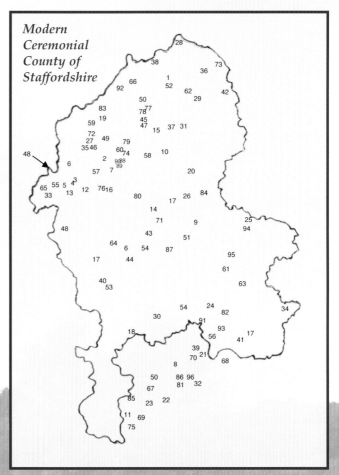

Modern Ceremonial County of Staffordshire

PLACE-NAME TABLE FOR THE TRENTHAM TRIANGLE

1 Abbey Green	2 Acton	3 Ashley	4 Ashley Dale	5 Ashley Heath
6 Aston[1]	7 Beech	8 Bentley	9 Booth	10 Boundary
11 Bromley	12 Bromley Hall	13 Broughton	14 Burston	15 Cellarhead
16 Cotes	17 Coton[2]	18 Coven	19 Crackley	20 Deadman's Green
21 Druids Heath	22 Dudley Port	23 Eve Hill	24 Farewell	25 Fauld
26 Field	27 Finney Green	28 Flash	29 Ford	30 Four Crosses
31 Foxt	32 Great Barr	33 Hales	34 Haunton	35 Hawthorns
36 Hayes	37 Hazles	38 Heaton	39 High Heath	40 High Onn
41 Hints	42 Hope	43 Hopton	44 Hyde Lea	45 Jack Hayes
46 Keele	47 Kerry Hill	48 Knighton[1]	49 Knutton	50 Ladymoor[1]
51 Lea Heath	52 Leek	53 Little Onn	54 Littleworth[1]	55 Loggerheads
56 Lynn	57 Maer	58 Meir	59 Miles Green	60 Oak Hill
61 Olive Green	62 Onecote	63 Overley	64 Ranton	65 Red Bull
66 Robin Hill	67 Roseville	68 Roughley	69 Round Oak	70 Rushall
71 Salt	72 Scot Hay	73 Sheen	74 Sideway	75 Silver End
76 Standon	77 Stanley	78 Stanley Moor	79 Stoke	80 Stone
81 Stone Cross	82 Stowe	83 Talke	84 The Heath	85 The Straits
86 The Woods	87 Tixall	88 Trentham	89 Trentham Lake	90 Trentham Park
91 Triangle	92 Wain Lee	93 Wall	94 Wood End	95 Woodmill
96 Yew Tree	[1] Place appears twice in Staffordshire; [2] Place appears three times in Staffordshire			

The Trentham Triangle –
A Staffordshire Shire-Ode Almanac

NAME (STATUS):	**ABBEY GREEN** (Village)
POPULATION:	c.50
DISTRICT:	Staffordshire Moorlands
EARLIEST RECORD:	The place was still referred to as Dieulacres Abbey (after which Abbey Green is named) on John Speed's map of 1610, but is then recorded as *Abbey Green* in 1611.
MEANING:	The grassy open place at the abbey.

Abbey Green Pub: The Abbey Inn

The Abbey Inn is a Grade II-listed building, and has a lintel over the entrance that is inscribed with the date 1702 along with the initials of the original tenant John Allen. However, initially it appears to have been a private house – and which had a bowling green laid around 1726. The house then became known as Bowling Green House in 1770 and probably wasn't converted to an inn until the early 19th century, but by 1834, it was known as the Bowling Green Inn.

Abbey Green Historic Trivia:
Dieulacres Abbey

Abbey Green was named after, and marks the position of, Dieulacres Abbey, founded in 1214 by Ranulph de Blondeville, 6th Earl of Chester. The abbey was founded for monks of the Cistercian order, previously based in Poulton, Cheshire but who sought sanctuary a little further into England where they would be less prone to attacks from Welsh raiders! De Blondeville also donated the manor of Leek, a mile to the south of the abbey, and the abbey eventually became the second largest monastic land owner in the county, after Burton Abbey. That said, there were numerous disputes over land and the collection of tithes with other monasteries such as Croxden Abbey and Trentham Priory, and which led to successive abbots deploying armed gangs for their protection! They certainly built up a reputation, with a royal commission of 1379 accusing them of "assault, maiming and murder", and indeed the abbot himself was arrested and imprisoned in 1380 following the beheading of a man allegedly at the abbot's command. By 1517, it was the turn of Abbot William Albion to maintain the tone, when he and eight other monks were accused of organising a major riot in Leek with the purpose of preventing the arrest of an abbey steward... also for murder!

Of course, the abbey eventually succumbed to the Dissolution of the Monasteries in 1538, but even the last abbot, Thomas Whitney, had a reputation for violently abusing abbey tenants and was also suspected of fraud! After the Dissolution, the abbey fell into disrepair, although much of its remains, including the gateway to the former abbey, were used as part of the build of a manor house in its place in 1612, by Thomas Rudyard. Originally known as Abbey Dieulacres, it was later converted into a farm known as Abbey Farm.

Abbey Green Quirk Alert:
Wholehearted Commitment

The Abbey of Dieu l'Acres literally means "the acres of God", although it is also reputed that it was named after the exclamation of the wife's founder "may God increase it", when informed by her husband, Ranulph de Blondeville, that he had been requested to move it in a dream – by his deceased grandfather! As was a common custom in those days, de Blondeville's heart was removed and buried at the abbey – after his death, of course – with his body buried elsewhere!

The main (and only) road through Abbey Green.

The Abbey Inn at Abbey Green dates from 1702.

NAME (STATUS):	**ASHLEY** (Village)
POPULATION:	508
DISTRICT:	Newcastle-under-Lyme
EARLIEST RECORD:	*Esselie*, 1086 (Domesday Book)
MEANING:	Clearing in an ash-tree wood.
DERIVATION:	From the Old English words *æsc* (ash-tree) and *lēah* (woodland clearing).

Ashley Church: St John the Baptist

Despite its medieval Gothic appearance, much of Ashley's parish church was rebuilt between 1860 and 1862 by J. Ashdown of London – although the tower is still the 17th century original. The church is home to a number of beautiful tombs in the Gerard Chapel on the north side of the church, including the alabaster tombs marking the passing of Sir Gilbert Gerard (1523-1593), his wife Anne Radcliffe (d.1608) and their son, Thomas Lord Gerard (c.1554-1618). On the opposite side is the Kinnersley Chapel with further monuments to the Kinnersleys of Clough Hall, including one by the famous sculptor, Francis Chantrey dedicated to Thomas Kinnersley (d.1819).

Ashley Historic Trivia: Rectors and Priests

One of Ashley's 17th century rectors was John Lightfoot, who had graduated with honours at Cambridge. On his return to Ashley as rector, he bought the field next to the rectory where he built himself a study, a parlour and a bedroom – all so that he would remain uninterrupted in his studies by any domestic distractions! It certainly paid off, though, as he then went on to become the finest Hebrew scholar of his day. After the Restoration in 1660, he returned to Cambridge University as vice chancellor.

In the late 18th century, emigré priests fleeing from the French Revolution had helped to bolster the English clergy, and one of those priests who settled in Staffordshire was Abbé Louis Martin de Laistre, and who eventually found his way to Ashley in 1796 where he took charge of the Catholic mission there. This, in turn, can trace its origins back to around 1760, when Mass centres, such as that at nearby Gerards Bromley, were serviced by Jesuits. By 1791, services were allowed in registered places, and one such place was

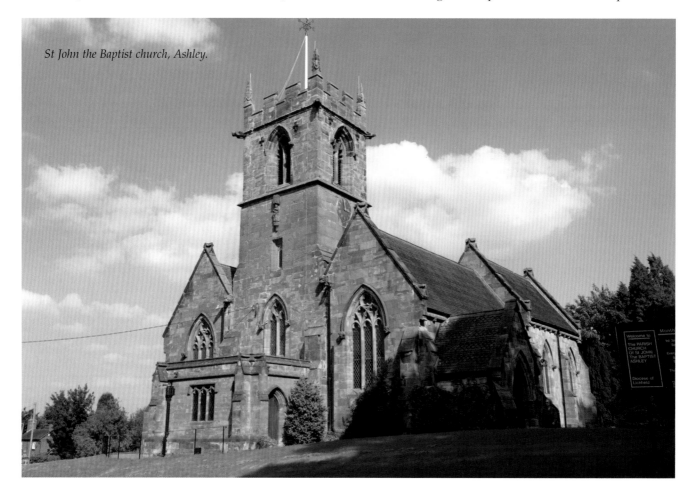

St John the Baptist church, Ashley.

The Catholic Church of Our Lady and St John the Baptist, Ashley, built in the 1820s.

Ashley Methodist church.

registered in Ashley and which was dedicated to St John the Baptist. Prior to this, de Laistre had been taking Mass at Farmer Brown's house in Napley Heath, whilst staying at the rector of Mucklestone's house. However, following the registration in Ashley, the local Catholics wrote to the bishop and successfully requested that de Laistre be appointed as their resident priest. By 1795, Father de Laistre had built a small chapel house in Ashley and was able to run it courtesy of the French lessons he gave and the small farm that he also ran. Alas, de Laistre died suddenly, aged sixty, under suspicious circumstances, with rumours abounding that he had been murdered by a local farmer over a dispute about land. Between 1813 and 1825, Ashley didn't have a resident priest, and was served by Swynnerton and Cobridge. However, in 1823, Father James Egan from Kerry, who was also an architect and skilled builder, oversaw the building of the current church, which was originally dedicated to St Bridgit. He then became resident priest in 1825, while the church was re-dedicated to the Blessed Virgin and St John the Baptist in the 1830s.

Ashley Quirk Alert: Largest In England

Earlier, we mentioned the Gerard Chapel within St John the Baptist church, and the beautiful alabaster monument to Sir Gilbert Gerard (d.1593). This monument, however, expanded over several generations with the initial main structure built under the supervision of Gilbert's son, Thomas, 1st Baron Gerard and which includes Sir Gilbert and his wife, Anne along with her dog. Beneath them is a cadaver, while the kneeling figure of Thomas himself was later added looming over his parents at the head end and what is thought to be the younger son, also Gilbert Gerard, 2nd Baron Gerard, is kneeling and praying at their feet. Sir Gilbert and Anne's four daughters are then depicted on a separate rear panel alongside Anne, while two smaller kneeling and praying female figures, probably from a later generation, have been positioned to the front of the main structure. The monument is then topped off by a large and heavily decorated alabaster canopy, displaying the arms of both the Gerards and the Radcliffes.

Anyway, the work was completed in around 1612, and John Betjeman describes it as "the largest Elizabethan monument in England".

The former Meynell Arms at Ashley is now an Indian restaurant. The building is over 400 years old.

The Peel Arms is a few yards further down Church Road.

Three's-Up!

	ACTON	**ASTON**	**BEECH**
STATUS:	Hamlet	Hamlet * 2	Hamlet
POPULATION:	c.150	c.30	c.40
DISTRICT:	Newcastle-under-Lyme	Stafford, Newcastle-u-Lyme	Newcastle-under-Lyme
EARLIEST RECORD:	*Acton*, 1689	*Estone*, 1086 (Domesday Book)	*Le Bech*, 1295
MEANING:	Farmstead near the oak tree(s).	Usually eastern farmstead or estate.	Place at the beech tree.
DERIVATION:	From the Old English words *āc* (oak) and *tūn* (farmstead).	From the Old English words *ēast* (east) and *tūn* (farmstead).	From the Old English word *bēce* (beech tree).

The main road through Acton.

Two shots of the main road through Aston (Newcastle-under-Lyme).

Three's Up Trivia!

The hamlet of **Acton** is located a couple of miles to the south-west of the outskirts of Newcastle-under-Lyme. Although being slightly larger than most hamlets, it has to be recognised as such as it doesn't possess a church – although it does have a Wesleyan chapel that dates from the late 19th century. Acton should also not be confused with the South Staffordshire village of Acton Trussell (*Actone*, 1086; *Acton Trussel*, 1481), which was differentiated from the Newcastle-under-Lyme Acton in the 14th century by applying the manorial affix of the landowning Trussel family.

Meanwhile, the linear hamlet of **Aston**, also known as Aston-by-Doxey, is situated a couple of miles west of Stafford, and comprises a handful of buildings, farms and Aston Livery Stables along the road known as Aston Bank. The other **Aston** is a pretty little hamlet that is located around a mile north-east of Pipe Gate.

The hamlet of **Beech** is slightly larger, and sits just off the A519 a couple of miles south-west of Trentham, and it is here on Beechdale Lane that you will find what is known as the Beech Caves. The caves are man-made, and date back to at least the 1630s when they were used for quarrying sandstone such as that which went on to be used in the building of Trentham Hall; indeed, a certain Roger Low paid 22 pence a score to remove 130ft of stone from Beech Caves in August 1633.

Much later, during World War II, it is rumoured that the caves were used as either a bomb store for the Royal Ordnance Factory at nearby Swynnerton, or it was in use by the Americans who were based at Trentham – rumoured because the site was "out of bounds" without any forthcoming explanation. As for when the caves became so-named, this happened sometime between 1901 when maps simply refer to the site as a quarry and 1924 when we first see the name Beech Caves appear.

Beech Caves, on Beechdale Lane. Man-made, they were quarried for sandstone as far back as the 1630s.

The woodland that covers a steep hill behind Beech Caves.

NAME (STATUS):	**BENTLEY** (Suburb of Walsall)
POPULATION:	6,371 (Walsall Middle Layer Super Output Area 023)
DISTRICT:	Walsall, West Midlands
EARLIEST RECORD:	*Benætlea*, 12th century
MEANING:	Woodland clearing where bent grass grows.
DERIVATION:	From the Old English words *beonet* (bent grass) and *lēah* (woodland clearing).

Bentley Historic Trivia: King in Disguise

In 1651, the future King Charles II was on the run, following the Royalists' defeat at the Battle of Worcester which took place on 3rd September. Desperately trying to avoid capture by Cromwell's troops, Charles was taken in on the 10th September by Colonel John Lane and his sister Jane Lane both of Bentley Hall. The next day, Jane Lane disguised Charles as her servant and they both set out for Bristol via Stratford, with disguise not an easy task, as at over 6ft, Charles was unusually tall for a man of the 17th century. On stopping over at the home of John Tomes in Long Marston, Charles was somewhat amusingly bullied by the cook because he didn't know how to wind up the roasting jack. Nevertheless, he eventually made it safely to Bristol, although his escape to France took around six weeks and 600 miles before he eventually arrived safely in Normandy on 16th October. As for Lady Jane, word got out that Charles had been aided in his escape by a lady, and so Jane and her brother had to escape to the continent themselves, again disguised as peasants, during their flight to take ship at Great Yarmouth.

Almost a century later, in 1743, Bentley Hall was owned by another John Lane, this one a Justice of the Peace. On October 20th he was greeted by an angry mob that had brought with them the famous John Wesley, founder of the Methodist Church. The great man had apparently been preaching that day in Wednesbury, at which point a number of the "congregation" became angered by his words. Allegedly egged on by the local Anglican vicar, Edward Egginton, the mob descended on Bentley Hall demanding that Lane prosecute Wesley. However, Lane refused to speak to them and his son merely told the mob to "go home and be quiet". The story then goes that the mob went on to Walsall, where a fight broke out with a rival gang, at which point Wesley managed to escape!

The Lanes held Bentley until 1748 when it was sold to Joseph Turton of Wolverhampton and then later, to Lord Anson of Shugborough. By the 19th century, the Jacobean Bentley Hall had been converted into a farm house, after which the estate was mined for ironstone and in the early 20th century for coal. It was the latter that eventually did for the hall, when subsidence led to its demolition in 1929. Today, stonework from the final hall has been worked into the landscaping around what is called Bentley Cairn.

Originally a village, Bentley was subsumed into the Walsall area in the 19th century where it became part of the Darlaston Urban District. However, it was between

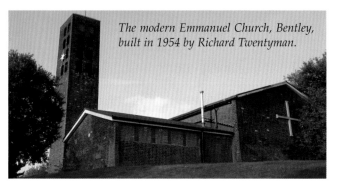

The modern Emmanuel Church, Bentley, built in 1954 by Richard Twentyman.

Bentley Cairn. One of the stones in the cairn depicts Jane Lane of Bentley Hall and her servant – who happens to be Charles II in disguise. The year was 1651 and the future king was fleeing to France with Cromwell's troops in hot pursuit.

The Guru Nanak Gurdwara Sahib, at Bentley – the first Sikh Gurdwara (House of God) in the borough of Walsall.

the late 1940s and the 1960s when the bulk of new local authority housing was built, with many of the roads on the estate taking their name from World War II heroes (i.e. Churchill Road), members of the British Royal Family (i.e. Queen Elizabeth Way) or former politicians (i.e. Attlee Road). Following its realignment to the Walsall Metropolitan District in 1974, further housing development took place between the late 1970s and the early 1980s.

Three's-Up!

	BOOTH	BOUNDARY	BROMLEY HALL
STATUS:	Hamlet	Hamlet	Hall, Hamlet, Mill and Pool (*above*)
POPULATION:	c.20	497 (Dilhorne parish)	c.20
DISTRICT:	East Staffordshire	Staffordshire Moorlands	Stafford
EARLIEST RECORD:	*La Bolde*, 1175	*Boundary*, 1836	*Bramelie*, 1086 (Domesday Book)
MEANING:	Either "house/dwelling place" or "place at the booth/shelter".	Usually place at the boundary.	Woodland clearing where broom grows.
DERIVATION:	From either the Old English word *bold* (house), or the Old Scandinavian word *bōth* (booth or shelter).	Because the place lies at the junction of three parishes.	From the Old English words *brōm* (broom) and *lēah* (woodland clearing); the place is part of Gerard's Bromley where the affix refers to the Gerard family, landowners here in the 16th and 17th century.

Three's Up Trivia!

Booth is located in the middle of nowhere, and pretty much at the centre of a rural triangle formed by Uttoxeter, Rugeley and Stafford. Booth, can only be approached on a northerly or southerly bearing along the single-track Booth Lane. At the northern end is The Blythe Inn and at the southern end is Dapple Heath (*shown top left*). Unsurprisingly, the hamlet is made up of a series of farms and the odd isolated house stretched out along the one and a half mile length of Booth Lane, while the road is bisected roughly half way down by the River Blithe and which flows into the Blithfield Reservoir a mile south of Booth.

Next, **Boundary** is located a couple of miles west of Cheadle, and is home to the Red Lion Inn, and its own chapel, Boundary Methodist church. There was also once a colliery on the northern outskirts of Boundary at Dilhorne known as Foxfield Colliery, and which was worked from 1880 to 1965. The first shaft was completed in around 1888 and went to a depth of 752ft while a second shaft was even deeper at 1,000ft. In its heyday, Foxfield Colliery employed around 390 men underground and another 150 on the surface.

Finally, **Bromley Hall** is located around 3 miles south-east of Ashley alongside the hamlet of Gerrard's Bromley. What is also known as Gerard's Bromley Hall

The Blythe Inn sits at the northern end of Booth Lane.

The River Blithe where it bisects Booth Lane roughly half way down.

Boundary Methodist church.

The Red Lion Inn at Boundary.

A number of the Gerard's have already been mentioned in the Ashley chapter, thanks to the stunning alabaster monument to their family at Ashley's church. This includes Sir Gilbert Gerard (d.1593) who was a prominent lawyer, landowner and politician, returned six times as an MP for four different constituencies; more significantly, he was also Elizabeth I's Attorney General from 1559 to 1581 and Master of the Rolls in 1581. His son, Thomas, was created the 1st Baron Gerard, of Gerard's Bromley in 1616, and who was succeeded as 2nd Baron by his younger brother, also called Gilbert Gerard, a year later. The barony of Gerard's Bromley passed down the family until the death of the 5th Baron in 1684 when it passed to his second cousin Charles. On Charles' death, succession passed to his brother Philip Gerard. However, as a Jesuit priest, he died without children in 1773 and the barony expired.

The Elizabethan Bromley Hall was demolished in the 1750s, but some of the farm buildings and the grand gateway survive today. Also here today is Bromley Pool and Bromley Mill Farm.

is actually a Grade II-listed building, and its grounds contain the earthworks of the formal gardens that were laid out to the south-east of the present house, and which date from around 1575. These gardens were then later adapted by John Rea (d.1681), for Charles Gerard, 4th Baron Gerard. John Rea was reputed to have the largest collection of tulips in England, while he also wrote a book in 1665 entitled *Flora, Seu, de Florum Cultura, Or a Complete Florilege*, dedicating the book to Charles Gerard's son. A copy of this book was recently auctioned at Christie's and sold for $2,750, where it was described as a "FIRST EDITION of one of the most important gardening books to be published in England during the second half of the seventeenth century."

Bromley Pool, which lies adjacent to Bromley Mill and Bromley Hall Farm.

The view from Commonside at Boundary.

Looking beyond the north-western edge of Bromley Pool. So is it common for cows to congregate on the summit of a hill? If not, perhaps this was a defensive formation in preparation for an attack from another herd!

NAME (STATUS):	**BROUGHTON** (Church and Hall)
DISTRICT:	Stafford
EARLIEST RECORD:	*Hereborgestone*, 1086 (Domesday Book), *Borchton*, 1258
MEANING:	Either "farmstead by a brook", or possibly "farmstead belonging to a man called Hereburh.
DERIVATION:	From either the Old English words *brōc* (brook) and *tūn* (farmstead), or the Anglo-Saxon personal name *Hereburh* plus *tūn*.

Broughton Church: St Peter's

St Peter's church was originally built as a private chapel by Thomas Broughton in 1630 on the site of an earlier medieval church. Initially, baptisms and marriage of anyone other than members of the Broughton family or those living or staying in the hall were forbidden except with the permission of the vicar of Eccleshall! Thomas Broughton also had the right to nominate a suitable chaplain, but they had to be a graduate with either a BA or an MA, while even the parish clerk was expected to be "a man of education".

St Peter's is constructed of local sandstone and the six crocketed pinnacles on its tower are still the 1630 originals, as is the main door and the priest's door, although the porch was probably added slightly later. Internally, the most striking feature of the nave is the high oak box pews that were probably installed sometime around 1711 – and which are probably contemporary with a brass plaque containing the names of thirty-five local people who had been allowed to worship at the chapel by gracious permission of the first baronet! Also worthy of note are the many memorials and monuments to the Broughton family, as well as the unusual-looking font – a recess carved out deeply from the wall of one of the tower piers. Finally, the glass in the chancel is much older than the church, most having originated from the chapel at Doddington Park in Cheshire (the main seat of the Broughton family) when Thomas Broughton had the hall and chapel demolished in order to build a new one.

St Peter's church actually remained a chapel of ease until 1907, when a district chapelry was assigned to it by Order in Council, while today it is part of the benefice of Ashley, Broughton, Croxton and Mucklestone.

Broughton Historic Trivia:
Broughton's, the Civil War and Tragedy

The manor of *Hereborgestone*, as Broughton was known in the late 11th century, was owned by the Bishops of Chester both during Anglo-Saxon rule and by the time Domesday Book had been compiled in 1086. However, by the 13th century, it was owned by the Broughton family – who, like so many other medieval families took the name of their manor as their surname. The family was actually descended from Richard Vernon, fourth son of the 3rd medieval Baron Vernon of Shipbrook, Cheshire, and it was his great grandson, Roger, who acquired the estate at Broughton in 1271.

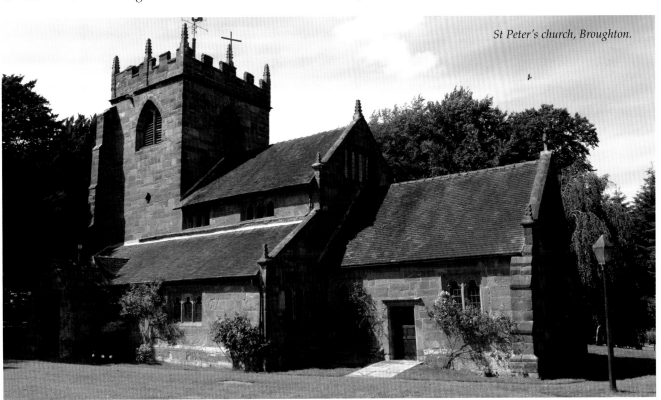

St Peter's church, Broughton.

Broughton Parish Room, a mile down the B5026 from Broughton in Wetwood. The plaque (inset) informs that Lady Broughton laid the building's foundation stone in October 1907.

LAUS DEO
THIS FOUNDATION STONE
WAS LAID BY
LADY BROUGHTON
OCTOBER 13TH 1907

Broughton Hall is a Grade I-list manor house that was built in the mid-16th century and still sports the Elizabethan black and white timbered style today, although the house was later stuccoed. Around a century later, Broughton Hall sheltered a Royalist fugitive from the Battle of Worcester (1651). His name was Colonel Blagg, and he had fled the battlefield allegedly with one of the crown jewels. The jewel then passed from Blagg to George Barlow, who passed it onto the great Isaak Walton who managed to avoid being discovered in possession of the jewel – which would have meant the Tower of London for him – and which is where Blagg ended up, having been arrested shortly after passing on the jewel to Barlow. However, Blagg managed to escape from the Tower, collected the jewel from Walton, and then managed to cross the Channel and reunite the jewel with Charles II. As for the owner of Broughton Hall during the English Civil War, this was Thomas Broughton (d.1648), a fervent Royalist and hence the £3,500 his family had to pay at the end of the Civil War to regain their estates after they had been sequestered by Parliament; indeed, Cromwell's troops had even billeted at the hall, while poor Thomas languished in Stafford jail. However, the Restoration saw Broughton family fortunes improve when Thomas's son, Sir Brian Broughton was rewarded with the Broughton baronetcy in 1661 along with the office of High Sheriff of Staffordshire.

The marriage of the third baronet in 1711 to Elizabeth Delves of Doddington Hall, in Cheshire, brought about the surname Delves Broughton, and which still survives today. By the time the title had passed down to the sixth baronet in 1766, the Revd Sir Thomas Delves Broughton, the family had removed themselves from Broughton and established Doddington Hall as their main seat. By 1914, the Broughton estate had been sold by the 11th baronet, Sir Henry Delves Broughton, to a Midlands industrialist called John Hall, and it was he who removed the stucco to re-expose the original timbers of Broughton Hall. He also extended the property and carried out significant restoration work. The 1940s then saw the house converted to a school for a short while until it was donated to the nuns of the Franciscan order of St Joseph

in 1952. The hall was then abandoned in the 1990s until bought privately in 2003 by the Stoke-on-Trent billionaire businessman John Caudwell, who founded the company Phones4U.

As for the Broughtons, their baronetcy still continues and is currently in its 13th incarnation, although succession is disputed and not currently proven. The seat is still at Doddington Park in Cheshire and is in possession of the family of Sir Evelyn Delves Broughton, the 12th Baronet who died in 1993. Tragically, Sir Evelyn Delves Broughton's only son, John, died aged only two after drowning in an ornamental pond. Equally tragic is the life of his eldest child, Isabella Delves Broughton, better known as influential fashion stylist Isabella Blow, and for whom the little boy's death had a profound effect. A magazine editor who forged a famous fashion relationship with hat designer, Philip Treacy, she was also credited with discovering the models Stella Tennant and Sophie Dahl as well as fashion designer Alexander McQueen. Alas, Isabella suffered terribly from depression, which presumably wasn't helped by being disinherited from her father's estate on his death in 1993. She took her own life in 2007, aged only forty-eight.

Broughton Quirk Alert: Haunted and Cursed

Broughton Hall is reputed to be haunted by a drummer boy, seen by several people who have actually mistaken him for a real person. The story goes that the boy opened a window and shouted his support for King Charles as a troop of Parliamentarians walked past – at which point, one of the soldiers promptly shot him with his musket. Mortally wounded, it took the poor boy two days to die and it is said that the floorboards are still stained by his blood. His ghost is nicknamed Red Socks… because of the red socks that he wears! Local folklore also has it that the hall is cursed, too, the curse being that no elder son will live to inherit it. Tragically, this isn't remotely amusing considering poor John Delves Broughton, drowning in 1964. As for Broughton Hall now, John Caudwell announced in 2015 that he is to build a railway in his grounds to ferry his family, friends and guests around his 28 acres!

NAME (STATUS):	**BURSTON** (Village)
POPULATION:	361 (Parish of Sandon and Burston)
DISTRICT:	Stafford
EARLIEST RECORD:	*Burouestone*, 1086 (Domesday Book)
MEANING:	Possibly farmstead of a man called Burgwine or Burgwulf.
DERIVATION:	From the Old English personal name of either *Burgwine* or *Burgwulf*, plus the Old English word *tūn* (farmstead).

St Rufin's chapel at Burston is named after the 7th century saint who was martyred very close to this spot. The chapel is also unusual in that it is adjoined to a house, shown here on its right-hand side.

The Greyhound Inn, Burston.

Burston Church: St Ruthin's

Burston's chapel of St Ruthin is one of the smallest chapels in Staffordshire, and is unusual in that it is attached to a house. Built in 1850, the chapel is also associated with a 1400-year-old legend that suggests that St Rufin and St Wulfad were martyred nearby; indeed it is thought that the chapel was built on or close to the site of the old Saxon shrine to Rufin, just to the south-west of the village and which is said to have marked the spot where he was killed. As for the chapel's predecessor, it was known to have been in use in the 16th century, but what remained of it was destroyed when the Trent and Mersey Canal was built through the village in the 18th century. Finally, a holy well on the Burston side of the canal is known as St Rufin's Well. As for Burston's parish church, that is All Saints' church at neighbouring Sandon.

Burston Historic Trivia: The Trail of the Mercian Saints

As a result of the local martyrdom of St Rufin, along with the other Staffordshire-related martyrs of St Wulfad, St Werburga and St Chad, Burston has recently become a key point of interest on the Trail of the Mercian Saints – also known as Two Saints Way. The trail runs for around 90 miles between the cathedral cities of Chester and Lichfield, and the Stone to Sandon stage is known as Stage 11. As for the legend, there are many in nearby Stone who would have you believe that the town was the early capital of Mercia on the east bank of the Trent and that it was therefore the first royal seat of Mercia rather than Tamworth. Just north of Stone is the site of the large Iron Age hillfort of Bury Bank which was later thought to have been the Royal Mansion of the Mercian King Wulfhere (658-674), son of Penda, and the most powerful monarch south of the Humber. Now legend has it that Stone owes its origin to the murder of two of Wulfhere's sons, at his own hand – these being the Saxon Princes, Rufin and Wulfad. Like his father, Penda, Wulfhere had

The picturesque millpond at Burston.

Cottages in front of the millpond.

been a Pagan, but on his marriage to Ermenilda, a Saxon princess of the Royal and Christian house of Kent, Wulfhere converted to Christianity. However, on returning to his home in Mercia, close to modern-day Stone, Wulfhere reverted to Paganism, plus he also refused to allow his two sons to be brought up in the Christian faith.

Anyway, as they grew up, the boys became very fond of hunting until one day when, as Wulfad was about to shoot a white stag, his hand was stayed by a hermit silently standing by his cave. The hermit was the future Saint Chad, the man who brought Christianity to Mercia, and over time, Wulfad and Rufin often returned to the cave to be taught by Chad, eventually secretly converting to Christianity. Meanwhile, back at the Royal Mansion, Wulfad and Rufin's sister, Werburga, had attracted the interest of Werebode, King Wulfhere's general. Wulfhere gave his consent for Werebode to marry Werburga, but she refused, claiming that she would only marry a Christian. Insulted, Werebode sought his revenge, which he duly delivered by following Rufin and Wulfad to one of their secret teachings with Chad. He immediately informed King Wulfhere, adding in the suggestion that the three Christians were plotting to overthrow him. The gullible Wulfhere ordered their immediate deaths, but on returning that day, the boys were tipped off and subsequently fled. Alas, Wulfhere pursued them and slaughtered them himself, Wulfad first at what is now Stone and Rufin shortly afterwards at Burston. A distraught Ermenilda and Werburga then gathered up their bodies and interred them "under a great sepulchre of stones", thus lending Stone its future name. Wulfhere was then

apparently filled with remorse for his actions and sought and received absolution from Chad. This time, Wulfhere renounced his pagan beliefs for good and became the first Christian King of Mercia. Ermenilda, meanwhile, built a priory on the site of Wulfad and Rufin's grave, and it soon became a magnet for pilgrims. Records don't state what happened to the duplicitous Werebode, but one would hope that he didn't get to marry Werburga!

So, that's the legend. Alas, there are many who dismiss the whole tale as the romanticisms of 12th century storytellers!

Burston Quirk Alert: Sideways Slant

The information panel at Burston millpond is very informative. It also includes William Kip's Staffordshire map of 1610 (*shown below*)… and which reads south to north, from left to right.

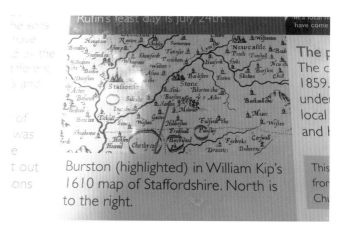

Burston (highlighted) in William Kip's 1610 map of Staffordshire. North is to the right.

Three's-Up!

	CELLARHEAD	COTES	COTON
STATUS:	Village	Hamlet	Hamlet * 2; suburb * 1
POPULATION:	150	c.20	c.20; c.20; 3,840
DISTRICT:	Staffordshire Moorlands	Stafford	Stafford (E), Stafford (W), Tamworth
EARLIEST RECORD:	*Sellarhead* (1736); Cellar Head (1775)	*Cota*, 1086 (Domesday Book)	*Cote*, 1086 (Stafford [E]); *Coten*, 1327 (Stafford [W]); *Coten*, 1313 (Tamworth)
MEANING:	See Three's Up Tivia	The cottages or huts.	Place at the cottages or huts.
DERIVATION:	See Three's Up Tivia	From the Old English word *cot* (cottage, hut or shelter).	From the Old English word *cot*, in its plural form of *cotum*.

Three's Up Trivia!

Cellarhead is a small village located to the east of Stoke-on-Trent in the Consall parish at the busy crossroads formed by the A52 and the A520. In the early 20th century, Cellarhead crossroads had a pub on every corner; on the western side was The Royal Oak and The

Red Lion while opposite were The Bowling Green and The Hope And Anchor. Today, none of these pubs survive! The Bowling Green (NE point) is now a health and wellbeing centre, The Hope and Anchor (SE point) is an Indian restaurant, The Royal Oak (SW point) is a hairdressers and The Red Lion (NW point) is a private residence. Of the four, the eastern pair survived as pubs until quite recently, but the western pair ceased serving alcohol many decades ago.

The pubs may well have influenced the place-name, too, for the word "cellar" is usually associated with land belonging to an ecclesiastical cellerar, but there isn't an ecclesiastical connection in Cellarhead's case.

Other definitions equate "cellar-head" to "a canopy" or "the high ground with the shelter" (Cellarhead is indeed located on high exposed ground), while the English Dialect Dictionary describes cellar-head as "the landing at the top of the stairs leading to the cellar". So the place-name may well be a combination of these definitions with a public house; certainly a pub is recorded here in 1798, and Yates' map of 1775 shows one building here at the south-eastern corner of the crossroads.

As for **Cotes**, the place is a tiny hamlet located down Cotes Lane, less than a mile to the east of the slightly larger Cotes Heath. Cotes consists of a couple of farms

The west-to-east cast-iron milestone marker at Cellarhead (left) and its north-to-south sister (right).

The busy Cellarhead crossroads, where the A52 and the A520 meet, used to have a pub on every corner. However, none of them survive today, with the former Hope and Anchor now an Indian restaurant (below) and the former Bowling Green now a wellbeing centre (above). The other two corners were occupied by the now long-gone Royal Oak and Red Lion.

St James's church at Cotes Heath.

Cotes Lane, the only road through the tiny hamlet of Cotes.

and a handful of buildings, whereas Cotes Heath has its own church, St James's.

Coton appears three times in Staffordshire. Two of them are tiny hamlets in the Stafford district; one on the border with East Staffordshire on the B5027, around 7 miles south-west of Uttoxeter, and the other over on the other side of both district and county, just west of Gnosall and 3 miles from the Shropshire border. The more easterly of the two has its handful of houses

augmented by the Green Lea First School, while the more westerly Stafford-based Coton can be found down a single-track lane. That leaves the largest of the three which is a suburb of Tamworth located on the north-western outskirts of the town. At the north-western tip of this Coton is the pub known as The Fox, while a few yards east of the pub is the intriguing street name of "Mariner"… and where you will find the Lichfield Road Industrial Estate.

The village of Coton, around 7 miles south-west of Uttoxeter.

Also at the more easterly-based Stafford Coton is this former pub, The Wheatsheaf, and which is clearly in a very sorry state today.

The Fox, at the Coton that is located on the north-western outskirts of Tamworth is in a much healthier state!

The junction between Coton Lane End and the A518 at the Coton that is located immediately west of Gnosall.

NAME (STATUS):	**COVEN** (Village)
POPULATION:	7,329 (Parish of Brewood and Coven)
DISTRICT:	South Staffordshire
EARLIEST RECORD:	*Cove*, 1086 (Domesday Book)
MEANING:	Place at the huts or shelters.
DERIVATION:	From the Old English for *cofa* (plural *cofum*), meaning "chamber, cave, cove or hut".

The Fox and Anchor, at Coven.

The Staffordshire and Worcestershire Canal at Coven.

Coven Pub: The Fox and Anchor

The Fox and Anchor can be found on the south-eastern outskirts of Coven alongside the Staffordshire and Worcestershire Canal. This quintessentially English pub dates back to the late eighteenth century when it was known simply as the Anchor Inn. However, the original was destroyed by fire and the current pub was built in the early 1960s.

Coven Church: St Paul's

Although St Paul's church is Grade II listed, it was built relatively recently, in 1857, by Edward Banks of Wolverhampton. It was built on land donated by George Monckton, who also contributed towards the cost. Built in the Early English style, it consists of a nave, two transepts and a 16ft square chancel. The church was also consecrated the same year (1857) by the Bishop

St Paul's church, Coven.

of Lichfield. As for today, St Paul's is one of a growing number of ecumenical churches working together with local Methodist and Roman Catholic congregations.

Coven Historic Trivia: Homage to Iron-Founding

Coven is recorded as *Cove* in Domesday Book (1086), and is listed as belonging to the Norman lord, William de Stafford, while it also informs us that the previously disenfranchised Anglo-Saxon was the unfortunate Ailric. By 1166, the village had lent its name to the family of Alan de Coven, who held a knights fee under Robert de Stafford, and indeed, this manorial right lasted until as late as 1956 when held by Major R. F. Monckton.

By the 17th century, the village was home to a furnace and two forges where iron-making was practised. It was also home to the building known as The Homage, built in around 1679 and thought to be the oldest brick-built house in Staffordshire. Meanwhile, by 1771, Coven was brushed on its eastern flank by the Staffordshire and Worcestershire Canal, one of James Brindley's earliest projects, and which ran for 46 miles from the Trent and Mersey Canal at Great Haywood, to the River Severn at Stourport.

By 1851, Coven had become a working village of around 800 people, and by 1860 it was dominated by an iron-smelting foundry founded by local resident John Smith, and which produced stationary steam engines and locomotives. The Smiths lived in Lawn Lane and their foundry was located in between their cottage and Brewood Road. Downstairs was the machine shop and alongside was the foundry and the blacksmith's shop, while the first floor pattern shop doubled up as a Sunday school – all perfectly logical, as John Smith was also the local preacher, presumably preaching in the Methodist chapel that had been part-built in his garden in 1839! In fact, to get to the chapel, the minister had to pass through Smith's cottage! The chapel is still there on Lawn Lane today.

Coven Quirk Alert: Eponymous Panthers

Burnt Mill in Coven was so-named because it, well, burnt down. As for Jackson's Bridge, that was so-named after a certain Mr Jackson hanged himself beneath the bridge. Finally, the stones for St Paul's church were provided by Thomas Giffard, whose family have owned the estate of Brewood and Coven since 1178 – and whose descendants still live at nearby Chillington Manor – where local legend has it that a panther was once killed in the grounds by a bow and arrow.

The Fox and Anchor, shown from the rear alongside the Staffordshire and Worcestershire Canal.

Three's-Up!

	CRACKLEY	DEADMAN'S GREEN	DRUIDS HEATH
STATUS:	Estate (of Chesterton)	Area to the east of Checkley	Heathland and Golf Course
POPULATION:	7,285 (Chesterton)	N/A	N/A
DISTRICT:	Newcastle-under-Lyme	Staffordshire Moorlands	Walsall, West Midlands
EARLIEST RECORD:	*Crackley*, 1960	*Dadelond*, 1317	*Druwode*, 1326
MEANING:	Unknown	Land of many dead men; "Green" affix applied by early 16th century.	Heath or wood belonging to a man called Dru (the diminutive of Drogo).
DERIVATION:	Unknown	Deadman's Green was the site of an ancient battle between Anglo-Saxon and Dane.	From the personal name Dru or Drogo, plus the Old English word *hæth* (heath, heather or uncultivated land).

Crackley is an estate on the north-western outskirts of the large village of Chesterton. Many of the estate's houses were built for the miners of the nearby Holditch Colliery in Chesterton, which was opened in 1912 but closed in 1989 due to cheaper foreign coal. Known locally as 'Brymbo', two shafts were sunk in 1912 and 1916, that each ran to a depth of around 2,000 feet and provided access to the Great Row and the Four Feet seams. At its height, the colliery employed 1,500 men who mined for ironstone as well as coal and, in 1947, output reached 400,000 tons of coal, while towards the end it was outputting 500,000 tons. Alas, like many collieries, it had its own disaster. Known as the Holditch Colliery Disaster, it occurred on 2nd July 1937 and was caused by the ignition of firedamp (methane gas) by a coal-cutting machine which, in turn, resulted in a fire which set off a series of explosions, killing 30 men, including four men from the Hanley Rescue Brigade. The story is a gripping one and commences at 05:45 with a coal cutter called William Beardmore noticing a flame, which quickly spread across the coalface into a lethal wall of fire. Of the 55 miners working in the vicinity, two were lost in the smoke and presumed dead, while the remaining 53 tried in vain to put out

A mile south-west of Crackley is the Apedale Heritage Centre. In the foreground is the monument to the 30 miners of Holditch Colliery who died as a result of the explosion on 2nd June 1937.

the fire. As the first of the explosions occurred at 06:50, a full evacuation was ordered, and the men began implementing two stoppings on solid ground – a method of building dams from sand, stone and dust to manipulate the air flow in order to dilute and render methane harmless. By 07:20, the night-shift was sent home, and the day-shift took over work on the stoppings. Alas, their plan was then overruled by the managing director, who despite opposition, made the fatal decision to place three stoppings in a position that would enable the coal seam to be saved – but which also placed them onto unstable ground. By 09:10, a sixth explosion occurred, but the 35 men of the day-shift continued work on their new stoppings. The seventh (and small) explosion didn't then occur until 10:10, but it was shortly followed by a massive and deadly eighth explosion, and which threw men to the ground who were standing 1,000 yards away. Of the men working underground, it killed thirty, and the remaining eight were badly burned. A later investigation was summarised by Inspector Wynne as follows: "It is my considered opinion that at the time the second plan was adopted, very dangerous conditions existed, and were known at the time to

Above: *The three Anglo-Saxon crosses in the churchyard at Checkley St Mary and All Saints, which are reputed to commemorate three bishops killed in an ancient battle at nearby Deadman's Green. The left-hand stone depicts the three bishops, complete with halo.*

Left: *The church of St Mary and All Saints at Checkley is deemed one of England's finest Norman churches, although the tower is 15th century rising from its Norman base.*

exist which made the attempt to follow this plan a matter of imminent peril to the lives of the unnecessarily large number of men required to execute it."

On a brighter note, on 19th October 1937, Scottish Football League champions Rangers played Stoke City at the nearby Victoria Ground in a benefit match for the victims of the disaster, raising £2,000 for the relief fund. On a not so bright note, though, another eleven lives were claimed between 1949 and 1967, mainly due to roof falls. Today, the former colliery site is occupied by a large business park.

Meanwhile, at Checkley in East Staffordshire, the Norman church of St Mary and All Saints is rated as one of England's best. However, in its churchyard you will find the fragments of three Anglo-Saxon crosses, and local legend has it that they commemorate three bishops killed in a battle between the Saxons and the Danes at **Deadman's Green** – and where the combatants are reputed to have fought naked! Deadman's Green is attached to the east of Checkley (*shown opposite, top centre*) and got its name because of the legend and the high number of casualties. As for those three crosses, the engraving on one of them certainly has rows of three human figures with what appear to be halos around their heads – and hence the theory regard-

ing the Christian bishops who are said to have died during the battle at Deadman's Green. Whatever their story, though, it is fairly certain that the crosses pre-date the Norman church.

Originally recorded as *Dadelond* in 1317, the place doesn't appear with its affix until 1514 when it is named as *Dadland Grene*, with the affix deriving from the Old English word *grēne*, meaning "green coloured, grassy place or a village green". On a more mundane level, Deadman's Green is now the site of a water treatment works!

Finally, **Druids Heath** is an area of heathland immediately east of Aldridge and which lends its name to Druids Heath Golf Club which opened in 1974. The place was named after a man called Dru or Drogo in the early 13th century, and there is certainly no evidence to suggest that Druids ever lived here. Over time, the *Druwode* of 1326 gradually morphs into Druids Heath, via *le Drewed field* (1592), *Drewed field* (1684), *Drewed Field* (1712) and finally *Druid Heath* (1798). As for the family Dru, they were Norman landowners who were the lords of Aldridge, and who derived their name from Dreux, in the department of Eure-et-Loir in Normandy. They owned this area of heathland that originally adjoined Cannock Forest to the east.

Years before the golf club appeared, the area was home to an orphanage that was actually known as Druids Heath Orphanage. It was opened in 1904 by the Royal Antediluvian Order of Buffaloes (RAOB) – a British charitable fraternity dating back to 1822. It was initially home to forty children – mainly orphans but also some children beyond the control of their parents. Druids Heath Orphanage was expanded to accommodate sixty children in 1912, and further wings were added in 1921. Alas, the ownership of the property had long been subject to dispute, and as a result, the RAOB orphanage was eventually moved to Harrogate in the 1930s. The building continued to be used, first as a Junior Approved School from 1940 to 1973, when it became a community home with education. The original school building was then replaced in 1980 by modern buildings and was renamed the Druids Heath Centre, but this only lasted until 1988 after which new housing was built on the site.

The 18th hole at Druids Heath Golf Club.

NAME (STATUS):	**DUDLEY PORT** (Built-up area attached to Tipton)
POPULATION:	12,834 (Tipton Green)
DISTRICT:	Sandwell, West Midlands
EARLIEST RECORD:	*Dudley Port*, 1802
MEANING/DERIVATION:	Named to reflect the large number of warehouses and wharves that emerged around the Birmingham Canal to serve industry in nearby 19th century Dudley. Initially known as Dudley's Port, it eventually evolved into Dudley Port.
FAMOUR RESIDENTS:	David Burrows (b.1968), former West Bromwich Albion, Liverpool, Everton and Coventry City footballer was born in Dudley but grew up on the Denbigh Estate in Dudley Port.

The Old Court House stands opposite the former St Martin's church at Dudley Port. The latter is now a stunning private residence that featured on Channel 4's Grand Designs.

Dudley Port Church: St Martin's

St Martin's church is on the east side of the Tipton Parish in the village of Horseley Heath, which adjoins Dudley Port to the south. It was built between 1795 and 1797 in a plain Georgian style, using bricks encased in cement. However, it still contains the standard nave, aisles and chancel, while its unusual feature is the tower with its belfry dome which is home to a peal of eight bells.

The church originally replaced the former Tipton parish church of St John's, which had fallen into disrepair. Alas, St Martin's in turn had become redundant by 1992, and soon became derelict, too. Step forward builder Dean Marks, who purchased the property in 1999 for a mere £12,750 and set about renovating it. The project eventually ended up on Channel 4's *Grand Designs* programme in 2007 where it won their runners-up prize for that year, but not before it cost Marks serious health problems caused by his demanding building schedule, and a series of mindless vandal attacks on the property. As for the church renovation, it included 11 miles of electric cable and 3½ miles of pipes, and was eventually converted into a private house of five bedrooms, four bathrooms, an indoor swimming pool, gym and library. Remarkably, the build cost Marks only £110,000 financially; it is now worth an estimated £1.5 million.

Dudley Port Historic Trivia: Disasters

Today, Dudley Port is a built-up area that is located half way between West Bromwich to the east, and Dudley to the west. It is part of the ward of Tipton Green in the county of West Midlands, but before April 1st 1974, it was part of Staffordshire.

Dudley Port Junction is also a major waterway junction of the Birmingham Canal Navigations between its Main Line and the Netherton Tunnel Branch. The first canal built in what was to become the Birmingham Canal Network (BCN), was the Birmingham Canal, built between 1768 and 1772 by the great James Brindley, while Dudley Port's section formed part of Thomas Telford's improvements in the 1830s. This section was also the scene of a disaster at around 02:30 am on Saturday 9th September 1899, when what is known as a "canal burst" occurred. The burst opened a hole 30 yards wide by 100 yards long, emptying the water from 6 miles of canal into the Dudley Port area. Amazingly, no-one was killed, although one boatman had to leap on to the towpath as his boat overtook the horse that was towing it! Thankfully for the horse (and his boat), he managed to tie the towline around a telegraph pole and saved them the fate of disappearing through the gaping hole. It was thought that subsidence caused the breach, with the nearby works of

In the foreground is the railway bridge which takes the main line from Wolverhampton to Birmingham over Dudley Port Road. The bridge behind is the Ryland Aqueduct which takes the Birmingham Canal over the road.

Samuel Barnett's Rattlechain & Stour Valley Brickworks deemed responsible thanks to the extraction of clay too close to the canal. The damage to Dudley Port property was estimated at £50,000, and took many months to repair.

A few decades earlier, in 1852, Dudley Port railway station was opened. Passenger services were run initially, but due to a declining number of passengers in the 1880s, it became a freight-only line in 1887, for which it was heavily used in order to service the highly industrialised area of the Black Country. Dudley Port Station was originally known as Dudley Port High Level Station in order to distinguish it from the Low Level Station on the South Staffordshire line (opened 1850) from Dudley to Walsall, and which passes beneath. The High Level affix was dropped in 1964 when the Beeching Axe put paid to the Low Level station, although it continued to be used for freight until 1993. Today, Dudley Port is served by London Midland's services between Walsall and Wolverhampton. However, Phase Two of the Midland Metro will see the former South Staffordshire line reopening between Walsall and the Merry Hill Shopping Centre via Dudley Port. This will be for trams on one track and freight on the other, with the Lower Level station re-opening as a Midland Metro tram stop.

The memorial to the 19 girls who died in the Tipton Disaster of 1922, when a spark and a pile of gunpowder triggered a massive explosion in a factory. They were all aged between 13 and 15.

One of Dudley Port's most famous landmarks is the Ryland Aqueduct, also known as Dudley Port Bridge. It was built in 1836, and carried the Birmingham Canal over what is now the A461, also known as Dudley Port Road. Today, it also takes the mainline rail service from Wolverhampton to Birmingham over Dudley Port Road alongside Dudley Port Station.

Moving into the twentieth century, and the year 1922 saw Tipton's greatest tragedy when what became known as the Tipton Disaster unfolded. Despite this being the 1920s, Victorian-style child labour still existed and, although legal regulations had improved conditions in the mining and textile industries, plenty of trades remained unaffected. One such business was Dudley Port, Phosphor Bronze Co., set up by a John Knowles in 1916, and which was located on Groveland Road, off the road called Dudley Port. In 1922, the company had bought 160 tons of cartridges left over from World War I with the intention of separating the lead bullet from the copper casing. The separation work was carried out by a number of young girls aged between thirteen and fifteen, and who earned between four and six shillings a week. They would empty gunpowder from the cartridge on to the floor, and this was swept up periodically, dampened and deposited into the nearby canal. This routine was acted out as normal on the morning of 6th March 1922 – except at around 11:45, a spark from an open fire ignited the gunpowder on the floor. The resulting blast blew the factory roof clean off and blew out all of its windows, while the building was soon a raging inferno. Shortly afterwards, witnesses reported seeing screaming young girls running wildly around the yard, their arms and legs scorched black. Passing vehicles were commandeered to take the injured and dying to the Guest Hospital at Dudley, but alas, one by one, the girls passed away as the degree of burns were so severe. The eventual death toll was nineteen, with many of the survivors horribly disfigured. A relief fund was set up for the bereaved in the wake of the tragedy with all local industries donating, while concerts were also held and football matches staged. As for John Knowles, he was found guilty of manslaughter and sentenced to "five years of penal servitude".

Dudley Port Quirk Alert: Reinvention
Earlier, we mentioned the recent renovation of St Martin's church. However, a particularly quirky feature is that the kitchen units were made out of the church's original pews, while the original stained glass windows have also been effectively incorporated, plus an observatory was built at the top of the former church tower.

NAME (STATUS):	**EVE HILL** (Estate of Dudley)
POPULATION:	14,213 (St James's Ward)
DISTRICT:	Dudley, West Midlands
EARLIEST RECORD:	*Eve Hill*, 19th century

St James's church, Eve Hill, built in 1840 for the growing population and now a Grade II-listed building.

View from Eve Hill across Grange Park towards tower blocks in Dudley.

Hilly House pub, a former Palladian mansion in Himley Road, Eve Hill, and set in 180 acres of grounds.

Eve Hill Geographic and Historic Trivia

Eve Hill is a residential area located just 2 miles to the south-west of Dudley Port, and is also therefore part of Dudley too. The area has only ever spent eight years in Staffordshire, though. Prior to 1966 it belonged to Worcestershire, until Dudley was ceded to Staffordshire, while eight years later, in April 1974, the majority of south-west Staffordshire, including Dudley and Eve Hill, was ceded to the new metropolitan county of West Midlands when the Local Government Act 1972 took effect.

As for Eve Hill, it began to expand in the mid-19th century, as the Industrial Revolution caused the population of Dudley to soar. Hundreds of houses were built in the area around Salop Street, while St James's church was opened in 1840 for the people of Eve Hill (the two existing churches of St Thomas and St Edmund were unable to meet the increased demand), and a new infants' school, also called St James's, was opened in 1842. The Eve Hill area was then further developed in the mid-20th century with a mixture of private and council housing built to the east of Salop Street towards the Priory Estate where the remains of Dudley Priory can also be found. The early 1960s, however, saw the demolition of much of the Victorian housing around the Salop Street area, with many families rehoused on new council estates, while the former Victorian site was redeveloped with three multi-storey blocks of council flats, 21, 19 and 16 storeys high, respectively. These only lasted for thirty years, though, having soon fallen into disrepair, and the two tallest tower blocks were demolished thanks to controlled explosions in July 1999 – and the wheel of development continued to turn as new housing was built in their place.

Going back to St James's church, it took its name from the patron saint of Dudley Priory, while the priory had been founded in 1155-60 by Gervase Pagnel, for the Cistercian order on behalf of Queen Maud. Although dissolved in the 1530s, fragments survive today on the eastern fringes of Eve Hill in Priory Park, including some of its medieval floor tiling. Back in 1282, though, the priory required Papal Arbitration when the Bishop of Worcester, William Cantilupe, claimed that both Dudley Castle and Dudley Priory should be within his diocese. The pope eventually agreed to a compromise, with the castle and priory going to Lichfield diocese and the town and its churches to Worcester. Remarkably, this unusual arrangement remained in place until 1928. Originally a chapel-of-ease to St Thomas's, St James's was created a parish in its own right in 1844.

Eve Hill Quirk Alert: Immortalised

Earlier, we mentioned the three Eve Hill tower blocks that were built in the 1960s. Anyone who owns a Led Zeppelin IV record will be more familiar with them than they think – as they appear on the back cover of the record. The front cover very cleverly shows a frame hanging on a wall with a picture of an old man carrying a bundle of sticks – but open it out, and you see that it is the wall of a demolished house, with Eve Hill flats revealed in the exposed city-scape beyond.

NAME (STATUS):	**FAREWELL** (Village)
POPULATION:	318 (Parish of Farewell and Chorley)
DISTRICT:	Lichfield
EARLIEST RECORD:	*Fagerwell*, 1200
MEANING:	Pleasant or pure spring or stream.
DERIVATION:	From the Old English words *fæger* (fair or pleasant) and *wella* (spring or stream).

St Bartholomew's church, Farewell.

Farewell Hall.

Farewell Church: St Bartholomew's

The Grade II-listed parish church of St Bartholomew is the descendant of Farewell Priory, although the current incarnation was largely a rebuild in 1745 that was built in red brick. However, the 13th century stone-built chancel was preserved and survives today along with the old altar rails and four 13th century oak stalls. The church was also restored in 1848 which included the addition of a new roof. One interesting discovery during the 18th century rebuild was of a series of earthen vessels or jars that had been built into the south wall in three rows around 6 feet off the ground. These would have been used to enhance the acoustics of the medieval church, a not uncommon practise which actually dates back to Roman times, and which also occasionally used horse skulls to achieve the same effect.

Today, St Bartholomew's serves the parish of Farewell and Chorley which is largely made up of the two villages of the same name, although Chorley is considerably larger than Farewell.

Farewell Historic Trivia:
Farewell Priory and Farewell Hall

Farewell Priory was originally a nunnery founded as an abbey by Roger de Clinton, Bishop of Lichfield and Coventry from 1129 to 1148. However, it later became a Benedictine priory but, like the majority of its contemporaries, it was dissolved – although this happened in 1527 and not during Henry VIII's Dissolution of the Monasteries in the late 1530s. This particular dissolution was conducted by Cardinal Wolsey, and Farewell Priory's income was granted to Lichfield

Cathedral to support their choristers. Later, in 1550, the Dean and Chapter of Lichfield granted the lands of the former priory to William, Lord Paget. Meanwhile, Farewell Hall dates from the 18th century, and includes an oak staircase and grand oak panelling.

Farewell Quirk Alert: Hello and Goodbye

There can't be too many places in the UK that greet you with a "goodbye" as you enter the place, but that is the case when you approach "Farewell" from the south-west! Both road approaches to the

village have interesting road names, too. The photo shown above can be found at the top of Shute Hill, while the entrance to Farewell from the south-east, having approached the village from Lichfield, is along Cross In Hand Lane. The latter was once the main road from Lichfield to Stafford, from the 13th century until around 1770. It is thought that it was named after a 15th century direction post that once stood at a road fork, and was fashioned as a cross with a pointing hand to direct travellers. However, an alternative theory suggests that it was so-named because either travellers seeking sanctuary at Farewell Priory, or pilgrims on their way to the priory, walked along the lane carrying a cross in their hand.

NAME (STATUS):	**FAULD** (Hamlet, Crater)
POPULATION:	c.40
DISTRICT:	East Staffordshire
EARLIEST RECORD:	*Felede*, 1086 (Domesday Book)
MEANING:	Probably fold or enclosure for animals.
DERIVATION:	From the Old English word *fald* (fold or enclosure).

Fauld Historic Trivia: A Cataclysmic Event

The tiny hamlet of Fauld is located around a mile and a half west of Tutbury, and has neither a church nor a pub. It does have, however, one of the most astonishing tales of the 20th century to tell. For on Monday, 27th November 1944, the RAF Fauld underground munitions storage depot was the scene of one of the largest non-nuclear explosions in history and the largest to occur on UK soil. Around 4,000 tons of ordnance exploded along with 500 million rounds of rifle ammunition, too. The resulting crater was 100ft deep (30m) and 300 yards across (270m) and is still visible today just south of the village of Fauld. Worse still, the explosion obliterated a nearby reservoir which proceeded to add 450,000 cubic metres of water to the disaster area, but which turned into an even more lethal surging tide of mud and water as it advanced, engulfing all in its path and thus bringing with it further death and devastation. Damage was sustained by all property within a 1,420 yard radius (1,300m), and those buildings and farms closest to the source of the blast were completely wiped out. This included Upper Hayes Farm which was located directly above the site, and which therefore completely disappeared along with the six people inside it, all blasted into the sky along with a million tons of rock and soil. The gypsum works to the north of the hamlet along with a row of cottages were also completely demolished. Also in the firing line for the devastating surge of water was a lime works which was wiped out, while the blast substantially damaged every house in nearby Hanbury, where the Cock Inn lost half of its roof. In nearby Tutbury, chimney pots and roofs were shattered while at Burton, two church steeples were cracked, one of which had to be taken down.

The first official report stated that 90 people had been killed or missing, including 26 at the munitions depot, 37 killed (mostly drowned) at a nearby plaster mill, and 7 farm workers who had been working nearby; 200 cattle were also killed by a combination of the blast and inundation from the burst reservoir. Eyewitnesses from a safer distance actually reported *two* distinct blasts after which they observed two distinct columns of black smoke that formed a double-stalked mushroom cloud 50 yards wide, ascending to several thousand feet and with an inferno raging beneath. It was also reported that mounds of earth, weighing up to a ton each fell to the ground after being lifted skywards, while in the aftermath, four inches of

Left: *Memorial at the southern crater rim to those who died in the catastrophic explosion at the Fauld munitions depot on 27th November 1944. It remains the largest ever non-nuclear explosion in the UK.* Right: *There are dozens of these signs all around the Fauld crater rim and which are very clear.*

fine dust settled upon the ground in the surrounding area. The explosion was thought to have released about one-fifth of the force felt when the atom bomb was dropped on Hiroshima, hence it is no surprise that the blast was heard as far afield as Birmingham and Daventry; indeed, only three larger blasts were recorded during World War II – those at Hiroshima, Nagasaki and at the New Mexico test site.

As to the cause of the blast, it was 1974 before an official explanation was supplied. At the time of the disaster, there were 189 inexperienced Italian POWs working in the mines, and so it was announced that the cause of the explosion was probably a site worker removing a detonator from a live 450kg bomb using a brass chisel rather than a wooden batten – and which would have therefore supplied the fatal spark. This would have set off the pile of similar bombs in the immediate vicinity which, in turn, set off the c.4,000 tonnes of high explosives stored in that part of the mine. Extraordinarily, there was no official count of the number of workers at the facility, therefore a later revised count of the dead put the figure at 70 and that has remained the official death toll ever since. This lack of an official roll call obviously comes over as an appalling rule-breach today, but this all happened in the middle of World War II when there was a shortage of quality manpower and an excessive demand for munitions – and hence corners were cut. This also explains why those munitions were stored in 180,000 square feet of underground concreted corridors, just 12ft high and 20ft wide, and fashioned out of a former gypsum mine. Small surprise, therefore, that the inquiry found the event to be an "avoidable accident". The report from the inquiry concluded that: "*An airman was permitted to perform a dangerous operation in the mine. This indicates negligence on the part of the supervising staff present in the mine due either to lack of knowledge, lack of a proper sense of responsibility, or lack of proper direction from senior authority.*"

Miraculously, only around one third of the RAF dump exploded, as rock pillars between No. 3 and No. 4 sections held and prevented the other munition storage areas from exploding in a chain reaction. This meant that, despite the magnitude of the blast, a number of the men working there actually survived and made it to the surface, albeit presumably deafened for life. However, the rescue work took three months and was hindered by pockets of gas, 6 million gallons of water from the reservoir which had turned extensive areas into a quagmire, and 10,000 tons of rubble – all of which meant that 18 of the 70 people killed were never found.

Despite the disaster, the surviving parts of the site actually continued to be used by the RAF for munitions storage until 1966, after which the US Army used the site between 1967 and 1973 to store US ammunition previously stored in France. Six years later in 1979, the site was fenced off and has since been reclaimed by nature, including over 150 species of tree and wildlife.

In the aftermath of the disaster, a local relief fund had raised £7,831 by December 1945, and the Trustees of the fund continued to lend vital financial assistance to those affected for another fifteen years. In addition, the Government agreed to pay for a period of ten weeks only, £2.10s.0d per week to families affected, 32s.6d per week for widows and 11s.0d for each child. Further grants were made for children's clothing, assistance with school fees and for doctors' bills (there was no NHS back then), but this was only scratching the surface of the needs of many. For example, some of the men had been so badly affected by gas that they were unable to work at all while the psychological effects on those living nearby were probably never addressed. For example, a rescue party visited a farmhouse to find an elderly couple still sitting at the dining table facing each other, with the remains of their meal intermingled with debris. On a more positive note, heroics were performed by local rescue parties, resulting in one OBE, one MBE, four BEMs, the George Medal and two gallantry awards.

Today, there are signs all around the 12-acre area warning walkers not to stray into the former site because of unexploded bombs. This is because although it took a year of delicate work to remove the thousands of tons of ordnance that *were* reachable, around 3,000 tons of unexploded bombs had to be left untouched within the collapsed mine. Somewhat quirkily, the path approaching the crater from the north east is paved with gypsum collected from the surrounding area after the blast, while any recently ploughed fields in the area are still likely to reveal small blocks of white gypsum which would all have originated 20m below the ground, but ended up in the fields courtesy of the blast. That said, the British Gypsum site at Fauld is Britain's leading source of anhydrite, but produces no gypsum at all.

The edge of the crater today is also home to the first memorial for the tragedy, where the names of those who lost their lives are carved. A service used to be held here every year until numbers dwindled and the service was dropped after the 60th anniversary in 2004. And finally, an extraordinary fact is that the devastating explosion that occurred at Fauld on 27th November 1944 occurred at exactly 11:11 a.m. – thus adding a fourth dimension to the 11th hour of the 11th day of the 11th month that is the watchword of Armistice Day, 1918, and which signified the end of World War I. It is certainly worth sparing a thought for the Fauld Seventy on Remembrance Day.

View from the southern edge of the Fauld Crater which is 300ft deep and a quarter of a mile across. It has been comprehensively reclaimed by nature, which somewhat disguises the huge scale of this disaster.

Three's-Up!

	FIELD	FINNEY GREEN	FORD
STATUS:	Hamlet	Hamlet	Hamlet
POPULATION:	c.30	c.30	c.30
DISTRICT:	East Staffordshire	Newcastle-under-Lyme	Staffordshire Moorlands
EARLIEST RECORD:	*Felda*, 1114	*Finney Green*, 1699	*Forde*, 1240
MEANING:	Place at the open land.	Either "marshy place", or "grassy place belonging to a man called Finney.	Place at the ford.
DERIVATION:	From the Old English word *feld* (field).	From either the Old English *fynig* (moist or marshy), or the Old English personal name Finney, plus the Old English word *grēne* (green-coloured, grassy place or village green).	From the Old English word *ford* (ford).

Three's Up Trivia!

Field is a hamlet situated where the B5027 is bisected by the River Blithe around 4 miles west of Uttoxeter. Part of the parish of Leigh which includes several other villages with a combined population of 975, Field is probably smaller today than it was between 1870 and 1872 when John Marius Wilson compiled his Imperial Gazetteer of England, as it lists 12 houses for Field and a population of 84. It also states that the manor was owned by the Pipes and passed to the Bagots, after which a rather quirky morsel of trivia is offered, as follows: "A wych-elm was felled here in 1680, so large that two able workmen took five days to cut it down. Its length was 120 feet; its girth, at the base, 52 feet; its girth, at the middle, 25½ feet. Its branches furnished upwards of 60 loads of fire-wood; and its timber weighed about 100 tons, and furnished 80 pairs of naves for wheels, and 8,000 feet of boards and planks".

Today, the north-western outskirts of Field is the location of Birchwood Park in which you will also find The Traditional Flower Company. Based on a 100 acre sheep farm, the flower business is, to quote their website, "a small scale outdoor operation of approximately 8,000 scented rose bushes, over 5,000 herb plants and acres of seasonal flowers and foliage". All of which go to make some pretty stunning bouquets

The River Blithe at Field.

Looking down Agger Hill, Finney Green.

judging by the examples supplied on the website. Meanwhile, on the eastern outskirts of Field is Ashcroft Park, the self-styled "very best in Corporate UK Events, Country Pursuits and Outdoor Team Building Activities in Staffordshire, Derbyshire and the Midlands", offering hen and stag weekends, while the activities include archery, paintball, quad biking, shooting, laser combat… and blind driving!

Meanwhile, **Finney Green** is a tiny hamlet located around 4 miles west of Newcastle-under-Lyme. It is known locally as Hollywood Bowl thanks to a two-day pop festival that took place in 1970 at Lower Farm and which was attended by 45,000 people and included such legendary bands as Black Sabbath, Mungo Jerry, Free, Grateful Dead (their first perform-ance in the UK), Family, Traffic, Colosseum, and Ginger Baker's Air Force. One of the pioneers of open air festivals, the event actually came about by pure chance when a bunch of students at Keele University bumped into farmer Ted Askey who was visiting the campus to collect pig swill! The result was the Finney Green festival where people came from as far afield as Holland and Germany, while organisers provided 270,000 meat pies, 190,000 sandwiches and five lorry loads of beer! It was also the first rock concert to be held in the northern half of England. The concert should have been aired on the BBC but local legend has it that the film crew were spiked with LSD by one of the bands! Finally, the bands waited in the wings at the festival at Highway Farm, also in Finney Green… and in December 1970, Free released an album called *Highway*, with the title track, *Highway Song*, all about messing around on a farm and carrying on with the farmer's daughter!

Memorial to the 62 miners who died at Fair Lady Pit on 21st January, 1880.

Half a mile north of Finney Green is Leycett, and it was here at 08:30 on 21st January 1880, that yet another mining disaster occurred, this one a gas explosion at Fair Lady Pit which claimed the lives of 62 men and boys, ranging from age sixteen to fifty-five, and which included two pairs of brothers. Only 10 men survived what was the second such incident to occur at Leycett Colliery inside six months, with 8 men killed in an explosion the previous September. Coincidentally, the manager – who perished in the January blast – had been summoned to the Newcastle Magistrates Court the Monday before the January disaster for neglecting to provide sufficient ventilation in the mine for the September explosion. Thankfully, a new ventilation fan had been installed between the two disasters, and which remained intact following the blast thus allowing the mine to be quickly cleared of gasses so that the rescuers could get below ground. The generally accepted theory for the explosion was that it was the result of a blown out shot which ignited the under-ground gases. Judging by the mutilation of the bodies, the force must have been terrific, killing the miners instantly. A memorial to the disaster can be found in All Saints' church at nearby Madeley.

Finally, **Ford** is a tiny hamlet in the Staffordshire Moorlands that comprises a dozen or so houses and two farms. The place is situated in a remote part of the Peak District, close to its south-western edge, and within 2 miles of the larger villages of Grindon and Butterton. The name clearly derives from the days when there was only a ford over the River Hamps here, although today, a stone bridge takes the single road through Ford over the river.

Two shots of the only road through Ford.

NAME (STATUS):	**FLASH** (Village)
POPULATION:	242 (Quarnford parish)
DISTRICT:	Staffordshire Moorlands
EARLIEST RECORD:	*Flasshe*, 1568
MEANING:	Place where rainwater lies.
DERIVATION:	From the Old English word *flashe* (where rainwater stands).

Ramshaw Rocks, viewed from the Roaches.

View along the Roaches towards Hen Cloud.

Flash Geographic Trivia: Highest in Britain?

At 1,518ft (463m) above sea-level, the village of Flash in the Staffordshire Moorlands claims to be the highest village in Britain – as proclaimed on the above village welcome sign. However, the claim had been disputed by Wanlockhead in Scotland, but was upheld by the Ordnance Survey in 2007, who measured the highest house in each village and Flash came out as the winner. More recently, though, the claim has been disputed again, this time by the inhabitants of Nenthead in Cumbria – which if upheld, would mean that Flash wouldn't even be the highest village in England, never mind Britain. One thing that is undisputed, though, is that the Methodist chapel at Flash is the highest in Britain! Meanwhile, Flash is also the northernmost place in Staffordshire, sitting neatly underneath a very distinctive point at the top of the county. Its altitude means that it is frequently snowbound in winter, and finds itself isolated at times. The main part of the village clings to the south-eastern side of Oliver Hill, and clusters around St Paul's church, with a few farms dotted about further afield and which are mainly sheep farms – although pony trekking is also available from Northfield Farm! As for Oliver Hill, at 1,684ft (513m), it is the highest point in Staffordshire.

Also within 3 miles of Flash are a number of the Peak District's premier beauty spots, including the source of the Rivers Dane, Dove, Goyt and Manifold, Axe Edge, The Roaches, Ramshaw Rocks, Three Shires Head and Lud's Church – the latter two of which show up again in the *Flash Historic Trivia* section. Flash actu-

ally sits on the southern slope of the highest ground on Axe Edge Moor while Axe Edge itself rises to a peak of 1,807ft (551m). Meanwhile, to the south of Flash is Morridge Top, while a trig point at 1,604ft (489m) at Merryton Low provides stunning sunset views across the Cheshire plain to the west and to the south-west where a spectacular range of rocky outcrops runs from Ramshaw Rocks to Hen Cloud to The Roaches – and with the latter also offering stunning views all around. Also famous in these parts is the "Winking Man", a combination of upright stones on Ramshaw Rocks which appear to wink as you drive along the A53. Other interesting features include caves on the west side of Axe Edge, including The Devil's Hole, named after the strange sounds that are emitted when the wind blows in a certain direction!

Flash Pubs: The New Inn and The Knight's Table

Despite being the (disputed) highest village in Britain, the New Inn at Flash (1,470ft) is actually only the fifth highest *pub* in Britain (and England), two places behind The Knight's Table (1,500ft) half a mile to the north of Flash, and three places behind the famous Cat and Fiddle Inn (1,690ft) which sits on the exposed stretch of the A537 between Buxton and Macclesfield, around 4 miles to the north-west of Flash. But three in the Top Five isn't bad for this remote area where the three counties of Cheshire, Derbyshire and Staffordshire meet! As for the New Inn, it may only be the fifth highest pub in Britain, but it is still definitely the

The New Inn at Flash, the highest village pub in Britain, but only the fifth highest pub!

St Paul's church, Flash.

And here is the third highest pub in Britain, The Knight's Table, located half a mile north of Flash at Flash Bar, also known as the Traveller's Rest.

highest *village* pub in Britain!

The nearby Knight's Table doesn't qualify for that accolade, even though it is at a slightly higher altitude, as it isn't in the middle of a village. It is located half a mile north of Flash on the A53 at what is known as either Flash Bar or The Traveller's Rest, but which has an address of Quarnford – even though there isn't a place of that name (Quarnford being the name of the parish). As well as The Knight's Table, there is also the Flash Bar Stores & Coffee Shop at the Traveller's Rest, along with one house and a craft shop known as the Craft Barn. Finally, inside The Knight's Table there is a medieval theme running throughout, based on the legend of Sir Gawain and the green knight – a legend which culminates at the Green Chapel, thought to be a mile or so to the south-west of Flash. Before Sir Gawain reaches this place, though, he describes the "land of the Peakrills" as being "a wild, uninhabited place which was unknown to him or any of Arthur's knights".

Flash Church: St Paul's

St Paul's is the parish church of Quarnford of which Flash part-comprises. Located on Brown Lane in Flash it is... you've guessed it... the highest village church in Britain! The current St Paul's church was completed in 1901, although records show that its construction was halted for several weeks due to heavy snow! The 1901 version replaced an earlier church that was built in 1744, but which by the end of the 19th century had fallen into disrepair. Alas, the current incarnation has also become run down in recent years, and an appeal to raise £35,000 for a new roof had to be launched in 2009. The biggest cause of damage is the rainwater after which Flash is named, and which had leaked into the church causing plaster to fall off the walls, while certain pews close to the leak became out of bounds every time it rained. The money for the repairs was gradually accumulated thanks to donations from parishioners and Flash's annual flower festival. Also used for raising funds is the village's annual Tea Service which dates back to 1846 (see *Flash Quirk Alert* for more).

Flash Historic Trivia: Prize-Fighting, Flash Money and Lud's Church

Flash doesn't appear in Domesday Book, while the 1568 recording of *Flashe* names the place as part of the parish of Alstonefield. Today, Flash is in the parish of Quarnford, and the latter actually dates back much further, with the first reference dating from 1227. The two names then become interchangeable over time, with the British History Online website referring to *Quarnford* as "a township in Alstonefield parish and later a civil parish". Hence this explains why the first record of coalmining dates from 1401 in what is termed "Quarnford township" – when a certain Thomas Smith took a year's lease on the "vein coal" of Black Brook, near Upper Hulme, some 5 miles south of Flash. There were a large number of other coal pits in the area, including Blackclough, Goldsitch, Hope, Knotbury and Orchard Common, and which continued to be worked throughout the 18th and 19th centuries, with some surviving into the early 20th century, for both commercial and domestic use.

Over the same time period, Flash became a haven for hawkers who occupied the open land here, travelling from fair to fair selling their wares. What is clearly tough country became a place for tough characters and it also became a hotbed for outlawed practises such as cock fighting and also prize-fighting, the latter continuing at Flash long after it was made illegal. This was where Flash's location came in rather handy, placed as it is in Staffordshire and around a mile or so from both Cheshire and Derbyshire – as the law-breakers could soon outrun officials, and later the police, into a neighbouring county where the officials had no jurisdiction. For this reason, another typical location for prize-fighting bouts was Three Shires Head, a mile or so north-west of Flash, where both combatants and gamblers could hot-foot it over the border in seconds! Given the brutality of the practise, though, it couldn't fly more in the face of the beauty spot where it was practised – as Three Shires Head is one of The Peak District's prettiest places.

However, the most infamous of these outlawed practises in the 18th century was the counterfeiting of money, and which soon became known as Flash Money. This counterfeiting practise piggy-backed onto button-making, which was a popular cottage industry in Flash between the 17th and 19th centuries – for in the eighteenth century, a gang began using the button presses to make counterfeit coins. Despite the apparent quick getaway option, though, a number of the gang were caught and were hanged at Chester – after a servant girl gave them away! As for their counterfeit coins, they ended up being distributed all over the Midlands and beyond via innocent merchants picking them up at markets.

As for the honest residents of Flash, life was tough, with farmers barely scraping a living from the land and having to find extra employment in local mills or from mining coal beneath the bleak moors. Nevertheless, the population of the Quarnford parish had grown to 783 by 1831, with the professions mainly comprised of agricultural labourers, silk workers and colliers, but complimented by blacksmiths, cordwainers, dressmakers, errand boys, game-keepers, house servants, grocers, pedlars, shoemakers, tailors and wheelwrights. These people were not wealthy though, and at one stage, 29 families were receiving weekly poor relief and 23 families occasional relief. As for today, the population is only 242 and the school accommodates only seven pupils!

Hopping back to the 18th century and despite the nefarious practises that abounded in the area, Flash also became a strong and early base for the Methodist movement, too. As a result, a Methodist chapel was built as early as 1784 to which 61 members were affiliated. From here, the movement spread out to neighbouring villages such as Hollinsclough.

Finally, a couple of miles west of Flash, a huge landslide on the hillside above Gradbach created a deep and narrow gorge known as Lud's Church. Over 328ft (100m) long and 59ft (18m) deep, it is mossy and overgrown, wet and cool even on the hottest of days. The place also became a secret place of worship as early as the fifteenth century, when the followers of early

Lud's Church, home to the church services of the 15th century Lollards, plus a whole host of other legends!

church reformer John Wycliffe (known as the Lollards) used it, primarily because they were being persecuted for their religious beliefs. It is thought that the place was named Lud's Church following the capture here of Walter de Ludank. In the nineteenth century, it is known that a wooden ship's figurehead was placed in a high niche above the chasm, and went by the name of Lady Lud!

Unsurprisingly, legends abound too, and each of Robin Hood, Friar Tuck and Bonny Prince Charlie are reputed to have hidden from the authorities in Lud's Church. The place is also believed to be the Green Chapel, owned by the Green Knight in the tale of Sir Gawain and the Green Knight. Meanwhile, another legend suggests that Lud's Church was named after a horse called Lud, which threw its hunter rider to his death in the chasm… thus leading to *another* legend which is that the hunter still haunts Lud's Church, covered from head to toe in moss and leaves… yet another legendary green man!

Flash Quirk Alert: Quarn in a Teapot

Flash is home to a tradition that dates back two hundred years and which is known as the Teapot Club. Almost certainly borne out of the hardship endured by the people of this remote place, members of the community would contribute regularly to a special fund that was kept in a teapot, and which was to be used whenever any of its members fell on hard times. Whenever this happened, it is said that a committee member would visit the house in need and empty the contents of the teapot onto the kitchen table. The collection process would then start again from scratch until the next recipient benefitted. Those in need of the financial support would perhaps have become too ill to work, or it might have been used to enable a member of the community to bury their dead; indeed, such sickness or burial clubs weren't uncommon in England in the years before the NHS existed.

The earliest record of the fund dates back to 1767 from what was then known as the Quarnford Club. By 1846, it had become known as the Flash Loyal Union friendly society and was based at what was then called the Traveller's Rest (now The Knights Table). It wasn't until 1906 that it became known as the Teapot Club and which had 700 members at its peak. As for today, the tradition continues and is now celebrated every year by a special teapot service at St Paul's church, followed by the blessing of the dressed wells at Flash, although this latter Peak District custom was only introduced to Flash as late as 2006. The celebrations then continue with a parade which starts from the village hall and then proceeds northwards along the A53 towards Flash Bar. The parade is generally led by drummers and a brass band, while also part and parcel of the parade is a giant teapot carried on a kind of stretcher affair. Of course, for the parade to proceed safely, the police close the A53 for the length of time it takes to head up to The Knights Table at Flash Bar, have a drink or two, and then make the short return journey to Flash.

The parade was probably started in the early nineteenth century, and it is thought that members had to either attend the parade or pay a fine. Even back then, the parade would proceed from either the parish or the Methodist church, out to the Traveller's Rest and back for a tea, including seed cakes and ham sandwiches!

As an addendum to this story, the Flash Loyal Union friendly society was actually dissolved in 1995 following new laws introduced in the wake of the Daily Mirror pension scandal. However, the villagers kept the custom alive and have continued to perform the parade ever since.

Three Shires Head is located a couple of miles north-west of Flash and marks the point where the counties of Cheshire, Derbyshire and Staffordshire meet. The packhorse bridge crosses the River Dane here above a plunge pool known as Panniers Pool. It was also a known meeting point for illegal prize-fighting.

Three's-Up!

	FOUR CROSSES	HAWTHORNS	HAYES (HAYES HEAD)
STATUS:	Hamlet	Hall of Residence	Hamlet/Farm
POPULATION:	c.50	c.600	c.10
DISTRICT:	Cannock	Newcastle-under-Lyme	Staffordshire Moorlands

Three's Up Trivia!

Four Crosses is a hamlet at a crossroads on the A5 a mile to the west of Cannock and is named after its 17th century pub, the Four Crosses. Originally built in 1636 from old shipping timbers that are almost 1,000 years old, the pub has ten bedrooms if you're brave enough to stay. For given its age, it is unsurprisingly haunted, and also contains a number of secrets, too. Several secret passages have been discovered but the most remarkable find was that of a coachman's uniform which had been preserved for over 150 years behind the chimney. Meanwhile, the hauntings may well be explained by the number of deaths that have occurred here over the years, ranging from a 19th century baby who died after falling from a table in the upper bar area, to a poor young boy who ran out onto the busy A5 in the 1980s and was killed instantly. Paranormal experiences include smashed glasses, unexplained footsteps, the piano playing itself and an apparition of a young girl, while shadowy figures, a black-eyed child, a drunkard called Charlie and the sounds of children crying have also been reported. One of the spookiest experiences occurred one morning in 2005, just before opening time. The manager was giving the pub the once-over when she found two roses in the shape of a cross on each toilet seat. Assuming it was someone from the previous evening she thought no more of it… until she turned around and found the exit blocked by a large candelabrum that usually belonged on the fireplace! There was no one else in the building at the time… and she was later to learn of the ghost of a broken-hearted damsel called Emily, who is often spotted crying in the Ladies' toilets! Meanwhile, the Gents appears to be the haunt of a Roundhead soldier, while a man in a long dark cloak regularly appears in the car park on rainy evenings, looking forlornly towards the pub. Then there was the experience of a staff member coming face to face with a teenage girl with unkempt hair and tatty clothes, who then promptly turned away and walked through a wall! The member of staff was so spooked that she quit shortly afterwards. Small surprise, therefore, that the owner of "Eerie Evenings", who runs ghost-themed events, stated that: "I have hosted events at haunted buildings throughout the country and I have to say the Four Crosses Inn is probably the most haunted." Finally, it is said that Jonathan Swift often stopped here when journeying from London to Ireland, where he developed a liking for the landlord's wife, and which moved him to scratch a verse into a window-pane: *"Thou fool, to hang four crosses*

The Four Crosses Inn at Four Crosses, near Cannock. The front of the building has the date 1636 inscribed.

Hawthorns House, built in the mid-19th century for the Sneyd family, but which is now part of the off-campus main halls of residence of Keele University, and which is also known as The Hawthorns.

at the door! Hang up thy wife! There needs not any more."

As for **Hawthorns**, this is an area to the north-west of Keele that comprises Keele University's Halls of Residence. The Hawthorns is located off-site of the university and provides accommodation for approximately 70% of all full-time students, while it is also home to Hawthorns House, built in the mid-19th century for the lord of the manor's agents, they being the Sneyds. The Hawthorns has also been the name of West Bromwich Albion's football ground since 1900, and which used to be in Staffordshire until 1st April 1974.

Finally, **Hayes** is a mile or so north of Warslow and includes Hayes Cottage, Hayes Gate Farm and Hayes Farm. The place was recorded as *Hayheade* in 1608 and as *Hays Head* on an 1842 Ordnance Survey map, with the former part of the name deriving from either the Old English word *hēg* meaning "hay" or the word *hecg(e)* meaning "hedge". Hays Gate also gets a mention as far back as 1593 when it is recorded as *Heysgate*.

NAME (STATUS):	**FOXT** (Village)
POPULATION:	c.200 (Foxt); 1,488 (Ipstones parish)
DISTRICT:	Staffordshire Moorlands
EARLIEST RECORD:	*Foxwiss*, 1176
MEANING:	The fox's den.
DERIVATION:	From the Old English words *fox* (fox) and *wist* (den).

The Fox & Goose Inn, Foxt.

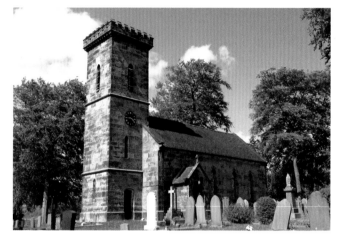

St Mark's church, Foxt.

Foxt Pub: The Fox & Goose

The Fox & Goose Inn dates from the 17th century and was originally two cottages and a blacksmith's forge. Today, the Fox & Goose is located, quite appropriately, on Fox Lane in Foxt, and has a great reputation for its food. Glad to say that the fox fetish doesn't extend to its menu, though… and which doesn't include goose pie for that matter, either!

Foxt Church: St Mark's

St Mark's church is relatively new, dating from 1839 – although it wasn't actually consecrated until 1899. It was initially used by the local Methodists before they built their own chapel in 1859, and was then used by the local school… until they, too, built their own school in 1877. The school lasted until 1984 when it was forced to shut due to the shortage of local children, and has since been used as a village hall.

Foxt Geographic and Historic Trivia: Copper and Tourism

Foxt is a village of over one hundred houses that straggle along a narrow country lane in the Staffordshire Moorlands. It lies on the eastern side of the Churnet Valley and is just 3 miles short of being in the Peak District. Its western approach rises steeply from the valley at nearby Froghall, climbing around 800ft around steep banks and sharp bends, to the top of a ridge on which it sits. Down in the valley, the Churnet Valley Steam Railway winds is way along its 5.5 mile stretch from Cheddleton to Kingsley & Froghall Station

a mile south-west of Foxt, and which is kept company by the Caldon Canal, originally built in 1776 and restored in 1974. The Caldon Canal was originally built to link the wharf at Froghall with Etruria in the heart of the Potteries where it joins the Trent and Mersey Canal (see *Staffordshire County History* for more on both railway and canal). Many of the residents at Foxt worked at the copper works in Froghall, or in the numerous limestone quarries in the immediate area, all of which were linked by a complex tramway network that ultimately delivered products to Froghall Wharf… and then onwards via the Caldon Canal and the Trent and Mersey Canal to a multitude of destinations. The Thomas Bolton Copperworks at Froghall and nearby Oakamoor, are famous as being the location where the world's first transatlantic telegraph cables were produced, while in the 20th century, the factories knocked out wiring components for British Spitfire fighter planes. It was also Thomas Bolton & Sons who built 24 houses at the lower end of Foxt in 1911, initially to accommodate a number of skilled workers from their Birmingham factory, which they were closing, having moved operations to Froghall. Alas, the industry declined in the latter half of the 20th century, and by the 21st century, much of the site was derelict before being largely demolished in 2011.

Meanwhile, a number of the stone-built houses in Foxt date back to the 17th century, while "Foxt Town" is a group of farms that may have been built as a grange to Croxden Abbey. The latter half of the 19th century then saw the ironstone and coal industries also increase

The Village Hall at Foxt.

Approach to the Fox & Goose Inn.

in importance in the area, although few signs of it remain today bar some now-grassed over spoil heaps in the Foxtwood area, around half a mile to the south-west of Foxt.

Today, Foxt looks more towards tourism as an industry, with a number of homes converted to holiday cottages – including Lucky Cottage, so named because it is house number 13. Clearly, these holiday homes look to exploit the location's proximity to the Peak District and Alton Towers, as well as celebrating the stunning Staffordshire Moorlands countryside too.

Foxt Quirk Alert:
"Vandalism Against Nature"

Earlier, we talked about the prevalence of fox-based names in Foxt. Alas, three animals that were shamelessly "hunted" in May 2015 were three deer in nearby Foxt Deer Park. The offenders clearly took two of the carcasses with them, leaving a third at the scene – but which had clearly been subjected to a dog attack as well

as being shot. Needless to say, the inhabitants of Foxt were appalled… as they had also been six months earlier when a mature beech tree in the centre of the village was felled by a well-known power company. The electricity distribution operator had earlier circulated letters to the villagers stating that as part of its extensive tree cutting programme it was going to "carry out work which included the removal of branches in close proximity to overhead lines, which would make the supply more reliable". Expecting a little bit of minor tree surgery, the villagers were horrified when contractors turned up and took the entire beech out, leaving only a stump – particularly as the tree was a memory tree planted for Norman Goodwin who had opened the village shop in 1938. A village spokesperson said that: "This was a magnificent tree, which was a standalone mature tree, possibly the best tree in the village of Foxt. This is an act of vandalism against nature."

The centre of Foxt village.

The Caldon Canal at Froghall Wharf, half a mile south-west of Foxt.

NAME (STATUS):	**GREAT BARR** (Built-up area of West Midlands)
POPULATION:	23,419 (Great Barr [12,409]; Pheasey Park Farm [11,010])
DISTRICTS:	Birmingham, Sandwell, Walsall (All West Midlands)
EARLIEST RECORD:	*Bearre*, 957; *Barre*, 1086 (Domesday Book)
MEANING:	Hill-top
DERIVATION:	From the Celtic word *barr*, meaning "hill-top". The name refers to nearby Barr Beacon.

Great Barr Geographic Trivia: Chopping and Changing

Today, Great Barr is a large area in the county of West Midlands which straddles the district boundaries of Birmingham, Sandwell and Walsall. As such, Great Barr is bounded by Junction 8 of the M6 motorway to the west, the Birmingham to Walsall railway line and Perry Barr to the south, Kingstanding to the east, and open countryside to the north, including Barr Beacon after which the place is named – all of which now resides comfortably within the boundaries of the county of West Midlands. However, before 1st April 1974, the majority of Great Barr was in Staffordshire, except for the part now known as Perry Barr which was in Warwickshire. Indeed, before World War I, it was also a largely rural area close to Staffordshire's county border with Warwickshire. It was only in the 1920s that private housing and council houses began to appear. The expansion continued up to and after World War II, and by the 1960s, Great Barr found itself sliced along its eastern edge by the M6, with Junction 7 serving the area, while a mile to the west, the M5 also started its lengthy journey down into the South West of England, commencing from Junction 8 of the M6.

Great Barr Pub: The Old Horns

The Old Horns is located on Queslett Road, Great Barr…but the current modern incarnation was preceded by a building with a little more character – and which is known in the area as the Old Old Horns! That said, there is an even older version for which you can see grainy photographs online with the old horse

and traps outside – and, naturally, this one is known as the Old Old Old Horns!

Great Barr Church: St Margaret's

Great Barr's Grade II-listed parish church is named after Saint Margaret of Antioch who was martyred for her faith during the emperor Diocletian's persecution of Christians in the fourth century. The church is located on Chapel Lane – now part of the vast urban sprawl of the county of West Midlands, but once very rural in the shadow of Barr Beacon after which the place is named. A church was first built on the site during the thirteenth century and it is first referenced in 1256 regarding the sale of land, while by 1563, the church was a chapel of ease annexed to Aldridge church. However, most of the medieval church was replaced during a rebuild in 1862, with the exception of the tower (although this was built slightly after the medieval period in 1677) and the 18th century spire that crowns it.

Great Barr Historic Trivia: Great Scott!

Great Barr once had a station on the Grand Junction Railway, one of Britain's earliest railways opened in 1837, although Great Barr station was later re-named to Hamstead station. Rather unusually, the railway passed through Great Barr before the canal did – the latter being the Tame Valley Canal which was opened in 1844. The canal is only 8.5 miles in length, and runs from Tame Valley Junction where it joins the Walsall Canal near Ocker Hill and Toll End, and includes an aqueduct at Great Barr that takes it over the M5.

The Old Horns, Great Barr.

St Margaret's church, Great Barr.

The war memorial on top of Barr Beacon, where you get an impressive 360 degree panorama over five counties.

Bishop Asbury Cottage on Newton Road, Great Barr. It was here that the famous 18th-century Methodist, Francis Asbury grew up.

One constant throughout these times was the Grade II listed Great Barr Hall, an eighteenth century mansion located at modern-day Pheasey. However, its predecessor, known as Nether House, was acquired in the mid-seventeenth century by Richard Scott and it wasn't until 1777 that his descendant, Joseph Scott demolished Nether House and built the Gothic Great Barr Hall in its place, a two-storey, nine-bay mansion. Joseph Scott was later knighted and made 1st Baronet Scott of Great Barr. However, the late eighteenth century saw the Scott family suffer from financial problems and this led to the hall being leased out from 1788 to Samuel Galton (1753-1832), who was somewhat bizarrely both a Quaker and an arms manufacturer! He was also a member of the famous Lunar Society, a dinner club and informal learned society of prominent Midland's industrialists, philosophers and intellectuals, who met regularly between 1765 and 1813, and whose numbers included Erasmus Darwin, Josiah Wedgwood, James Watt, James Brindley and Joseph Wright. They were so-named because they would meet during the full moon, as the extra light made for a safer journey home (in 1999, stone memorials or "Moonstones" to the Lunar Society were erected at the nearby Asda supermarket). Back under the control of the Scott's under Sir Francis Scott, 3rd Baronet, the house was altered and extended in the early 1840s, while a chapel was added to the grounds in 1863, probably designed by architect George Gilbert Scott (no relation) who also built two lodges in the grounds.

The widow of Sir Frances (d.1863), Mildred, lived at the Hall until her death in 1909. Without an heir, the estate was purchased by a local hospital board in 1911 and, by 1918 it had become St Margaret's Mental Hospital. Much later in the 1980s, the grounds became a nature reserve managed by the Staffordshire Nature Conservation Trust, but the Hall had already been abandoned by this stage. Other hospital buildings in the grounds continued to be used but also sequentially fell by the wayside with the last one closed in 2004. Today, Great Barr Hall is in a very poor state of repair and is on the Buildings at Risk Register, while a number of schemes to re-develop it have all fallen through.

The later years of the twentieth century saw Great Barr in the news for the wrong reasons. The first was when in August 1975, eight-year-old schoolgirl Helen Bailey was found dead from a single knife wound, in woods near Booths Farm. Her killer was never found. Seventeen years later in January 1992, Michael Sams famously abducted estate agent Stephanie Slater from a house in Turnberry Road, Great Barr before holding her for eight days. Sams released her after receiving a ransom of £175,000, but was arrested three weeks later. He was sentenced to life imprisonment for abducting Slater and for murdering Julie Dart from Leeds.

Finally, we'll just hop back to the 17th century, for this was when Francis Asbury, the first American Methodist bishop, grew up at what later became known as Bishop Asbury Cottage on Newton Road. Asbury was born in nearby Hamstead in 1745 and the family moved into the cottage the following year. Brought up as a strict Methodist, Asbury worshipped at nearby Wednesbury before becoming a full-time preacher at the age of twenty one. However, Asbury left England for America in 1771 and never returned, going on to become instrumental in the founding of the Methodist Episcopal Church (now The United Methodist Church) in the United States. His family remained at the cottage in Great Barr until the death of his mother in 1802. Grade II listed in 1955, the cottage is now a museum, furnished in 18th- century style, and includes memorabilia and information relating to Francis Asbury's life in Great Barr and later in the United States.

Great Barr Quirk Alert:
Say it enough times…
As just mentioned, Bishop Asbury Cottage on Newton Road was the childhood home of famous Methodist, Francis Asbury. However, the cottage was part of a terraced pair, and in 1964 the more southerly of the pair was demolished when Newton Road (the A4041) was widened. At that time, there was a common joke doing the rounds, suggesting that the bungling developers had knocked down the wrong cottage. Over the years, the joke evolved into serious doubt, and so it had to be formally disproven by scrutinising documentary evidence in Sandwell Museum… and which clearly shows that the Asbury's house is indeed the last cottage standing!

NAME (STATUS):	**HALES** (Village)
POPULATION:	c.100
DISTRICT:	Newcastle-under-Lyme
EARLIEST RECORD:	*Halas*, 1086 (Domesday Book); *Hales*, 1291
MEANING:	The nooks or corners of land.
DERIVATION:	From the Old English word *halh* (nook or corner of land), but in its plural form.

Hales Church: St Mary's (and Hales Hall)

Two buildings that survive in Hales today are St Mary's church and Hales Hall. The latter was built in 1806 overlooking the River Coalbrook, and the entire village of Hales was part of its estate, with every house or farm belonging to the squire. One such squire was the Reverend Alexander Buchanan, one of a number of 19th century men who doubled up as both squire and parson – and hence the term "squarson". However, despite being a Reverend, his estate didn't possess a church, as the original wooden church of Hales had been destroyed by fire. The Reverend Buchanan there-fore paid for St Mary's church to be built in 1856, and which was designed by George Gilbert Scott. The church silver of its wooden predecessor still survives, though, and the paten, goblet and two chalices have 1833 and the Buchanan crest on them.

St Mary's church, Hales, built in 1856 by the local squarson, the Reverend Alexander Buchanan.

Hales Historical Trivia: Romans, Normans and the Wars of the Roses

Hales is a tiny village in the north-western Staffordshire parish of Loggerheads, close to the Shropshire border. Historically, it was the site of a Roman corridor villa, probably dating from the late first century, and a bath-house perhaps built a little later in the first half of the 2nd century. Around one thousand years later, the Normans built Tyrley Castle here, although nothing remains of it today. One thing that does survive, though, is the Audley Cross and which is located just to the north of Hales on Blore Heath. The cross marks the site of the second great battle of the Wars of the Roses, the Battle of Blore Heath (1459), and is named after Lord Audley, who commanded the Lancastrian forces here. However, despite having 10,000 men to the Earl of Shrewsbury's 5,000 Yorkists, Audley's men lost the battle and he himself was mortally wounded. Originally there was a wooden cross here to mark the site of the battle, but this was replaced in 1765 by the current stone memorial.

Finally, Hales was home to the medieval industry of glass-making, and which is marked today to the east of the village by Glass House Farm which dates from around 1550. Also here is Burnt Wood, the largest acreage of woodland belonging to the Hales Hall estate. Originally part of the Forest of Blore, it was so-named because of the charcoal which was made to provide the fuel for the glass-making, and to this day within the

Hales and District Club, donated to the parishioners of Hales in 1924, but which today is a private members club. It is also home to darts, snooker and cricket teams as well as Hales WI and Loggerheads Parish Council.

wood, charcoal can still be found lying in heaps just below the surface.

Hales Quirk Alert: Ooh err Missus...

Hales and District Club (*shown above*) was originally just a cottage. However, it was expanded by a former squire of the Hales estate to house his organ – the exten-sion taking the form of a huge panelled room under which was a cellar connected to the main room by a spiral iron stairway. Apparently, Squire Buchanan frequently left his wife in the cottage next door and retired to the extension... with his manservant!

NAME (STATUS):	**HAUNTON** (Village)
POPULATION:	c.120 (parish of Clifton Campville is 912)
DISTRICT:	Lichfield
EARLIEST RECORD:	*Hagnatun*, 942; *Hauneton*, 1271
MEANING:	Farmstead of a man called Hagena.
DERIVATION:	From the Old English personal name, *Hagena*, plus the Old English word *tūn* (farmstead).

St Michael and St James's church, Haunton, built in 1902.

The centre of Haunton.

Haunton Hall, an 18th- century building that was converted into a nursing home in the late twentieth century.

Haunton Church: St Michael and St James

Domesday Book (1086) mentions the chapel of St James the Greater at Haunton, as in those days, Haunton was a chapelry of the parish of St Andrew's of neighbouring Clifton Campville. This lasted until the English Reformation of the 16th century when the Church of England broke away from the Catholic Church. Conversely, the only church today in Haunton is the Roman Catholic church of St Michael and St James. The next section explains why…

Haunton Historic Trivia: Haunton Hall

Haunton was a township of Clifton for many centuries, and even today, it is still part of the parish of Clifton Campville. The largest building in the village is Haunton Hall, which dates from the 18th century. By the 1840s, the Hall had been inherited by Charles Edward Mousley, and in 1845, he added a Catholic chapel to the hall which was dedicated to the Immaculate Conception. By 1885, services were moved from the chapel to the newly-built church of St Michael, built with the support of Henry Pye, the squire of Clifton Campville, and who was also the son-in-law of the Anglican bishop Samuel Wilberforce. An Anglican rector himself, of the Clifton parish – and therefore yet another Staffordshire village squarson – Pye had later converted to Catholicism. St Michael's church was soon extended, and this particular extension re-used some of the masonry taken from the ruins of the chapel of St James the Greater – and which also led to the church dedication being re-assigned to both St Michael and St James. However, this particular incarnation of St Michael and St James didn't last long, as it was replaced by a new one in 1902, designed by Edmund Kirby, and supported by Lady Frances Mostyn of Haunton Hall. Lady Frances was also the mother of Francis Mostyn who went on to become the Roman Catholic Archbishop of Cardiff between 1921 and his death in 1939. The 1902 incarnation of the church is still going strong today, having been built in a neo-gothic style, including a small timber bell tower.

Sticking with the Catholic scene in Haunton, and 1904 saw a group of French nuns, the Sisters of St Joseph of Bordeaux, set up a convent in Haunton Hall. The convent later became the St Joseph Convent School for Girls, but was eventually closed in 1987. The Hall also became a nursing home in the latter part of the 20th century, and the nuns moved to a new, purpose-built convent in the village.

Three's-Up!

	HAZLES	**HIGH HEATH**	**HIGH ONN**
STATUS:	Farm, Wood	Housing Estate	Hamlet
POPULATION:	c.10	11,871 (Rushall-Shelfield Ward)	680 (Parish of Church Eaton)
DISTRICT:	Staffordshire Moorlands	Walsall, West Midlands	Stafford
EARLIEST RECORD:	*Haseles*, 1302; *Hazeles*, 1356; *Hazles*, 1836	Unknown	*Othnam*, 1081; *Otne*, 1086 (DB); *Great Onne*, 1253
MEANING:	The hazel trees	High heathland	A kiln
DERIVATION:	From the Old English word *hæsel* (hazel-tree).	From the Old English words *hēah* (high) and *hæth* (heath).	From the plural of the Celtic word *odn* (kiln).

Three's Up Trivia!

Hazles is an area at the northern end of the hamlet of Hazelscross which, in turn, is half a mile north of the village of Kingsley. The area is also marked by Hazles Wood, a wooded area on the western bank of the river Churnet, and where, as well as hazels, you will also find oak, birch and holly trees – all of which are part of Consall Nature Park. The place on the maps marked as Hazles is represented by Hazles Farm (*top left*) and Hazles Cross Farm, with the latter also home to a nursery and what is described as "a national collection of hellebores" and which are held under the National Plant Collections scheme designated by Plant Heritage. The whole area around Hazles, and indeed all the way along the Churnet Valley is considered to be amongst Staffordshire's most beautiful landscapes.

Meanwhile, **High Heath** is an area at the north-eastern tip of Walsall and is therefore now part of the county of West Midlands – but lies just over a mile south of Staffordshire to which it belonged before 1st April 1974. The area is largely built-up, but does possess High Heath Park, a green recreational area. It also possesses a pub called The Four Crosses (*above, centre*), and which is only the second pub in Walsall to be added to the borough council's list of assets of community value (ACV) – and it went on the list largely thanks to the work of The Four Crosses Preservation Society. This now means that the pub must be maintained within the community, and thus prevents developers from converting it into something else or demolishing it – which had been the intention, as plans for demolition and replacement with a new 30-bed care home had actually been approved! Any future development now has to preserve and incorporate The Four Crosses as a pub.

Finally, the twin hamlets of **High Onn** and Little Onn are located in west Staffordshire close to the border with

Shropshire. High Onn consists of a handful of homes and farms and the High Onn Caravan Club, and sits alongside the Shropshire Canal. Opened in 1835, there is also a wharf at High Onn. As for the *Earliest Record* reference above, that came in 1081 courtesy of Roger de Montgomery, first Earl of Shrewsbury, when he gave the manors of *Othnam* (High Onn) and *Mereston* (Marston) to the Abbey of St Ebrulf at Utica in Normandy.

View towards Hazles Wood from Hazles.

The Shropshire Canal at High Onn Wharf. The canal was opened in 1835 shortly after the death of its creator, the great Thomas Telford, and was originally called the Birmingham and Liverpool Canal.

NAME (STATUS):	**HEATON** (Village)
POPULATION:	262 (Heaton parish including Danebridge)
DISTRICT:	Staffordshire Moorlands
EARLIEST RECORD:	*Heton*, 1230
MEANING:	The high farmstead.
DERIVATION:	From the Old English words *hēah* (high) and *tūn* (farmstead).

The Knot Inn at neighbouring Rushton Spencer.

St Lawrence's church in Rushton Spencer has served the Heaton parish since at least the 18th century, while Heaton was still part of the Rushton chapelry until 1865.

View from Heaton towards The Cloud.

The centre of the tiny hamlet of Heaton.

Heaton Pub: Heaton House Farm

Heaton doesn't have a pub *per se*, but Heaton House Farm, which offers Bed & Breakfast and Self Catering is also used as a wedding reception venue in what used to be the farm's barns... and hence has a licensed bar! Interestingly, back in 1824, Heaton House was a doctor's surgery before eventually becoming a farm. The nearest traditional Staffordshire pub to Heaton, is the Knot Inn a mile to the west in Rushton Spencer.

Heaton Quirk Alert: Madrenaline

A few yards down the road from Heaton House Farm is Madrenaline Activities. This is the first and the only Segway PT venue in the UK to have an off-road obstacle course – Segway being a two-wheeled, self-balancing, battery-powered electric vehicle which takes its name from the word segue (meaning smooth transition) and PT which stands for Personal Transporter. Madrenaline Activities also offers Archery, Body Zorbing (think Gladiators Atlas Spheres), Clayzar (Laser Clay Pigeon Shooting), Segway Safari, Sphering (rolling downhill in a large inflatable ball), and Sky Bow (moving target archery).

NAME (STATUS):	**HINTS** (Village)
POPULATION:	355
DISTRICT:	Lichfield
EARLIEST RECORD:	*Hintes*, 1086 (Domesday Book)
MEANING:	Place on the road or paths.
DERIVATION:	From the Welsh word *hynt* (road). The road in question is the former Roman road, Watling Street (now the A5).
FAMOUS RESIDENTS:	Sir John Floyer (1649-1734), physician and author.

Hints Church: St Bartholomew's

The current St Bartholomew's church dates from 1883 and was designed by John Oldrid Scott, the youngest son of the more celebrated Victorian architect, Sir George Gilbert Scott. The cost of £5,000 was largely met by the local squire of Hints Hall, James Chadwick, and who had made his money as a cotton merchant. A renowned benefactor, Chadwick also provided the £4,000 finance for the vicarage (now Chadwick House). However, the 1883 version of St Bartholomew's was at least the third incarnation of the church on this site. A topographical book from the early 19th century helps to visualise both predecessor churches, as the second incarnation was built in around 1800. The book

St Bartholomew's church, Hints.

In Hints' churchyard, this 20th century memorial cross, stands on the base of a cross that is many centuries older.

comments that the early 19th century church had been built in "the prevailing neo-classical style" and that it was a "truly elegant specimen of Grecian architecture upon a small and simple scale, picturesquely situated upon a bold eminence". However, the author is also familiar with its predecessor, and describes this as "very ancient", and "consisting of a nave and two small side-aisles divided by round arches and large pillars ornamented at the capitals".

Hints Historical Trivia: Hints Hall

Throughout the 13th and 14th centuries, the manor of Hints was held by the de Meynhill family, after which it passed to Ralph Bassett of Blore. By the 16th century, the Bassets had sold land and property, including the former Hints Hall, to Ralph Floyer whose family held on to the estate until 1793 when it passed to William Humberston Cawley. The hall was then remodelled in Queen Anne style, and throughout the 19th century, the park became landscaped along with a fish pond and water gardens, the latter including an ornamental waterfall. However, the Hall and estate were sold at auction in June 1949, and the Hall demolished in the 1960s.

Hints Hall was also the birthplace of John Floyer in 1649, the third child of Richard Floyer and Elizabeth Babington. After graduating at Oxford University, John Floyer went on to practice as a physician in Lichfield, and it was following his advice in 1714 that Dr Johnson, when a child, was taken by his mother to be touched by Queen Anne to cure him of "the king's evil", a disease in the lymph nodes also known as scrofula. Despite this somewhat backward belief, Floyer was very much a forward-thinking physician, too, and he was the first doctor to take regular observations of pulse rates. He was also an advocate of cold bathing, and wrote an early account of the pathological changes in the lungs associated with emphysema.

Hints Quirk Alert: The Hints Pig

The "pig" in question is actually a large ingot of lead that was dug up by labourers on Hints Common in 1792. Around two feet long and weighing around 150 pounds, it originated from Flintshire, while today, it can be found in the exhibition at Tamworth Castle. However, we know that it dates from 76 AD exactly, as it refers to the consuls Vespasian and Titus, courtesy of this inscription: IMP. VESP. VII. T. IMP. V. COS.

NAME (STATUS):	**HOPE** (Hamlet); **ALSTONEFIELD** (village and parish)
POPULATION:	c.50 (Hope); 304 (Alstonefield parish)
DISTRICT:	Staffordshire Moorlands
EARLIEST RECORD:	*Hope*, 1371
MEANING:	Small enclosed valley or enclosed plot of land.
DERIVATION:	From the Old English word *hop* (small enclosed valley or enclosure in marsh or moor).

The Watts Russell Arms at Hope dates from the eighteenth century.

The George at Alstonefield.

Alstonefield Church: St Peter's

Hope doesn't possess its own church; the nearest in the parish is half a mile to the east in Alstonefield. Part of St Peter's dates from Norman times, including the Norman south door, but the church has been altered many times in the 900 years since then. The largest alterations occurred in 1590 when most of the chancel was rebuilt, with further major restoration carried out in 1870. From pre-Conquest times, the church possesses the bowl of a Saxon font, which was dug up in the churchyard, while fragments of Anglo-Scandinavian crosses are built into the wall, near the porch. The church is also renowned for its woodwork, which comprises a set of low 17th century pews with their original brass-work, a double decker pulpit (originally a three decker) and a painted Beresford pew at the east end of the north aisle. The Beresford connection is courtesy of the Cotton family who owned Beresford Hall and the family pew bears their coat of arms on the back. Also part of the church woodwork was a huge 10ft-long chest and which was inscribed with the date 1713. The chest had three locks and the vicar and the churchwardens each had a key, making the presence of all three a necessity for opening it. Alas, the past tense has been used because, almost inconceivably, the chest was stolen from the church in 1995. Worse still, three years ago, the lead was stolen from the church roof, and required £10,000 to be raised by the villagers to help replace it. Perhaps a new law should be passed: violate a priceless medieval relic, and suffer medieval punishment! Most church roofs would probably remain intact!

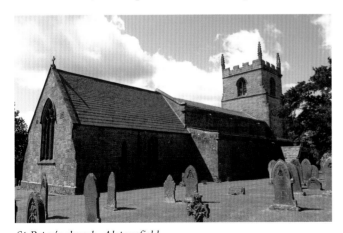

St Peter's church, Alstonefield.

Inside St Peter's church, looking through the nave towards the chancel.

Alstonefield village green.

Hopedale lies at the foot of the hill that on which Hope and Alstonefield sit.

Hope Historical Trivia:
Biblical Words and Cheese

The 19th-century curate and topographer Jonathan Eastwood (1824-1864), lived in Hope at the time of his premature death, aged only forty. Having graduated from St John's College, Cambridge, with both classical and mathematical honours, he was initially appointed curate of Ecclesfield, Yorkshire in 1847 before switching to the curacy of Eckington in north-east Derbyshire. He devoted his leisure to the study of local history and antiquity and his literary works include the *History of the Parish of Ecclesfield in the county of York*, published in 1862. His other main work remained unfinished, this being *Notes on Scriptural and Liturgical Words*, an alphabetic glossary of biblical words for which he only got up to the letter "H". However, as Eastwood had proposed to complete the book in collaboration with William Aldis Wright of Cambridge, the latter was able to steer it through to publication in 1866 – by which stage he had changed the title to the *Bible Word-book: a Glossary of Old English Bible Words*. A second edition, revised throughout and greatly enlarged by Wright, was issued in 1881 without Eastwood's name!

In 1874, Hope became the site of England's first co-operative cheese factory. This followed the setting up of the Alstonefield Dairy Association by twenty local farmers, and the factory was soon producing Derby

cheese. Trade was good until the latter half of the 20th century by which stage better transport and the emergence of larger dairies took the trade away. Finally, Hope's pond is said to have never run dry, while to the west of the village is Steep Low, a prominent barrow that is one of the last places in England where a gibbet was used!

Alstonefield Quirk Alert:
Leadenboots and Gargoyles

Neighbouring Alstonefield may well be a small country village, but it certainly has its fair share of sports interests. Among the village's inhabitants is the man who organises the annual Leadenboots Challenge, a marathon around the Peak District that takes in 5,800ft of ascent. Meanwhile, the village cricket team are known as the Gargoyles – apparently named after some of St Peters' church gargoyles and a number of its members' care-worn faces!

Left: *My Dad will appreciate this one! He researched our ancestry several decades ago before genealogy became fashionable and found that we originated from Alstonefield. This plaque appears on the wall of the south aisle.*

The double decker pulpit inside St Peter's church.

NAME (STATUS):	**HOPTON** (Hamlet)
POPULATION:	1,615 (parish of Hopton and Coton)
DISTRICT:	Stafford
EARLIEST RECORD:	*Hotone*, 1086 (Domesday Book); *Hoptuna*, 1167
MEANING:	Farmstead in a small enclosed valley or enclosed plot of land.
DERIVATION:	From the Old English words *hop* (small enclosed valley or enclosure in marsh or moor) and *tūn* (farmstead).

St Peter's church, Hopton, which Arthur Mee describes in his 1937 King's England Staffordshire volume as "fashioned out of a barn".

Hopton's beautiful village green.

Hopton Church: St Peter's

Annual rent records confirm that there was a chapel of St Peter at Hopton in 1587, and which belonged to St Mary's Collegiate Church in Stafford. This particular chapel, which has long-since disappeared, was located just to the west of Hopton in a field still known as Church Hill. Meanwhile, the current church of St Peter is located across the road from the village green, and according to Arthur Mee's 1937 Staffordshire volume of *The King's England*, it was fashioned out of a barn!

Hopton Historical Trivia: The Battle of Hopton Heath

Hopton is most famous for being the site of the Battle of Hopton Heath in 1643 during the first phase of the English Civil War. The battle was fought between Parliamentarian forces led by Sir John Gell and Sir William Brereton and a Royalist force commanded by Spencer Compton, 2nd Earl of Northampton. The lead-up to the battle involved the capture of Lichfield by Gell, at which point they turned their attention towards Stafford. However, the Earl of Northampton, having arrived too late to prevent Lichfield's capture, joined forces with Colonel Hastings' local Royalists to assist Stafford's defence – and which also included the legendary 29 pound cannon known as "Roaring Meg"! Gell, meanwhile, was marching towards Stafford with his army of 500 cavalry, 1,000 infantry, 14 cannon and a mortar; Brereton weighed in with 300 cavalry and 200 infantry. By the morning of Sunday 19th March, Gell had reached Hopton Heath, where he was joined at 2pm by Brereton's forces. Northampton's Royalists arrived at 3pm, and took up a position where today, MoD No. 6 Site stands. When battle commenced, most of the Parliamentarian cavalry was defeated, while Roaring Meg's first shot beheaded six of Gell's pikemen and wounded four more. However, Royalist cavalry charges on Parliamentarian defensive positions proved rash, and many officers were killed or wounded. One such officer was Northampton himself, who was unhorsed and surrounded. However, he refused to surrender, and took out a few more Parliamentarian soldiers before his helmet was knocked off, after which he was killed by a halberd chop to the head and a deep sword cut to the face. Angered at the death of Northampton, Sir Thomas Byron took over command, but went for an all-out attack on Gell's infantry before his cavalry had been properly re-formed following earlier assaults. Byron himself was severely wounded and the Parliamentarians were driven off. His replacement, Colonel Hastings, attempted to mount another attack, but with men and horses exhausted on both sides, both forces made camp for the night – or rather the Parliamentarians gave the impression that they had made camp, thanks to a number of fires. In reality, they had retreated, Brereton to Nantwich, and Gell to Derby. At 4am, the Royalists found the Parliamentarian positions deserted and declared themselves the winners of the battle. In reality, neither side had won, although Parliamentarian losses far outweighed Royalist losses (around 500 men captured or killed vs. around 45 Royalists – although most of the latter were important officers). As a result of the impasse, the Royalists continued to hold Stafford, while Prince Rupert re-captured Lichfield on 21st April 1643. However, a surprise Parliamentarian attack on 16th May 1643 saw them take Stafford and it remained in their hands until the end of the war.

As an addendum to this tale, Lord Northampton's son, Lord Compton, was also seriously wounded during the battle, but when he wrote to his mother, he mentioned nothing of his own injuries, stating of his father: "Pray, Madam, let this be your comfort, that it was impossible for anyone to have done braver than he did."

Moving forward to the 19th century, and consecutive censuses reveal that Hopton and Coton had a population of 468 in 1851, but that this had risen to 1,174 by 1861. However, this population increase was courtesy of the enlargement of the parish's lunatic asylum, and the erection of a new lunatic asylum at Coton Hill; the census of 1861 reveals that these two institutions had 540 and 162 inmates, respectively.

Hopton Quirk Alert: Home Advantage

We've already talked about the Battle of Hopton Heath at length, but by a remarkable coincidence, the Parliamentarian forces were commanded by Sir John Gell, and who was lord of the manor of…Hopton in Derbyshire! So maybe the odds were somewhat stacked in his favour!

BEAUTIFUL HOPTON – A SERIAL BEST VILLAGE WINNER

Three's-Up!

	HYDE LEA	**JACK HAYES**	**KERRY HILL**
STATUS:	Village	Lane	Hamlet
POPULATION:	451	c.200	c.40
DISTRICT:	Stafford	Staffordshire Moorlands	Staffordshire Moorlands
EARLIEST RECORD:	*Hida*, c.1187; *la Hyde*, c.1225; *Hydeley*, 1601	*Jack Hay*, 1816; *Jack Hays*, .1836	*Kery*, 1194; *Kerealhull*, 1434; *Kerealhyll*, 1537; *Kerry Hill*, 1803
DERIVATION:	From the Old English words *hīde* (hide of land) and *lēah* (woodland clearing).	Likely to be named after a man called Jack Hay or Jack Hays in the early 19th century.	Possibly from Celtic/Welsh origins dating from the end of the 6th century.

Three's Up Trivia!

Hyde Lea is a village located a couple of miles south-west of Stafford town centre. As indicated above, it was originally known only as *Hide*; the addition of "Lea" occurred when *la Hyde* was merged with *la Leye*, with the latter first recorded as such in 1261. By 1840 Hyde Lea was home to a handful of cottages, while in 1863 a school opened using the building that is today the village hall. The Crown Inn was also up and running by 1861 and which originally occupied the whole of the building that it is now only the right-hand side; the left-hand side was initially converted into a shop and a private home, whereas today, it is all a private home. Moving forward to 1881, and Hyde Lea had become part of Castle Church parish and it wasn't until 2003 that Hyde Lea became a parish in its own right, when a large part of the former Castle Church parish was absorbed into the Borough of Stafford. The nearest church is St Lawrence's, half a mile down the road in Coppenhall, and dates from the 12th century; in fact, it is of particular interest as it has remained largely unaltered since then. Hyde Lea is also home to Stafford Grammar School which was founded in 1982, but utilises yet another Hyde Lea Victorian building.

Meanwhile, **Jack Hayes** is effectively a road known as Jack Hayes Lane (*shown top centre*) which is located a mile south-west of the village of Bagnall in an area known as Light Oaks. However, Jack Hayes Lane is fairly long and includes lots of attractive residential housing before heading off into the countryside.

By sheer coincidence, if you carry on down Jack Hayes Lane, you eventually arrive in the tiny hamlet of **Kerry Hill** – which essentially comprises a handful of houses, three farms and Kerry Hill Nurseries (*entrance shown top right*). Carry on a few yards further south, and you get panoramic views over Stoke-on-Trent which lies to the west and south-west.

The Crown Inn at Hyde Lea and which is first mentioned in the census of 1861.

Hyde Lea village hall also dates from the 19th century and was originally the village school.

NAME (STATUS):	**KEELE** (Village)
POPULATION:	4,129
DISTRICT:	Newcastle-under-Lyme
EARLIEST RECORD:	*Keel*, 1156; *Kiel*, 1169
MEANING:	Hill where cows graze.
DERIVATION:	From the Old English words *cŭ* (cow) and *hyll* (hill).

The Sneyd Arms, which is located on the road known as "The Village", Keele.

Houses a little further west on "The Village", Keele.

Keele Pub: The Sneyd Arms

The Sneyd Arms was built in 1846 on the road which is now called simply "The Village". However, in order to accommodate the build, a number of cottages were demolished and their inhabitants moved to the work-house!

Keele Church: St John the Baptist

St John the Baptist is a Grade II-listed church which was built in the Decorated Gothic style between 1868 and 1870 by local architect, Thomas Lewis. The current version succeeded its Georgian predecessor which had been completed in 1790, but which, in turn, had also incorporated the medieval tower of its own predecessor – and which was believed to have been built by the Knights Templar in the 12th century. Nothing remains today of either the medieval or the Georgian churches. As for the current church, its most striking component is its 130ft spire as well as a fine iron screen, built by the village blacksmith, Mr Cheadle, and which is dedicated to the church's long-serving 19th century rector, the Reverend Henry Sutcliffe.

Keele Historical Trivia: Keele University

As already alluded to above, along with their 12th century church, the medieval manor of Keele was owned by the Knights Templar, a Christian military order who were also a prominent presence in the Crusades. It wasn't until the mid-16th century that the Keele estate came into the possession of the Sneyd family, a prominent Staffordshire family dating back to at least the 13th century. It was the Sneyds who built the first Keele Hall in 1580. Two centuries later, and the

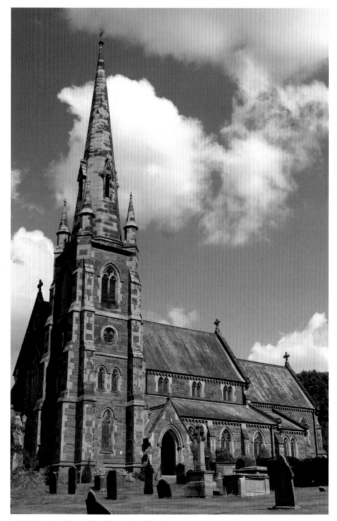

St John the Baptist church, Keele.

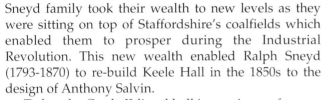

Keele Hall seen from the south-east (above) and from the south-west (large photo below). The hall was built in the 1850s by Ralph Sneyd, but today forms part of the Keele University campus.

The Old School at Keele, built in 1858.

Sneyd family took their wealth to new levels as they were sitting on top of Staffordshire's coalfields which enabled them to prosper during the Industrial Revolution. This new wealth enabled Ralph Sneyd (1793-1870) to re-build Keele Hall in the 1850s to the design of Anthony Salvin.

Today, the Grade II-listed hall is a major conference, wedding and banqueting venue, while the estate is also home to Keele University's campus. Spread across 617 acres of woodland, gardens, lakes and parkland, Keele's campus is the largest integrated university campus in the UK, so with only around 6,000 students, the ratio of student to campus grounds is therefore one of the best in the UK. The university was initially founded as the University College of North Staffordshire in 1949 and it was 1962 before it received its Charter as the University of Keele. By the 1980s,

there were four halls of residence, Barnes, Horwood, and Lyndsey on campus, along with The Hawthorns in Keele village.

Keele Quirk Alert:
Restored in the place of Fleet Street

The church of St John the Baptist in Keele is home to the sculpted figures of the Elizabethan lord of Keele manor, William Sneyd and his wife. However, the two figures were somewhat bizarrely interred under the church floor when the church was rebuilt in the late 18th century. Happily, they are now back in repose, having been reunited with their original altar tombs! Meanwhile, Keele is also featured on the 2007 UK "Here and Now" edition of the board game Monopoly, with Keele taking the place of Fleet Street in the traditional version.

NAME (STATUS):	**KNIGHTON** (Village * 2)
POPULATION:	c.200 (Knighton, Newcastle-under-Lyme); c.150 (Knighton, Stafford)
DISTRICT:	Newcastle-under-Lyme; Stafford
EARLIEST RECORD:	*Chenistetone* (Newcastle-u-Lyme), 1086 (Domesday Book); *Chnitestone* (Stafford), 1086 (Domesday Book)
MEANING:	Farmstead or village of the young men or retainers.
DERIVATION:	From the Old English words *cniht* (youth, servant or retainer) and *tūn* (farmstead).

Knighton Geographic Trivia: Protuberances

The more northerly of the two Staffordshire Knightons is located on the Shropshire border in the parish of Loggerheads (Newcastle-under-Lyme). This particular Knighton sits in a protuberance of Staffordshire that is surrounded to the west, north and east by Shropshire. The other Knighton is around 9 miles to the south, in the parish of Adbaston (Stafford), and sits just to the north-east of *another* Staffordshire protuberance into Shropshire.

Knighton Church: Methodist Chapel

Although both Knightons have a pub, neither has a church. The closest to having one is the Newcastle-under-Lyme Knighton, which used to have a Methodist chapel that was originally founded in 1834. Located on the eponymous Chapel Lane, the church was later converted into a residential home.

Knighton Quirk Alert: Denizen's Advice

Knighton (Stafford) is subject to a royal decree which states that all denizens shall be free of tax and tithe for ever more. Alas, today, this means that only denizens living within Knighton and engaged in agriculture can take advantage of these rights – so, just Knighton farmers, basically!

On Smithy Lane, Knighton (Newcastle), you will find a beautiful Grade II-listed, timber-framed house that dates from the 17th century. However, *during* the 17th century, the house wasn't located in Knighton; it was situated more than ten miles to the east in Stoke-on-Trent! Known as The Brookhouse, it was moved from its former location in the 1970s – where it was in a pretty bad state and due to be demolished. Once installed on Smithy Lane, Knighton, the restoration

work began and included the build of new foundations using sandstone recovered from a 13th century abbey.

The White Lion (above) can be found in the more northerly of Staffordshire's two Knightons, while The Haberdashers Arms (below) is located in the other Knighton in the borough of Stafford. The latter has hosted the annual potato show for more than sixty years which makes it the oldest horticultural show in Staffordshire, while it is also home to a large collection of oil lamps, many of which are used around once a month to transport the pub interior back in time.

Looking down Smithy Lane in Knighton (Newcastle). The timber-framed house in the foreground is the Grade II-listed Brookhouse, which dates from the 17th century.

The former Methodist chapel in Knighton (Newcastle).

NAME (STATUS):	**KNUTTON** (Residential area [Newcastle-under-Lyme])
POPULATION:	4,313 (ward of Knutton and Silverdale)
DISTRICT:	Newcastle-under-Lyme
EARLIEST RECORD:	*Clotone*, 1086 (Domesday Book); *Cnoton*, 1212
MEANING:	Either Cnut's farmstead, or farmstead on a hillock.
DERIVATION:	From either the personal name Cnut (possibly King Cnut), plus the Old English word *tūn* (farmstead), or the Old Scandinavian word *cnotta* (hillock) plus *tūn*.

St Mary's church, Knutton

The Masons Arms, Knutton.

Knutton Pub: The Masons Arms

In 1880, a certain James Shields was fined for leaving his horse and cart unattended outside the 19th century Masons Arms. Alas, while he sat inside enjoying his pipe and a beer or two, it was deemed by local magistrates to be irresponsible of him to leave his horse unattended as it was liable to bolt without anyone controlling it!

Knutton Church: St Mary's

Knutton's parish church was built between 1872 and 1874 by the architects, Thomas Lewis and Son, of Newcastle-under-Lyme. As a result, Knutton became an ecclesiastical parish in 1875. Kelly's *Directory* of 1872 also notes that there were places of worship for Wesleyans, Free Church and Primitive Methodists, too. Meanwhile, the 19th century vicarage was known as Knutton House, and accommodated successive vicars from 1874 until 1957 – by which time subsidence had taken its toll and it was replaced by a new vicarage.

Knutton Historical Trivia: Pounding Hammers and Knutton Halt

Formerly a rural township in the ancient ecclesiastical parish of Wolstanton, Knutton was transformed in the 19th century by the development of the iron industry. However, iron had been mined at Knutton since at least the 14th century with a mine recorded here in 1314 while in 1686 there was a forge on Knutton Heath at which flat round iron plates were hammered out to make frying pans. Knutton Forge prospered in the 19th century and was identified from miles around by its

three large chimneys, known locally as Faith, Hope and Charity; the foundry was also *felt* for miles around, too, thanks to the constant pounding of its steel hammers!

The early 19th century also saw several pits open in the Knutton area which provided iron ore and coal for the blast furnaces. One of those who prospered from the coal was a certain Mr Gordon of Oakhill Hall, proprietor of the School Ground Colliery, and who became a generous benefactor of education in Knutton. He financed existing local schools and also contributed financially to the new National School which was built at Knutton in 1872 and opened in March 1874. Alas, the pits were largely worked out by the 1920s, thus delivering a hammer blow to the local forges and ironworks! Knutton Forge was one victim, closing in 1929, with Faith, Hope and Charity demolished the following year. As an addendum to 19th century Knutton, among its societies was the Knutton Association for the Prosecution of Felons!

In 1905, Knutton Halt was opened as a station on North Staffordshire Railway's (NSR) Stoke to Market Drayton Line. The NSR then introduced a railmotor service between Silverdale and Trentham – this being a railway carriage pulled by a steam traction engine. The station was situated between Knutton village and Knutton Forge, but was relatively under-utilised. It was therefore no surprise that the station was closed in 1926, three years after the NSR became part of the London, Midland and Scottish railway.

Finally, Newcastle races were held on Knutton Heath in the 18th and early 19th centuries.

Three's-Up!

	LADYMOOR/LADY MOOR	LEA HEATH	LITTLE ONN
STATUS:	Residential area; Moorland	Hamlet	Hamlet
POPULATION:	13,363 (Bilston East ward)	c.30	680 (Parish of Church Eaton)
DISTRICT:	Wolverhampton; Staffordshire Moorlands	Stafford	Stafford
EARLIEST RECORD:	*Ladymoor*, 1810 (Wolves); *Ladie More*, 1547, *Ladymoor*, 1799 (Staffs Moorlands)	*Lee*, 1248;	*Anne*, 1086 (Domesday Book); *Little Onne*, 1253
MEANING:	The moorland dedicated to Our Lady, the Virgin Mary (Staffs Moorlands).	Woodland clearing on the heath.	A kiln.
DERIVATION:	From the personal name Mary, plus the Old English word *mōr* (moorland).	From the Old English words *lēah* (woodland clearing) and *hæth* (heath).	From the plural of the Celtic word *odn* (kiln).

Three's Up Trivia!

Ladymoor is a built-up residential area to the south-east of Wolverhampton, sandwiched in between Bilston, Bradley, Coseley and Ettingshall, and is represented by housing along Ladymoor Road as well as Ladymoor Recreation Ground, Ladymoor Pool and Ladymoor Brook. The southernmost stretch of the road sees it cross the Wednesbury Oak Loop Canal, part of James Brindley's original Birmingham Canal (later termed the Birmingham Canal Navigations), but which later became a loop following Thomas Telford's improvements of the 1830s. Sticking with the Industrial Revolution, a pit was sunk here in 1834 that became known as Ladymoor Colliery and which is thought to be responsible for Ladymoor Pool, this being a swag – a shallow, water-filled hollow produced by subsidence resulting from underground mining. Today, Ladymoor Pool is a haven for Canada geese during the day along with ducks, swans, mallards, coots, moorhens, doves, pigeons and seagulls, while at night you are likely to spot bats. The edges of the pool are comprised of banks of spoil along with large boulders of furnace slag, but which have been reclaimed by nature and now support diverse habitats suitable not only for the aforementioned birds, but also to great crested newts as well as rare plant species such as hawkweeds, common spotted orchid, southern marsh orchid and grass-wrack pondweed, which grows in the open water of the pool.

As for the other **Lady Moor**, this was an area of moorland to the north-west of the village of Endon in the Staffordshire Moorlands, and was first recorded here in 1547. The place-name then appears many more times over the centuries (*Ladie Moore*, 1568; *Ladymoor yate*, 1625; *Ladymoor Gate*, 1659; *Ladymoor Gate*, 1799; *Lady-Gate*, 1836).

Next up, **Lea Heath** is a tiny hamlet consisting of a few houses and a couple of farms. One of those houses also used to be The Wicket Inn on Lea Road, but this closed a few years ago and is now a private residence. The inn was formerly known as The Hanging Wicket, and before that, The Gate Inn (a wicket is a term for a small gate set within a larger one). Despite its tiny size, Lea Heath dates all the way back to 1248 when it was recorded as *Lee*. The name changed over time, from *La Le* in 1256, to *La Lee* in 1293, eventually arriving at *Lea* in 1834. The "heath" suffix was added later to differentiate it from other Leas and to indicate that the place is situated on relatively high ground.

Finally, **Little Onn** is a tiny hamlet in the parish of Church Eaton along with its twin, High Onn. It is also the location of the former Second World War airfield known as RAF Wheaton Aston which operated between 1941 and 1947 as a training school. The airfield has been long-since abandoned, although many of its former buildings remain; the site is now largely occupied by a pig farm!

Both Great Onn and Little Onn are located on the route of a now-defunct Roman road and which may

Ladymoor Pool can be found at the northern end of Ladymoor Road.

The main road through Lea Heath.

have accounted for the construction of the first kilns after which the villages were later named. Many centuries later, Little Onn Hall was built in the early 1870s, and was located close to a medieval moated site which is a Scheduled Ancient Monument. The initial gardens were laid out by Thomas Mawson in the last quarter of the 19th century. They were completed in 1898, and include terraces, a tennis court, a rose garden, yew hedges, walls, borders and some woodland; Messrs Bakers of Wolverhampton laid out the rest of the garden in the 1920s. At the same time (between 1920 and 1929), the owners, Major William Dickins Haywood and his wife made alterations to the house and extended it, while a few years earlier in 1917 they added a summerhouse and a dog bone-shaped pond.

One of the warehouses at Little Onn used in World War II, and which were part of an airfield and training school known as RAF Wheaton Aston.

The Shropshire Union Canal at Little Onn.

NAME (STATUS):	**LEEK** (Town)
POPULATION:	20,768
DISTRICT:	Staffordshire Moorlands
EARLIEST RECORD:	*Lec*, 1086 (Domesday Book).
MEANING:	Place at the brook.
DERIVATION:	From either the Old English word *læcc* (stream, brook or bog), or the Old Scandinavian word *lækr*, meaning the same thing.

Leek Geographical and Etymological Trivia

Leek prides itself as the Queen of the Moorlands, and given its location, it is pretty difficult to dispute. A historic market town situated at 600ft (180m) above sea level, it is also located only 4 miles south of the stunning scenery around The Roaches, a gritsone escarpment which rises steeply to 1,657 feet (505m); the town is even closer to Tittesworth and Rudyard Reservoirs which are popular with tourists and day-trippers. Leek is also the principal town of the Staffordshire Moorlands and, indeed, the most important on the south-western edge of the Peak District. As for the town's name, the two most proffered derivations have been captured above. However, there have been many more theories offered over the centuries, while the name itself took around 600 years to mutate from *Lec* in 1086 to *Leek*. The table below captures some of the older references; all references subsequent to the 1676 entry consistently name the place as *Leek*. However, some of those names in between have prompted a number of alternatively proposed derivatives. Picking up on the *Lech* references, one theory (Sleigh, 1833) suggests that the name is derived from the Welsh word *llech*, meaning "rock, crag or flat stone" – and there are plenty of these a few miles up the A53. Another theory (Duignan, 1902) proposes the brook derivation, given the Old English word *lece* (also meaning a brook), and he theorises that the brook in question was an upper arm of the River Churnet. Others suggest *lecan* (Old English to drip or to leak) or *leka* (Old Scandinavian meaning the same thing). Sticking with Old Scandinavian, *lækr* also means a brook or stream, maybe referring to Spot (Spout) Water, which transformed into Spout Lane in Leek, this deriving from the Middle English word *spouten* (to discharge liquid). However, the two main theories are that it relates to a brook that fed the River Churnet, or that it does exactly what it says on the tin – a leaky tin in this particular case!

No.	Name	Year
1	*Lec*	1086
2	*Lech*	1100
3	*Lecu*	1165
4	*Lech*	1188
5	*Lech*	1199
6	*Lec*	1199
7	*Leech*	1220
8	*Leych*	1240
9	*Leik*	1244
10	*Leke*	1247
11	*Leike*	1298
12	*Leck*	1318
13	*Lake*	1425
14	*Lyk*	1426
15	*Lyek*	1474
16	*Leke*	1532
17	*Leike*	1577
18	*Leek*	1583
19	*Leeke*	1637
20	*Leek*	1676

Leek Pub: The Blue Mugge

Leek has some very interesting pub names, such as The Bird In Hand and The Quiet Woman. However, The Blue Mugge wins this particular contest, primarily due to its unique name and the story behind it. The pub actually underwent a name change to The Blue Mugge as recently as 1979; before that it had been The Queen's Arms. The trigger for the name change occurred when the landlord discovered the original 'Blue Mugge' in the attic, after which he learned of its story. For the Blue Mugge spent its life in the 'Blue Mugge Room', which turned out to be a room for gentlemen only! Any visitors wishing to join the regulars in the Blue Mugge Room had to first buy all of the occupants a drink – and if he agreed, the occupants would then produce a glass that was only a third of a pint, given the newcomer had passed the test!

The Blue Mugge, Leek.

The Red Lion is located in Leek's Market Place alongside the Butter Market.

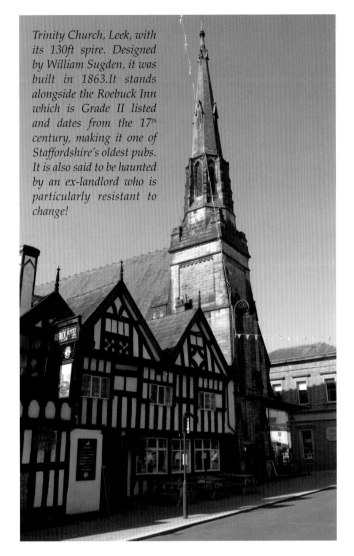

Trinity Church, Leek, with its 130ft spire. Designed by William Sugden, it was built in 1863.It stands alongside the Roebuck Inn which is Grade II listed and dates from the 17th century, making it one of Staffordshire's oldest pubs. It is also said to be haunted by an ex-landlord who is particularly resistant to change!

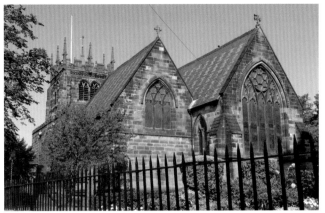

Leek's parish church, dedicated to St Edward the Confessor.

The two ancient Anglo-Saxon crosses in St Edward's churchyard. The cross on the left is widely deemed to be 10th century while its partner (right) has been variously dated from the 8th to the 11th century.

Leek Church: St Edward the Confessor

Leek actually has six churches, but this section features the parish church, the Grade II-listed St Edward the Confessor. The church dates from many different centuries, with the oldest parts possibly 13th century, while the tower dates from the 14th century. The aisles were then added in the 15th century, the clerestory in the 16th century, the gallery at the west end of the nave in the late 18th century and the north porch in 1838, while the church also underwent extensive restoration in the 19th century, initially by Ewan Christian, and later by Street in 1867. Most of the windows were replaced at this time, too, while Christian restored the nave roof in 1857 and Street lengthened the chancel in 1867; the marble font is 19th century, too, dating from 1867. The other feature worth mentioning is the church's rose windows one of which is a memorial to Dame Elizabeth Wardle (d.1902).

Leek Historic Trivia:
From William I to William Sugden

Although Leek is mentioned in Domesday Book, it is clear that there was a settlement there for many centuries before, witnessed by two ancient crosses in St Edward's churchyard. One of them is consistently deemed to be Mercian and dates from the 10th century – although sadly it is quite damaged. The other specimen is in superb order though, but there is some dispute as to its age. It has been dated as far back as the 8th century, while others consider it may be 11th century and of Danish origin.

Following the Norman Conquest, William I took possession of the manor of Leek. However, throughout most of the Norman period, the manor was owned by the Earls of Chester, with the 6th earl, Ranulf de Blondeville, founding Dieulacres Abbey a couple of miles north of Leek in 1210 (see *Abbey Green* for more). Three years earlier, in 1207, King John had granted Ranulf the right to hold a weekly Wednesday market and an annual seven-day fair in Leek; the town was granted its royal charter in 1214.

In 1666, Thomas Parker was born in Leek, and he went on to become Chief Justice and Lord Chancellor, while he also founded the grammar school in Leek in 1723. However, in 1725, he was impeached for corruption and fined £30,000 – a huge amount of money in those days – after which he retired to a private life.

During the Industrial Revolution, Leek was transformed from a small market town into an industrial hotbed as several large silk and textile mills were built.

Left: *York Mill, a former silk mill built in 1898. One of many surviving mills in Leek, this one on Ashbourne Road hasn't been as fortunate as the others on this page in terms of 21st century re-deployment.*
Centre: *Waterloo Mill, Leek, was built in 1894 for William Broster & Co who manufactured silk sewing threads. It now accommodates modern apartments.*
Right: *The former Print Works and a surviving part of the Belle Vue Silk Mill complex on Belle Vue Road, and now also home to a number of modern apartments.*

Left: *Myatt's Mill on Earl Street was built in 1864, one of many of Leek's most impressive buildings built by architect William Sugden (1821-1892).*
Centre: *Sugden House built in 1882 by Larner Sugden of the famous Sugden & Son (Architects). Today this building also includes a number of modern apartments.*
Right: *The Sanders Building, another design from Sugden & Son and built in 1894. Today it is home to apartments and a shop selling vintage toys.*

Also of note is that, although born in Tunstead, Derbyshire, the great James Brindley spent much of his life in Leek, while William Morris, founder of the Arts and Crafts movement, also lived and worked in Leek between 1875 and 1878.

Sticking with the 19th century, and many Victorian buildings still survive in Leek, with many built by the Sugden family. Their considerable contribution to Leek commenced in 1849 when architect William Sugden came to live in the town from Keighley in Yorkshire while he designed and oversaw the building of a number of railway stations for the Churnet Valley Railway. William Sugden's son, Larner, became an apprentice architect to his father in 1866 and Sugden & Son (Architects) was formed. Leek buildings designed by the company included the Congregational church with its 130ft spire (now Trinity church), built in the Victorian Gothic Revival style (1863), Myatt's Mill (1864), Mill Street Methodist chapel and Ragged School (1870), the Cottage Hospital (1871), their own houses in Queen Street, West Street School (extended in 1881), the District Bank (1882), the Sanders building (1894), the Leonard Street Police Station (1891), and the Technical Schools and the Co-operative Society Hall (1899). The finest Sugden building, though, is probably the Nicholson Institute, built in the Queen Anne style, in 1882, and where Larner Sugden worked the busts of Newton, Shakespeare, Reynolds and Tennyson into the building, thus representing 400 years of artistic and scientific achievement from the 16th to the 19th century. It was also around this time (1856) that the Britannia Building Society was founded in Leek – although it was originally known as The Leek and Moorlands Permanent Benefit Building Society.

Leek Quirk Alert: The Noisy Peace Memorial, The Double Sunset and Beating the Corn

Leek's impressive 90ft clock tower was erected in 1925 in memory of the fallen of World War I, with the fallen of World War II added later. The clock tower, also known as The Peace Memorial, also claims to be the tallest war memorial in England. It was commissioned by manufacturer Sir Arthur Nicholson and his wife in tribute to their son, Lieutenant Basil Lee Nicholson, who was killed in action at Ypres in 1915. However, the town council have recently had to change its chiming hours because a new Premier Inn has been built close to it, and the hotel company wish to make good on their promise of a great night's sleep! The Peace Memorial,

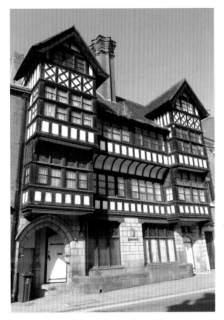

One of many ancient Leek buildings.

The Peace Memorial, Leek – and which doesn't chime as often as it used to!

The Bird in the Hand pub in Leek's Market Place.

as it is known in Leek, has therefore had its first chime modified from 6.15 am to 8.15 am. It will then ring every quarter of an hour until 10pm – although The Premier Inn tried to get that modified to 8pm, but the council dug their heels in on that one, also pointing out that, prior to electronic timers, it once used to chime every 15 minutes, 24 hours a day! To be fair to The Premier Inn, though, their hotel brought jobs to the town and helped to rescue the Talbot Inn in the process, which the hotel was built around.

Leek is also the home of an annual phenomenon known as the "Double Sunset". This occurs when the sun appears to set behind The Cloud (1,125ft; 343m) and which is sited around 6 miles to the north-west of Leek. The sun remains eclipsed by The Cloud until it reappears in the hollow of the hill's vertical northern side, before setting for a second time. It occurs on the 20th, 21st and 22nd June each year – a fine nod to the

summer solstice – and is such an ancient and famous phenomenon that it also appears on Leek's coat of arms, appearing at the top on either side of the Staffordshire Knot. In fact, the phenomenon is first recorded in Robert Plot's book from 1686 called *The Natural History of Staffordshire*.

Finally, St Edward the Confessor's churchyard is home to a stone memorial to a certain William Trafford (d.1697). The memorial is carved with a man, a flail, a sheaf of corn and the words "Now Thus"… and here is why. Because during the English Civil War, Trafford – a fervent Royalist – was discovered at his home by Parliamentarian soldiers, whereupon he immediately feigned idiocy by beating his corn with a flail, while his answer to every question was "now thus, now thus". The ploy worked a treat, too, for the soldiers left him alone, flail, corn and all.

Brough Park, Leek.

Vintage House, Leek.

NAME (STATUS):	**LITTLEWORTH**
STATUS:	Suburb (Stafford); Suburb (Hednesford)
DISTRICT:	Stafford; Cannock Chase
EARLIEST RECORD:	*Littleworth*, 1794 (Stafford); *Littleworth*, 1834 (Hednesford)
MEANING:	Either a little enclosure, or a derogatory term for poor land.
DERIVATION:	From the Old English words *lȳtel* (little) and *worth* (enclosure).

Littleworth Historic Trivia: Staffordshire General and Dorman Diesels

There have actually been four Littleworth's in Staffordshire in the past, but you will only find two of them on the map today, one – a former village – which is now an eastern suburb of Stafford, and the other which is at the south-eastern edge of Hednesford. The others, apparently, were on the south-western side of Woodseaves, 2 miles west of Rocester and on the western side of Stafford. Of the two featured Littleworth's, the one to the east of Stafford includes Staffordshire's major hospital, County Hospital. Alas, it has recently been in the news for all the wrong reasons. It opened in 1983 and went by the name Stafford District General Hospital, but faced its first crisis two years later thanks to an outbreak of Legionnaires' disease. It then became Staffordshire General Hospital in the 1990s when Staffordshire General Infirmary closed, with the latter's services transferred to Staffordshire General Hospital. It was in this guise that the hospital found itself under major public scrutiny following a Care Quality Commission inspection in October 2011. The commission found a lack of suitably trained nursing staff on duty in the accident and emergency department and, as a result, the department was closed at night for three months while members of staff were trained up to a suitable level. Then in January 2013 a police investigation followed the discovery that a dummy had been taped to a baby's face, while in July 2013 two nurses were struck off the nursing register for falsifying A&E discharge times – the aim being to avoid breaches of four-hour waiting targets. At around the same time, the hospital's regulator also warned that the trust was close to insolvency, due to a 67% drop in patient numbers over the previous five years – mainly due to lost confidence from the general public – and as a result, annual income had fallen by nearly £4 million. Continuing the tale of woe, the hospital also found itself accused of substandard care by numerous newspapers, which estimated that between 400 and 1200 more patients died between 2005 and 2008 than would be expected for this type of hospital. In June 2010, therefore, the coalition government opened up a full public inquiry, which resulted in 290 recommendations for improvement.

Contrast all of that with 2015, and what is now called the County Hospital (changed due to the stigma and reputation of its former name), has one of the lowest mortality rates in the West Midlands. Furthermore, even during the traumatic year of 2013, the hospital received lots of support from locals, with campaigners leading a 50,000-strong march through the centre of Stafford in April 2013, waving banners like "Stafford saved my dad" and "Stafford looks after my son". The group were also fearful that the facility on their doorstep was about to lose its intensive care facilities and its 24/7 A&E service, asserting that increased journey times for patients making the trip from Stafford to other hospitals could risk lives, not to mention increase the burden elsewhere.

View from Wimblebury towards Littleworth – this being the Littleworth just east of Hednesford, and at the southern edge of Cannock Chase.

As well as the hospital, the other major source of employment in Littleworth was the Perkins factory which made engines for marine and other applications. The company was formerly known as Dorman Diesels, founded by Henry Dorman in 1869 on Foregate Street, Stafford, initially manufacturing cutting tools for the footwear industry. It was 1903 when they produced their first internal combustion engine for the early motor car industry. In between making a significant contribution to the two World Wars, the company first moved out to a new 20 acre site at Littleworth in 1929. By 1979, Dorman Diesels was a subsidiary of GEC but was eventually purchased by the Perkins Engines Company of Peterborough… who then sold the business in 2010 along with the rights to the older engines to Lincoln Diesels Ltd.

Threes-Up!

	LOGGERHEADS	LYNN	OLIVE GREEN
STATUS:	Large civil parish, ward & village	Hamlet	Hamlet
POPULATION:	4,480 (parish); 4193 (ward)	c.25	313 (Hamstall Ridware parish)
DISTRICT:	Newcastle-under-Lyme	Lichfield	Lichfield
EARLIEST RECORD:	*Loghead*, 1657; Loggerheads, 1775; *Loggerheads*, 1798	*la Lynd*, 1262; *Lynda*, 1274; *Lynde*, 1311; *Lynne*, 1592	*Gallows Green*, 1741; *Olive Green*, 1775
MEANING AND DERIVATION:	See *Three's-Up Trivia*	Place at the lime-tree. From the Old English word *lind* (lime-tree).	See *Three's Up Trivia*

Three's Up Trivia

Loggerheads almost certainly derives its name from a pub that pre-dates the present one – which is known simply as "The Loggerheads" today, but which was formerly known as "The Three Loggerheads". The original pub here was an 18th century coaching inn that was also known as The Three Loggerheads, and for a couple of centuries was the only building here, at what was a busy crossroads then, and which now marks the busy crossroads of the A53 and the B5026.

As for the meaning of the word loggerhead, it simply means a fool, or perhaps "blockhead" would be a better description – so there were three of them represented here! The derivation is presumably from the word *logger* (a heavy block of wood). Certainly other pubs of the same name were known to adorn their public house signs with the words "We three logger-

The Loggerheads public house which sits at the crossroads of the A53 and the B5026, and which also lends the village and parish its name.

heads be..." along with two wooden heads, the spectator being the unwitting third head! It is believed that the original sign at Loggerheads also depicted two clowns or fools and the words "We three loggerheads be..." but which was replaced by a triangular inn-sign in the gable of the building portraying three jovial bumpkins – and thus missing the irony of the original! Of course, the other meaning of loggerheads suggests two parties in disagreement, and first appears in that sense in the *Chambers Dictionary* of 1831 where it is described as "to fight or to squabble".

The village of Loggerheads was also home to the Cheshire Joint Sanatorium between 1923 and 1969, an institution for sufferers of tuberculosis. It was built here because Loggerheads is on a hill, and fresh air was deemed to be an effective treatment, particularly at Loggerheads which was above the damp air of the lowlands and far enough away from the industrial soot and smoke of the Potteries. It therefore wasn't uncommon for the patients to be outside... in their beds!

Meanwhile, the tiny hamlet of **Lynn** can be found on Lynn Lane between the Lichfield district villages of Shenstone and Stonnal. It is part of the parish of Shenstone although historically it is usually referred to in documents about Stonnall, as it is closer to the latter. Lynn Hall, which is at the western end of Lynn where it runs into Lower Stonnal, used to be known as the Coach House, while Lynn Lane used to be known as Fighting Cocks Lane. Finally, the 18th century memoirs of Reverend Sanders reveal that local Quakers were buried in the graveyard immediately to the west of Lynn. The hamlet is also close to Quebb Lane and the Quebb Brook, where *quebb* is Old English for a marsh and, sure enough, the Rev. Sanders describes "The

Lynn in the district of Lichfield is a hamlet consisting of a handful of houses.

The stunning 17th century Sycamore Cottage in Hamstall Ridware is Grade II listed.

Quebb" as "a little water which rises near the Wall."

Finally, **Olive Green** (*shown previous page, top right*) is a tiny hamlet consisting of a handful of houses located a few yards south-east of the village of Hamstall Ridware. As to the origins of the place, there is some confusion, as the place is alternately recorded as both Olive Green and Gallows Green throughout the 18th and early 19th centuries. As well as the 1741 and 1775 records shown earlier, the name reverts to *Gallows Green* again in 1798, but then goes back to *Olive Green* in 1801, only to revert to *Gallows Green* again in 1806 and retains that name for an 1834 Ordnance Survey map. The assumption, therefore, is that the place was originally the site of the manorial gallows, and perhaps its other name was seen as a more palatable alternative.

As for the manor house, that was located at Hamstall Ridware – although all that remains of Hamstall Hall today is what is called The Watchtower and the Hall's distinctive Grade II-listed gateway, known as The Pepperpots. Had Hamstall Ridware been featured in the Shire-Ode, it would have got its own chapter, as it has a Grade I-listed church (St Michael and All Angels, the oldest parts of which date back to around 1130), an attractive pub (The Shoulder of Mutton, which dates back to 1827), and a series of beautiful historic houses… plus an awful lot of history, too. However, we'll restrict ourselves to mentioning that the surviving tower is actually older than the final Hamstall Hall, with the former dating from the turn of the 16th century, while the Jacobean Hall was built in around 1620.

St Michael and All Angels' church at Hamstall Ridware is Grade I listed.

The Shoulder of Mutton, Hamstall Ridware, dates from 1827.

Left: *In the churchyard at Hamstall Ridware is this cross which is considerably newer than the medieval base on which it stands. Part of the original shaft stands on its own nearby.*

NAME (STATUS):	**MAER** (Village)
POPULATION:	489 (Maer parish)
DISTRICT:	Newcastle-under-Lyme
EARLIEST RECORD:	*Mere*, 1086; *Mare*, 1198, *Meer*, 1291; *Mayer*, 1471; *Meire*, 1586
MEANING:	Place at the lake or mere.
DERIVATION:	From the Old English word *mere* (lake or mere).

The Swan With Two Necks is located a mile west of Maer.

St Peter's church, Maer.

Maer Church: St Peter's

St Peter's church stands splendidly above Maer Hall, halfway up a hillside with superb views to the west. The original church here probably dated from the Norman period but much of it now dates from the 17th century when it was rebuilt in 1610 – including the tower and most of the nave and chancel. The church was also heavily restored in 1877, while old photographs from the late 19th and early 20th century show the tower to be completely covered in ivy.

Maer Geographic and Historic Trivia: The Origin of Maer Hall

Maer is a rural village that sits in the shadow of the Maer Hills alongside the Maer Pool, while the settlement is dominated by Maer Hall. In fact, it is the first thing that you see on the right-hand side when you emerge from the tunnel at the entrance to the village. The hall, in turn, stands on a slope above the small lake (or mere) that Maer was named after – and which is all that remains of a very large Ice Age lake which once covered the whole of the valley. Maer Pool also marks the source of the River Tern. As for the Maer Hills, they are reputed to be the site of a battle in 642 when Oswy, King of Northumbria was killed. He is rumoured to have been buried at Kings Bank, which is located in the Maer Hills.

Historically, a manor house has existed on the site of the current Maer Hall since at least 1282 when it belonged to William de Mere, while the year 1532 saw

Another angle on St Peter's church with Maer Hall in the background.

Looking towards the chancel inside St Peter's church.

that particular Maer Hall recording five hearths as part of the Hearth Tax returns. That hall was replaced in 1680 by the current Jacobean Maer Hall which was built by the Macclesfield family, while the 18th century saw the gardens re-laid by Capability Brown with the pleasure grounds expanded to include Maer Pool. The hall was then bought in 1802 by Josiah Wedgwood II, the famous potter whose business was located around 7 miles to the east at his Etruria works. Wedgwood then had the grounds and park further landscaped by John Webb, and in 1807 Josiah and his family moved in.

A frequent visitor to Maer Hall during the early 19th century was a young Charles Darwin, Josiah Wedgwood's nephew. Apparently, it was while at Maer Hall that young Charles first became interested in the effects of earthworms, and which became the subject of an early paper presented to the Geological Society. He also spent a lot of time at Maer following his return from the *Beagle* voyage (1831-1836), and he continued his research in the surrounding countryside, discovering the nearby Butterton Dyke, a geological fault, formed by volcanic activity. It was also at around this time that Darwin proposed to Wedgwood's daughter, Emma, at Maer Hall, and they were married in January 1839 at St Peter's church – naturally! Their marriage is commemorated on the wall below the church (*shown above*), while they also appear on the Maer sign at the northern end of the village (*shown previous page, top left*), walking arm-in-arm out of St Peter's church; an older Darwin is also portrayed on the sign holding his famous book, *The Origin of the Species*. Darwins' wife – who was also his cousin – helped her older sister Elizabeth with

Maer Hall, taken from St Peter's churchyard.

the Sunday school which was held at Maer Hall and gave sixty village children their only formal training in reading, writing and religion.

When Josiah Wedgwood II died in 1843, the house and estate were bought by the pottery manufacturer William Davenport, of Davenport Pottery in Burslem. Davenport's additions to the house included a huge clock tower and more stables – although the latter were knocked down in the 1960s. The house was then next acquired by the Harrison family in 1893, owners of the Liverpool-based Harrison Shipping Line, and they added late Victorian wings to the house – but which were later demolished in the 20th century. The Harrisons also had the gardens re-laid by Thomas Mawson.

Today, Maer Hall is Grade II listed and includes a Grade II listed lodge and a Grade II listed gatehouse.

This beautiful war memorial is located at the top of the northern approach to Maer.

The next chapter includes the Meir Tunnel – so let's call this one the Maer Tunnel – which you drive through to enter the village from the north.

The grand entrance to Maer Hall.

NAME (STATUS):	**MEIR** (Suburb)
POPULATION:	4,756 (Meir Hay), 5,763 (Meir North); 4,941 (Meir Park); 5,791 (Meir South)
DISTRICT:	Stoke-on-Trent
EARLIEST RECORD:	*Mere*, 1242;
MEANING:	Place at the lake or mere.
DERIVATION:	From the Old English word *mere* (lake or mere).
FAMOUS RESIDENTS:	Dennis Smith (b.1947), footballer.

Meir Geographic Trivia: Wards of Wisdom

The population section above reveals that Meir is split up into a number of different wards. Of these, the Meir Park housing estate was built on the site of the former Meir Aerodrome (which closed in the early 1970s), while the southernmost of these wards sits just to the north of Meir Heath – outside of the Stoke-on-Trent unitary authority and part of the Stafford district, but thought to be the highest conurbation area in Staffordshire.

Meir Pub: The Windmill Inn

It is also in Meir Heath that you will find The Windmill Inn, and which still has the original and now-Grade II listed windmill in its car park. Probably dating from the mid-18th century, it is certainly on Yates' map of 1775 where it is specified as a corn mill, while throughout the 19th century it was brewing beer as well milling corn, but eventually fell into disuse in 1896. The mill tower was then sold to Staffordshire Potteries Water Board in 1908 and they installed a water tank in the tower, while much later, in 1940, the Home Guard used it as a look-out post. Thereafter, the windmill fell into disrepair until members of the local history group formed the Meir Heath Windmill Group in 2002 and which had become the Meir Heath Windmill Preservation Group Charity by 2006. As part of the windmill restoration, a £6,000 roof, or boat cap – so-called as it resembles an inverted boat – was added in 2010. The ultimate aim is to turn the wind-mill into a heritage centre looking back over the history of the immediate area. As well as a number of grants and charitable donations, the owners of the land, the Mitchells & Butlers Brewery, have leased the land to the preservation group at a peppercorn rent for twenty-five years!

Meir Church: Holy Trinity

Holy Trinity is a relatively modern church, built in the 1890s – although in those days, Meir was still a small village. However, a regular visitor to this new village church was a certain William Havergal Brian (1876-1972), who was later to become one of the most prolific writers of classical music in British history, composing 32 symphonies during his lifetime. Back at the turn of the 20th century, though, he used Holy Trinity's brand new organ chamber to hone his musical skills for around three years. Later, he would count Sir Edward Elgar and Richard Strauss amongst his friends, dedicating his Gothic Symphony to the latter in 1927.

Meir Historic Trivia: Stations and Tunnels

During the Roman occupation, Meir was on Ryknield Street, which ran from Little Chester in Derby to Uttoxeter and then onto Chesterton, via Meir, eventually terminating at Chester. Centuries later, the road is recorded as a highway in the 13th century and was then turnpiked 500 years later in 1759 with a toll house originally located at Meir, although it was moved to the

The Windmill Inn, Meir Heath.

Holy Trinity church, Meir. The classical composer, Havergal Brian (1876-1972), who completed 32 symphonies during his lifetime, was organist here aged thirteen.

boundary with Longton in 1763.

In 1894, Meir Station was opened by the North Staffordshire Railway on its line from Stoke to Derby and was situated in a cutting to the east of Meir Tunnel and close to the crossroads of the A50 and A520. However, following the Beeching cuts and subsequent railway closures of the 1960s, the station was closed in 1966 and no trace of it remains today.

Finally, one other impressive resident of Meir is the Meir Tunnel – constructed in the late 20th century and which largely resolved the previously notorious traffic hotspot at the junction of the A50 and the A520.

Meir Quirk Alert:
FRED and the Short Straw

The last official flight from the previously-mentioned Meir Aerodrome was on 16th August 1973 when Fred Holdcroft flew a Piper Tri-Pacer carrying a Stoke Sentinel journalist to Manchester. However, the last *unofficial* flight occurred a couple of years later when local man Eric Clutton took to the sky in a home-made folding machine, which was *also* called FRED (Flying Runabout Experimental Design), and which he apparently towed around behind his car!

Earlier, we mentioned the former Meir railway station. Research tells me that the building was made of timber and included a booking office with a cast iron coal burning stove, a waiting room, a small store room for cleaning and bike storage… and an Elsan – which turns out to be a bucket-style toilet! Apparently, the Junior Porter drew the short straw – I think you know what I'm saying – and which involved a dug-out hole in the small wooded area behind the station!

The partly-restored windmill which sits in the Windmill Inn car-park. Dating back to before 1775, the windmill actually ceased milling in 1896.

Three's-Up!

	ROUGHLEY	ROUND OAK	SCOT HAY
STATUS:	Former hamlet, now built-up	Built-up area	Hamlet
POPULATION:	24,025 (Sutton Four Oaks ward)		c.200
DISTRICT:	Birmingham, West Midlands	Dudley, West Midlands	Newcastle-under-Lyme
EARLIEST RECORD:	*Roughley*, early 20th century	*Round Oak*, early 19th century	*Skotteshay*, 1410; *Scott Heyes*, 1566
MEANING:	Woodland clearing on rough ground.	Unknown	Probably named after the Scot or Scott family who may have lived here in the 14th century, or perhaps meaning "a tax or payment".
DERIVATION:	From the Old English words *rūh* (rough) and *lēah* (woodland clearing).	Unknown, but likely to have derived from the Old English word *āc* (oak-tree).	From the Middle English word *scot* (tax or payment) and the Old English *hæg* (fence or enclosure).

Three's Up Trivia

Roughley was a South Staffordshire village until it was absorbed by Sutton Coldfield in the early 20th century, after which it became part of the West Midlands metropolis. Then, on 1st April 1974, it switched counties from Staffordshire to the newly-created metropolitan county of West Midlands, and became part of the Birmingham metropolitan district – albeit in the district's most northerly tip and still only half a mile from its former county's new boundary. As for the place-name, the rough clearing suggested opposite probably referred to uncultivated land cleared from the forest, or perhaps land already cleared before Anglo-Saxon times but later reclaimed by nature. Having said that, there is also another local theory about the name, but which is realistically set several hundred years after Roughley was first named. However, it is definitely worth an airing, for it is said that the highwayman, Dick Turpin, had his hideout at Muffins Den in Roughley where he is said to have stayed before waylaying travellers! Muffins Den was probably also the site of the first inn in Roughley, perhaps close to today's Plough & Harrow. As for the place-name link, it is thought that as well as Muffins Den, it was also known as Ruffians Den, named after thieves and high-waymen who allegedly frequented it!

The Fox & Dogs, Roughley.

Chase Farm at Roughley. Behind the farmhouse there is a thriving business, including Chase Farm Café, Chase Farm Shop and Roughley Limousin – another shop, named after the pedigree cattle bred on the farm.

Finally, there was also once a Roughley Farm, but that has since been demolished and a new housing estate built on its land. However, Chase Farm Shop on Weeford Road, Roughley, does survive. It started out as an egg shed selling the farm's own eggs. Gradually, the product line expanded to include Christmas turkeys, as well as potatoes and other vegetables from local farms, before eventually moving into the former dairy building and growing into today's thriving business.

Next up, **Round Oak**, is located just to the south-west of Dudley and was the site of a terrible railway disaster in August 1858. Round Oak had a railway station on the Oxford to Wolverhampton line that went via Worcester, and was opened in 1852. The disaster occurred when a coupling broke on an excursion train at Round Oak Station and the rear portion of the train – seventeen coaches containing around 450 passengers, plus one brake van – rolled back down the gradient from Round Oak Station towards Brettell Lane where it collided with another train, killing fourteen passengers and injuring more than fifty. Tragically, the two trains were part of the same excursion, comprising 42 four-wheeled coaches and four brake vans. However, prior to climbing the 1 in 75 ascent from Brettell Lane to Round Oak, the train had been subdivided for safety reasons due to its extreme length. At the time, the Board of Trade accident inspector, Captain H. W. Tyler, said that it was "decidedly the worst railway accident that has ever occurred in this country". It was later revealed that Guard Cooke, in the rear brake van, had been allowing passengers to work the van handbrake, but which resulted in three separate breakages. However, he only repaired two of them, and so when the first train of 28 coaches and two brake vans (pulled by loco-motives) ascended successfully to Round Oak, and then ground to a halt, the action caused the decoupling on the eleventh coach – leaving the trailing 17 coaches and Cooke's van rolling back down the incline to smash into the second train. The sturdy locomotive at the front of the second train was only superficially damaged; all of the real damage was done to the careering first train and its passengers, with Cooke's brake van and the first two carriages smashed to pieces. Despite protesting his innocence, it was proven that Cooke had left his post and had also not screwed down the brakes. He was therefore found guilty of manslaughter. Round Oak Station was eventually closed by British Rail in 1962. However, the station is set to be revitalised as part of the £1.1 million regeneration project that will include the station as part of the prospective local tram network with the line reopening between Walsall and the Merry Hill Shopping Centre alongside Round Oak.

Of the two alternatives for place-name derivation suggested opposite, **Scot Hay** may well be the *hæg* listed in a charter relating to Madeley as far back as 975. Moving forward to 1829, this was the year that the Independent Order of Oddfellows, Manchester Unity, set up their "Farmer's Glory" Lodge No 374! And the significance – it held its first meeting in the former

Cross Keys public house in Scot Hay – although by 1843, they had moved a mile or so up the road to the Boughey Arms at Alsagers Bank. By 1860 the lodge had 190 members.

It was also in 1860 that the nearby Lycett Colliery was opened and many of its miners lived in Scot Hay. The mine is infamous for the Fair Lady Pit Explosion on

21st January 1880, one of the region's worst-ever disasters and which claimed the lives of 62 men and boys, ranging from age 16 to 55 and left a number of others horribly mutilated. Many of the dead and injured came from Scot Hay. The disaster is covered in more detail in the *Finney Green* chapter. The mine was eventually closed in 1957.

This is Dudley No. 1 Canal demonstrating the recent redevelopment of this area on what was the former site of Round Oak Steel.The steelworks were closed in 1982 after 125 years of operation and around 1,300 employees were made redundant. Today, the area is known as The Waterfront and also includes the Merry Hill Shopping Centre, the fourth largest in the UK.

Also incorporated into the new development on the old steelworks site is The Brewer's Wharf, which itself incorporates an authentic Banks's Bitter chimney.

Below: *This is the memorial to the 63 miners who lost their lives during the Leycett pit disaster on 21st January 1880, many of whom lived in nearby Scot Hay. Leycett Colliery operated from 1860 to 1957.*

NAME (STATUS):	**ONECOTE** (Village)
POPULATION:	220
DISTRICT:	Staffordshire Moorlands
EARLIEST RECORD:	*Anecote*, 1199
MEANING:	Remote cottage.
DERIVATION:	From the Old English words *āna* (isolated, remote or lonely) and *cot* (cottage, hut or shelter).

The Jervis Arms, Onecote.

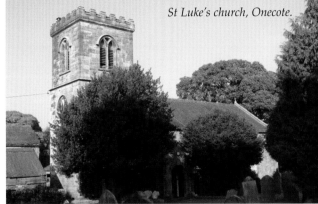

St Luke's church, Onecote.

Onecote Church: St Luke's

It is likely that the predecessor to the current 16th century St Luke's church, developed out of the monastic grange at Onecote that existed here in the 13th century. There are numerous references to a chapel here during the 16th and 17th centuries, and there was certainly a minister incumbent in the 1640s and 1650s, but the chapel appears to have fallen into disuse by the end of the 17th century; indeed, by 1751 when building of the current church commenced, the previous building didn't even exist! However, although the first baptism was recorded in 1755, it was 1782 before the first burial could be carried out, following the consecration of St Luke's by the Bishop of Lichfield. At this time, the church was still a chapel of ease to its mother church at Leek, and it was 1862 before Onecote with Bradnop became a parish separate from Leek. Much later in 1975, the parish was united with those of Ipstones and Berkhamsytch.

Onecote Historic Trivia: Anecote Grange

It is highly likely that the "remote cottage" after which Onecote is named, is the outlying farm referred to as "Anecote Grange" in Lord Audley's charter of 1223. The farm belonged to Hulton Abbey, and was run by its own lay brothers, but it is not clear if a pre-existing settlement lent its name to the farm or vice-versa.

In the *Conventional Staffordshire* section, it is mentioned that the Staffordshire Moorlands was a hot-bed for non-conformism in the 17th century, and Onecote seems to fit this bill – for the curate of 1604, Ralph Salt, was described as neither a preacher nor properly ordained, but that he was "a lewd young man… out of all good order, [who] weareth a feather in his hat"! Finally, the year 1872 saw the opening of a church school, and which lasted until its closure in 1984; the building has since become the village hall.

The nave of St Luke's church.

The western entrance to Onecote.

NAME (STATUS):	**RANTON** (Village/hamlet)
POPULATION:	382
DISTRICT:	Stafford
EARLIEST RECORD:	*Rantone*, 1086 (Domesday Book)
MEANING:	Farmstead where rams are kept, or settlement on the boundary.
DERIVATION:	From the Old English words *ramm* (ram) and *tūn* (farmstead or settlement), or the Old English words *rand* (edge) and *tūn*, perhaps referring to Ranton's location on the border between the Anglo-Saxon hundreds of Pirehill and Cuttlestone.
FAMOUS RESIDENTS:	Ozzy Osbourne

Ranton All Saints' church, much of which dates from the 13ᵗʰ century.

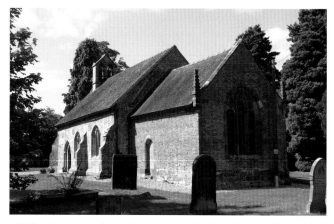

All Saints' church from the reverse angle showing the 18ᵗʰ century chancel.

Ranton Church: All Saints

All Saints' church in Ranton dates largely from the 13ᵗʰ century, although the chancel was added in 1753, while a gallery was erected in 1840. Meanwhile, the bell turret was removed in 1889, and was eventually re-erected in the 1940s in memory of two local men, Frank Russell and John Owen Timms, who gave their lives during World War II – although the turret wasn't initially strong enough to support the bells, which had to be stored in the church shed. According to Arthur Mee in 1937, these bells "are believed to have rung the monks to service in the great days of the priory". He was, of course, referring to Ranton Abbey (see *Ranton Historic Trivia* for more). At a later stage, the turret was strengthened and the bells re-mounted.

Ranton Historic Trivia: Ranton Abbey

Ranton Abbey or Ranton Priory was built for the Augustinian order of canons in the mid 12ᵗʰ century, by Robert Fitz-Noel, and was affiliated as a cell to Haughmond Abbey near Shrewsbury. Situated around a mile to the west of Ranton in around 700 acres of land, the priory was initially endowed by its founder with a number of properties, including nearby Coton Clanford Mill. The priory certainly prospered during the 13ᵗʰ century, but apparently became subject to a number of disciplinary issues and financial mismanagement during the 14ᵗʰ century. Like the majority of its peers, it was dissolved in the late 1530s, although by this stage, it only housed five canons. Thereafter, the usual scrap for its buildings and land ensued, with the Harcourt family eventually winning out. By the mid-17ᵗʰ century, Ranton Abbey was a sizeable family home owned by the Copes, and fashioned out of a number of the former priory buildings. As for Ranton Abbey today, only the 15ᵗʰ century tower remains along with part of the nave wall complete with Norman doorway, although the cloisters are known to have still been standing in 1663.

Located adjacent to the abbey ruins are the remains of Abbey House, built in 1820 by Thomas Anson, 1st Earl of Lichfield, following his purchase of the Ranton Estate from the Copes in 1819. The house was built in red brick, Regency style, and served as a second seat for the Anson family, whose main seat was at Shugborough Hall. Thomas Anson was a Whig politician, and between 1830 and 1841, he served as Master of the Buckhounds and Postmaster General. He spent large sums of money improving both the estate and the house, which he used as a weekend retreat and for hunting parties for distinguished guests including, Sir Francis Grant (President of the Royal Academy) and Lord Melbourne (Prime Minister). However, his lavish entertaining, coupled with his gambling, resulted in heavy debts, and he was eventually forced to sell off the entire contents of his Shugborough Hall estate.

The tower shown here is part of the remains of Ranton Abbey, built in the mid-12ᵗʰ century by Robert Fitz-Noel for the Augustinian order of canons. The red-brick structure is what remains of Abbey House, built in 1820 by Thomas Anson.

As for Abbey House, that survived up until 1942 when it was the victim of a devastating fire whilst being occupied by troops of the bodyguard of Queen Wilhelmina of the Netherlands. Since then, the estate has been bought on numerous occasions, firstly by the Wedgwood porcelain company in the 1950s. However, Patrick Lichfield, the 5th Earl, bought it back in 1987 with a view to restoring the house or building a replacement. Unfortunately, these plans were persistently put on hold for many years due to objections from English Heritage, and when permission finally arrived in December 2005, it came a month after Lichfield's death.

Ranton Quirk Alert: Ozzy's Pies

In the 1970s, Black Sabbath frontman, Ozzy Osbourne, used to regularly visit Ranton's village pub, the Hand and Cleaver – as he lived for a while in a farmhouse on the outskirts of the village. More recently, the pub changed hands, and apparently, the last owners ran a Pie Fest back in 2011 which ran for twelve days to allegedly show diners "64 different ways to eat our delicious pies". I wonder if one of them was a bat pie…

The former Hand and Cleaver at Ranton used to regularly host Ozzy Osbourne when the Black Sabbath singer lived here in the 1970s. However, its days as a pub are now over and it is now up for sale as a private house.

NAME (STATUS):	**RUSHALL** (Former village, now a residential area of Walsall)
POPULATION:	11,871 (Rushall-Shelfield ward)
DISTRICT:	Walsall, West Midlands
EARLIEST RECORD:	*Rischale*, 1086 (Domesday Book)
MEANING:	A place or nook of land where rushes grow.
DERIVATION:	From the Old English words *rysc* (rush) and *halh* (nook or corner of land).

Rushall Pub: The Manor Arms

The Manor Arms is a canal-side pub that is actually designated by CAMRA as "A Pub Interior of Outstanding National Historic Importance" – this in an effort to identify and help protect and promote the most important historic pub interiors in the country. The Manor Arms is listed because it is an exceptionally rare example of a pub without a bar; all of the optics, taps and hand pumps for the beer are set against the back wall of the lounge, beneath rows of shelving for glasses and bottles. The pub therefore has an odd but convivial ambience with no "segregation" of customers from staff, such as you find in a traditional bar-type pub. There is also a hatchway to serve drinkers in other parts

The Manor Arms, Rushall.

The interior of The Manor Arms is a real rarity – as it doesn't have a bar which is one of the reasons why it is designated by CAMRA as "A Pub Interior of Outstanding National Historic Importance".

of the pub, while many regulars favour the central corridor for drinking!

Prior to 1895, The Manor Arms had been a farmhouse owned by the Anson family, but in that year, they opened their front room as a beerhouse, with John Anson selling beer to the occupants of narrow boats negotiating the Rushall Canal to the rear of the house. That said, the Anson family had been selling beer since the 1860s as a sideline to their farming business, but it was 1895 before they acquired their first full publican's license. However, the building is much older than that, with one well-known website suggesting a rather unlikely build date of 1102 – this courtesy of local legend which also suggests the building was inhabited by monks. This explains why the pub stakes a claim for being the oldest pub in Britain. However, with its timber beams and quirky layout, it is certainly an old building, but its brickwork is mainly 18th century – although it does contain stone from a previous structure dating from either the 15th or 16th century.

Rushall Church: St Michael the Archangel

The current church of St Michael the Archangel was built in the Early English style between 1854 and 1868. It replaced a 15th century church built on the same spot by John Harpur and his wife Eleanor and which was consecrated by William Heyworth, Bishop of Coventry and Lichfield, on 19th January 1440. However, there was an even older church that is recorded as being appropriated in 1220 to the newly founded Premonstratensian abbey at Halesowen; the same document records Rushall church as a chapel of Walsall. Alas, nothing remains of this church and, in fact, it may not have even been on the site of its two successors, but perhaps closer to Rushall Hall. Meanwhile, the tower from the 15th century build actually remained standing until 1867.

As for today's church, its oldest internal possession is its font which dates from around 1200, while in the churchyard is the base of an ancient preaching cross of indeterminate age, situated on three steps. A bench seat in the chancel bears the inscription "RA 1661 CF" while there are also two 18th century memorial tablets in the south transept. More recent additions were the peal of six bells, installed in 1900 and the murals over the chancel arch and along the east walls of the transepts which were painted by E. Reginald Frampton in 1905.

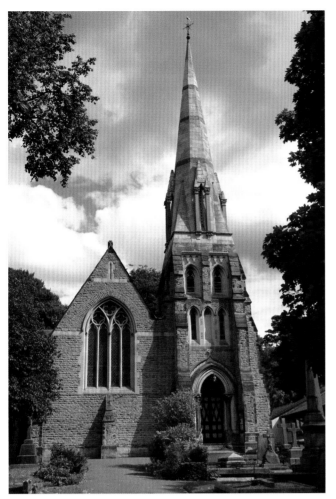

The church of St Michael the Archangel at Rushall.

Rushall Historic Trivia: Leighs and Limestone

When Rushall was recorded in Domesday Book, it was a hamlet of eight households and a mill. Prior to that, the Saxon settlement here was probably to the north of Rushall Hall where there are the remains of a moated site, while 19th century excavations unearthed Saxon coins nearby.

During the English Civil War, Rushall Hall was fortified and became an important stronghold. By this time, the manor of Rushall had passed from the Harpur family to the Leigh family and at the start of the English Civil War in 1642, Edward Leigh was an MP and soon became a Roundhead colonel. However, in 1643, Leigh left his wife in command at Rushall Hall, and it was during this time that the Royalists, led by Prince Rupert, took the fortified manor house for the Royalists – although they were also ejected a year later after a short siege. As for Rushall Hall today, much is comprised of the 19th century build, although this did incorporate walls from the previous building, while the medieval fortified gatehouse also survives.

The area around Rushall has been mined for coal and high quality limestone for centuries, with the limestone mines located to the south of Rushall at Daw End and the coal mines in the Ryecroft area. Here, they could take advantage of the Rushall Canal which was constructed in 1840 as a branch of the Wyrley and Essington Canal which, in turn, was part of the Birmingham Canal Navigations. A new settlement was born during the Industrial Revolution around the large-scale limestone works at Daw End. Later, the quarries in the grounds of Rushall Hall were flooded and became the Park Lime Pits and which is a nature reserve today, while the Arboretum lakes were also formed by the limestone quarrying. As well as Daw End, the main settlement at Rushall was centred on Lichfield Road at the junction of Pelsall Lane, while at Coalpool Lane a toll bar was set up after the main road was turnpiked in 1766. The limestone and coal industries also resulted in a trebling of Rushall's population between 1834 (c.700) and 1854 (c.2000). The number of pubs in Rushall also went up from four to eight during this period, too!

Rushall Quirk Alert: Spot the Ball

In the Rushall Historic Trivia, we mentioned that Rushall Hall changed hands twice during the English Civil War, while in between it was bombarded by both Royalists and Parliamentarians. And indeed, some of those cannon balls can still be seen in the ruins of the medieval house!

The Boat House, which is also located on the Rushall Canal.

Rushall top lock on the Rushall Canal. The waterway visible at the top left of the photo used to link the Rushall Canal to the Hayhead Lime workings at Daw End, but is now used as moorings for Longwood Narrow Boat Club.

	NAME (STATUS): **SALT** (Village)
	POPULATION: 333 (parish of Salt and Enson)
	DISTRICT: Stafford
	EARLIEST RECORD: *Selte*, 1086 (Domesday Book)
	MEANING: A salt-pit or a salt works.
	DERIVATION: From the Old English word *selte* (salt).

The Holy Bush, Salt.

The church of St James the Great at Salt.

Salt Pub: The Holly Bush Inn

The Holly Bush Inn at Salt is yet another pub claiming to be one of England's oldest. However, in this particular case, the Holly Bush has a reasonable claim as it is widely thought to have been only the second licensed pub in the country. Given that licensing of public houses began during the reign of Charles II (1660 - 1685), the Holly Bush must have been well established at the time it received its license – but whether that supports the local view that it dates back to 1190 is another matter!

Salt Church: St James the Great

Salt's church is dedicated to St James the Great and, along with its vicarage, it was built in the early 1840s on land donated by, and largely paid for by the Earl of Shrewsbury; in fact, even the stone that was used during its construction came from the Earl's own quarry at

Salt Village Hall.

Weston Bank. Externally, interesting points include a large circular stained glass east window, an unusually tall south porch and an open stone bell turret housing two bells. Internally, St James' church is also home to a wooden rood screen designed by well-known Victorian architect Augustus Pugin and which had previously been in situ at the private chapel at Alton Towers, one time home of the Earls of Shrewsbury.

Salt Historic Trivia: Schools and Stage Coaches

As well as the church, the Earl of Shrewsbury funded Salt School and a schoolmaster's house in 1858 – this in memory of his daughter who died in Naples in 1856. A decade later, Salt railway station was built on the Stafford to Uttoxeter line – although the line was eventually closed to passengers in 1939 and to goods traffic in 1951. Salt School lasted a little longer, but closed in 1981. Meanwhile, a century before the railway arrived, Salt was situated on the stage coaching route from London to Liverpool.

Salt has won the Staffordshire Best Kept Village on a number of occasions, as commemorated by the memorial shown right.

Two's-Up!

	SIDEWAY	STONE CROSS
STATUS:	Suburb	Residential Area
POPULATION:	1,770	1,545 (Sandwell 010B)
DISTRICT:	Stoke-on-Trent	Sandwell, West Midlands
EARLIEST RECORD:	*Sydewey*, 1327; *Sideway*, 1836	*Stone Cross*, 1626
MEANING:	Track on the side of the hill.	Named after a wayside cross.
DERIVATION:	From the Middle English word *side* (perhaps the side or slope of a hill) and the Old English word *weg* (way, track or road).	As above.

Two's Up Trivia

Pronounced "Siddaway", **Sideway** is an area located in the southern part of Stoke-on-Trent. It includes Stoke City's Britannia Stadium, which was built in the mid-1990s and which has hosted Premiership football since 2008. The stadium was actually built upon a spoil tip for the former Hem Heath Colliery, which had closed a couple of years earlier. Also located in Sideway is the head office of the UK Michelin Tyre Company Ltd. A French-based company, the UK Michelin branch was incorporated as long ago as 1905, albeit in South Kensington back then. The factory at Stoke-on-Trent was opened in November 1927, boasting its own branch line from the London to Manchester mainline. It is still going strong today, and has also boasted its own Michelin Athletics Club since the late 1940s and still has a Sports and Conference facility in Sideway.

Stoke City's Britannia Stadium is also located in Sideway. It was openend in 1997 and has hosted Premiership football since 2008.

This is the Michelin Island, located alongside the Michelin Tyre Company's UK head office. On the island are three Bibendums, also known as Michelin Men, the symbol and trademark of Michelin for over 100 years.

The Stone Cross at... well, Stone Cross! Or at least it used to be. For the former pub that went by that name for many decades is now part of the Curry and Grill House group.

There are actually two places called **Stone Cross** within the boundaries of the historic county of Staffordshire, although only one of them can be found on the AA *Close-Up Britain Road Atlas*. This particular Stone Cross swapped Staffordshire for the new metropolitan county of West Midlands on 1st April 1974 – and so today, it is a residential area of West Bromwich in the metropolitan borough of Sandwell. However, it was originally named after a wayside cross which stood here until the 18th century, while its base survived as part of a signpost until the late 1890s; a replica was created in 2002. The area expanded rapidly in the 1920s and 1930s with hundreds of both private and council houses built. The focal point of Stone Cross is its roundabout and which includes at its centre, the Stone Cross pub. Meanwhile, during World War II, Stone Cross was hit by a German bomber which dropped a bomb on Walsall Road and damaged several houses, but missed its target of a nearby anti-aircraft gun factory. Finally, Stone Cross is also home to the country's largest St George's Day parade, which runs between Stone Cross and Dartmouth Park in West Bromwich, and which regularly attracts around 15,000 people.

As for the other **Stone Cross**, this one can be found at Penkridge on the Stafford to Wolverhampton road. The earliest recording of this particular Stone Cross, pre-dates the other, as it was recorded as *Stone crosse yate* in 1598. Once again, the meaning is the same, and this one was mounted on circular graded steps. However, the cross is no longer there with perhaps its last map entry appearing on a map of 1754.

NAME (STATUS):	**SHEEN** (Village)
POPULATION:	234
DISTRICT:	Staffordshire Moorlands
EARLIEST RECORD:	*Sceon*, 1002, and 1086 (Domesday Book)
MEANING:	The sheds or shelters, or beautiful place.
DERIVATION:	From the Old English word *scēo* (shelter) in its plural form, *scēon*, or from the Old English word *scēne* (bright or beautiful).

Sheen Pub: The Staffordshire Knot

Sheen's pub is named after the Stafford Knot, the famous emblem of Staffordshire. The Stafford Knot is a distinctive three-looped knot – and hence the local legend that it was invented by a certain sheriff who wanted to hang three criminals in one go using just one rope! This is almost certainly not true for the knot probably pre-dates medieval times. Indeed, one of Staffordshire's oldest relics – an Anglo-Saxon cross in St Peter's churchyard, Stoke, dating from around 800 AD – has a pattern of the knot carved onto one side, while the design also appears on one of the 7th century Anglo-Saxon objects from the recently discovered Staffordshire Hoard. However, the earliest proven appearance of the Stafford Knot is on a seal in the British Museum which originally belonged to Lady Joan Stafford. The Knot was passed down through generations of the Earls of Stafford, but it was also gradually adopted by the citizens, Freemen and Burgesses until, ultimately, it was included in the Stafford Borough

The Staffordshire Knot Inn, Sheen.

St Luke's church, Sheen.

Coat of Arms.

As for the pub, it was formerly known as the Horse Shoe, and was run by the Woolley family, a family of blacksmiths, from 1834 to 1868. The name-change to the Staffordshire Knot occurred in 1872 – although it was known as Ye Olde Spinning Wheel for a time in the 1970s before reverting to its former and current title. Most of the building dates from the 19th century, although there is a lintel dated 1666 on the part of the building that now operates as a cottage.

Sheen Church: St Luke's

Sheen is known to have had a church since at least 1185 when it was a possession of Burton Abbey, while the oldest grave slab in Sheen churchyard dates back to 1200. Sheen's church is then referenced again in 1255 when it is described as a dependent chapel of Ilam church which, in turn, was also a possession of Burton Abbey. It is thought that this particular church at Sheen was destroyed in the late 1530s during the Dissolution of the Monasteries, perhaps due to its association with Burton Abbey. Certainly, Sheen chapel was granted to a William Paget in 1546 and was then rebuilt in 1552. The medieval church, and which was by the 18th century known as St Luke's, was then largely replaced by a new build between 1828 and 1832, with only a large part of the north wall surviving from its predecessor. However, this particular church was later described by Benjamin Webb as "a well meant but wholly unecclesiastical structure", so it was no surprise when only a couple of decades later, in 1850, Beresford Hope rebuilt it at his own expense in 14th century style. Once again, the new church retained most of the north wall, while the former church's tower was remodelled, buttressed, and a belfry added to the top. The intended spire was never erected, though, due to fears over the foundations, and so a short wooden spire was added a little later in 1864, and which is still in place today, albeit encased in copper. There was local opposition to the rebuild, but Hope responded by stating that the former church was unconsecrated and unlicensed, and therefore marriages conducted here were "of doubtful validity". The new church was duly consecrated in 1852.

Also surviving from medieval times are some of the former church's medieval gargoyles, while internally, the church boasts a number of features originally belonging to Margaret Street chapel in London, which Beresford Hope was also rebuilding.

Sheen Historic Trivia: Sheen Manor

The 1002 reference to Sheen comes from the will of Wulfric Spot, whose endowment of Burton Abbey included Sheen. By the 12th century, though, the estate had passed to Bertram de Verdun (d.1192), who granted the manor to Hugh of Okeover whose descendants kept the manor throughout the 13th century. The Pole family then owned the manor for most of the 14th and 15th centuries before it passed to Edward IV in 1476, but by 1506, it was held by the Duchy of Lancaster. The 18th century then saw the Sleigh family own the manor from 1709 to 1724 and the Bateman family from 1724 to 1825, while by the late 19th century, it was owned by the resident farmers.

In terms of the actual manor house of Sheen, this was originally on the other side of the Dove in Derbyshire at Hartington, from the 15th century to the early 17th century. Thereafter, Broadmeadow Hall became the manor house with the current hall dating from the 1660s.

Quirk Alert: The Sheen Farmers

Sheen is reputed to have the best tug of war team in Britain, with the Sheen Farmers made up of a group of extremely strong… well… farmers! Over the years, they have taken on some of the strongest tug of war teams in the world, and they have also appeared on television.

Above: *This building is currently the Village Hall, but it used to be a school, originally built in 1851 by Beresford Hope.*

Side by side in front of the Village Hall, are this 15th century cross (below) and a tree planted in 1994 by Sheen Parish Council (left) to celebrate the centenary of the establishment of civil parishes in 1894.

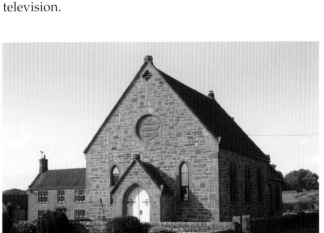

This Wesleyan chapel at Sheen was built in 1878.

View towards Sheen Hill from Sheen village.

NAME (STATUS):	**STANDON** (Village)
POPULATION:	879
DISTRICT:	Stafford
EARLIEST RECORD:	*Stantone*, 1086; Standon, 1190
MEANING:	Stony Hill.
DERIVATION:	From the Old English words *stān* (stone, rock or boundary stone) and *dūn* (hill).

All Saints' church, Standon.

Standon Mill, which today is home to Youngs Animal Feeds.

Standon Church: All Saints

The Grade I-listed All Saints' church was largely rebuilt in 1847, except for the tower and the central aisle. The tower is therefore still largely medieval, although the Norman doorway still survives while the base of the tower still has its original Norman stones, too. The nave arches with their octagonal pillars date from the 13th century, while the chancel is home to early 16th century alabaster monuments to a priest and to Francis Rose, his wife and their ten children.

Standon Historic Trivia: Standon Home

In 1885, Standon Home was established in Standon as part of the Waifs and Strays' Society. Initially home to 50 boys, the home was extended in 1892 in order to accommodate 90 boys. The home was also a purpose-built farm including over 50 acres of land, where the boys were trained in various agricultural skills, while their produce was good enough to be sold at local markets, including a regular stall at Stoke-on-Trent market. The home closed in 1947.

The western entrance to Standon.

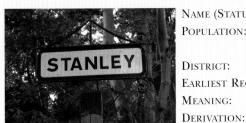

NAME (STATUS):	**STANLEY (and STANLEY MOOR)** (Village)
POPULATION:	3,221 (Parish of Endon and Stanley)
	1,591 (Ward of Bagnall and Stanley)
DISTRICT:	Staffordshire Moorlands
EARLIEST RECORD:	*Stanlega*, 1130; *Stanle*, 1273
MEANING:	Either "stony clearing" or "stony mound or tumulus".
DERIVATION:	Most Stanleys are derived from the Old English words *stān* (stone) and *lēah* (wood or woodland clearing), but this one may be derived from *stān* and *hlāw* (mound or tumulus).

The Travellers Rest, Stanley, dates from the 1860s when it was built along with rows of cottages for the mill workers at Stanley Mill.

The Rose and Crown, Stanley Moor.

Stanley Church: St Luke's

Stanley doesn't have a church. Its parish church (for the parish of Endon and Stanley) is St Luke's church in Endon. However, by 1851 occasional evening services were held at Stanley, eventually resulting in a mission room being opened in the village in 1868 and which, by 1872, had become known as St Agnes's Mission. A few decades prior to this, a Methodist preacher called Mary Dunnell took a service at Stanley in 1810 and shortly afterwards a Primitive Methodist society was formed – although it only lasted for four years before it was disbanded.

Stanley Historic Trivia: Stanley Mill

In the 19th century, Stanley expanded with the growth in importance of its flint mills – and hence the mill cottages and the Travellers Rest public house on Tompkin Lane that were built in the 1860s. However, there had been a mill in Stanley as early as the 16th century, while a flint mill was built here in the 1770s which was still there in 1835 and was powered by Stanley Pool. However, it was submerged five years later when the reservoir was extended. There was also a corn mill in the village in 1816, and by 1835 another mill had appeared in between the corn mill and the flint

St Luke's church at Endon is the parish church of Endon and Stanley.

This former chapel in Stanley was opened in 1868 and became known as St Agnes's Mission. The chapel held services until 1991.

Stanley Pool sits at the southern edge of the village of Stanley. It was dammed from a stream in 1776 and became a feeder reservoir for the Caldon Canal which was opened in 1778. The pool was then increased from 8 acres to 33 acres in 1840 when a new dam was built to the north.

Looking down from the dam that separates Stanley from the reservoir.

mill – this one used as a flint, glaze, and colour mill. It survived as a flint mill until the late 1870s, but by the late 1890s it had been turned into a gelatine works – after which it fell into disuse and was eventually converted into a house. As for the corn mill, it was this mill that was to later double up as a corn and flint mill. What became known as Stanley Mill was rebuilt in 1887 by Harrison & Son, who used it for grinding potters' materials such as black manganese. The mill eventually closed in around 1970 and by 1991 the mill and associated buildings were occupied by small commercial businesses.

By the 1880s, a post office had opened in the village, but the largest village expansion occurred in the 20th century between the two World Wars and throughout the 1960s. Today, Stanley is part of the parish of Endon and Stanley, and has been since 1894. Prior to that the parish also included Longsdon, and before that Stanley was a township in the Leek parish.

Stanley Quirk Alert: Almost Just William

It is thought that there was an estate at Stanley in the late 12th century, while by 1272 the estate was owned by a certain Walter of Stanley. Remarkably, the manor then stayed in Stanley hands for a further twelve generations until 1660, when William Stanley sold it to Thomas Fernihaugh. Even more remarkable, is that ten of those twelve Stanleys were called William! Three of them were knighted. Today, it is thought that Lower House Farm, which dates from around 1700, was built on the site of the former manor house.

Looking across the remains of the old mill pond that served Stanley Mill and which probably dates back to the 16th century.

	NAME (STATUS):	**STOKE** (City)
	POPULATION:	249,008
	DISTRICT:	Stoke-on-Trent
	EARLIEST RECORD:	*Stoche*, 1086 (Domesday Book)
	MEANING:	Outlying farmstead or hamlet or secondary settlement.
	DERIVATION:	From the Old English word *stoc* (place, outlying farmstead or hamlet, secondary or dependent settlement).

Nearside is The Glebe, a Grade II listed pub which sits alongside Stoke Town Hall, both having been built in the mid-19ᵗʰ century.

St Peter's church, also known as Stoke Minster.

Stoke Pub: The Glebe

The Glebe finds itself in distinguished company on Glebe Street alongside the town hall and more-or-less opposite Stoke Minster while it is itself a Grade II-listed building. It was built at the same time as the town hall in the mid-1830s which explains its classic design, period architrave, its original central rounded mahogany bar counter and the unique leaded glazing by the studio of William Morris.

Stoke Church: St Peter's

The full title of St Peter's church at Stoke is St Peter ad Vincula, meaning Saint Peter in Chains, and is derived from the Basilica of San Pietro in Vincoli in Rome. The church was also formally named as Stoke Minster in 2005 at a ceremony conducted by the Bishop of Lichfield, this in recognition of the important role that St Peter's plays in the civic life of Stoke-on-Trent and North Staffordshire, and thus mimicking the title reserved for important mother churches since Anglo-Saxon times. And indeed the first Anglo-Saxon church built on this site was seen as a formal minster church, too. It was built in 670 and would have been made of wood. A stone church then replaced the wooden one in 805 and this incarnation became a collegiate church; the Saxon font probably dates from this period, too. Remarkably, some of the second Saxon church survives in the form of two arches in the churchyard, while the arches inside the church date from the 13ᵗʰ century when the chancel was rebuilt. The remainder of the church dates largely from the late 1820s when much of it was rebuilt. There are also ceramic memorials in the church to many of the great potters of the district, while the church is the burial place of both Josiah Spode and Josiah Wedgwood. One of the memorials to Josiah Wedgwood is an alabaster tablet commissioned by his sons, and sculpted by the master, Francis Chantrey.

The remains of an Anglo-Saxon preaching cross in St Peter's churchyard.

Stoke Historic Trivia: Strimmed Stoke

A huge part of Stoke's significant history has already been covered in the *Staffordshire County History* part of this book, particularly with respect to industry, especially pottery and the life and works of Josiah Wedgwood (1730-1795). However, one other pottery giant of Stoke was Josiah Spode (1733-1797) who also founded a china works in the town in 1770. Spode is credited with the establishment of blue underglaze transfer printing in the early 1780s, and with the creation of an improved formula for bone china which thereafter became the industry standard. His success was all the more remarkable for having been born a pauper's son and orphaned at the age of six. However, he was later apprenticed to yet another of

Left: The Grade II-listed Victorian station at Stoke-on-Trent, built in 1848. It is located opposite Winton Square (right), which is thought to be Britain's only piece of major town planning undertaken by a railway company – this being the North Staffordshire Railway (NSR). Pictured right is the Grade II-listed North Stafford Hotel in Winton Square, built in 1849 by the NSR, with a statue in the foreground of Stoke-on-Trent's most famous son, the potter, Josiah Wedgwood (1730-1795), born in Burslem and laid to rest in Etruria.

Stoke's famous 18th century potters, Thomas Whieldon (1719-1795), who eventually became Josiah Wedgwood's business partner in 1754. Josiah Spode II (1755-1827) continued his father's business, while today, the Spode name is owned by the Portmeirion pottery company which is still based in Stoke-on-Trent. Other famous Stoke potters include Thomas Minton (1765-1836) who, having been apprenticed to Josiah Spode, formed his own company in 1793 which produced earthenware, while his son, Herbert Minton, effected a huge expansion of the business in the 19th century – which was also when John Aynsley (1823-1907) built the Portland Works in Longton in 1861.

Stoke Quirk Alert: Polycentric and 112

What has Stoke-on-Trent got in common with Randstad in the Netherlands, the Ruhr area in Germany, the Gold Coast in Australia, and San Francisco Bay in the USA? Answer: they're all polycentric – this meaning a region formed by the grouping of several political, social or financial centres. In Stoke's case, this is the "Six Towns" of Tunstall, Burslem, Hanley, Stoke-upon-Trent, Fenton and Longton, formed on 1st April 1910 when they were federated into the county borough of Stoke-on-Trent. It was also the first such union in the UK and remained the only one until the 1960s. Finally, the churchyard of St Peter's includes a tomb to Sibil and Henry Clarke, who both died in 1684, both at the alleged age of 112!

It is thought that part of the stone used in the slender pillars of these arches in St Peter's churchyard may date from the Anglo-Saxon church originally built in 805. The arches were re-erected here in the 13th century.

NAME (STATUS):	**STONE** (Town)
POPULATION:	16,385
DISTRICT:	Stafford
EARLIEST RECORD:	*Stanes*, 1187
MEANING:	Place at the stone or stones.
DERIVATION:	From the Old English word *stān* (stone).
FAMOUS RESIDENTS:	Richard Barnfield (1574-1620), poet; John Jervis (1735-1823), Admiral of the Fleet; Peter de Wint (1784-1849), landscape painter.

Stone Pubs: Loads

The Three Crowns is a former 18th century coaching inn on the road from London to Holyhead, as is The Red Lion Inn, a little further up the main road through Stone. Also used as coaching inns in those days were the Crown & Anchor and the Black Horse Inn. As for the Red Lion, a predecessor building with the same name existed here in the 16th century. Meanwhile, the building of The Swan Inn started life in 1771 as a warehouse servicing the Trent and Mersey Canal wharf; it wasn't until the mid-19th century that it was converted into a pub.

As to why there are so many pubs in Stone, this is largely down to the main road through Stone (the modern A51) being turnpiked in the 18th century, and thus Stone became an important stopping-off place for stagecoaches, with an 1851 directory stating that: "Stone is a very lively town and a great thoroughfare for coaches, carriers and travellers". And, indeed, 38 stage coaches passed through the town daily back then.

The Crown and Anchor was originally an 18th century coaching inn.

The Star sits alongside the Trent and Mersey Canal. The pub is set on five different levels.

The Three Crowns was also an 18th century coaching inn.

The Poste of Stone used to be Stone's main post office. The first resident postmaster (known as The Poste of Stone) was William Nicholson in 1575.

Stone Church: St Michael and St Wulfad

The current church of St Michael and St Wulfad was built between 1753 and 1758 on the site of the 12th century priory church of St Mary and St Wulfad. The former was one of the first churches to be built in the Gothic Revival style that would become so fashionable in the 19th century, and was designed by William Robinson of Greenwich. As for the naming of the church, St Wulfad was an Anglo-Saxon prince who allegedly died at the hands of his paranoid father, the Mercian King Wulfhere (657-674). The story goes that Wulfad was slaughtered at Stone, while his brother, Rufin, was killed a little further south at Burston. The boys were buried at Stone by their heartbroken mother and sister "under a great sepulchre of stones", thus providing the town with its future name, while the first church at Stone was also built on this spot by their mother, Ermenilda. For a detailed account of this story, see *Burston Historic Trivia: The Trail of the Mercian Saints*.

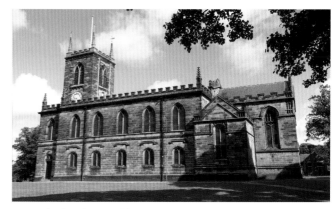

St Michael and St Wulfad's church, Stone.

The Anglo-Saxon church then flourished until the marauding Danes sacked it in the late 9th century. A new church was then built on the same spot in around 1135 by Geoffrey de Clinton, and was named as the Priory Church of St Mary and St Wulfad. Initially dependent upon its parent house, Kenilworth Priory, Stone Priory prospered to the point that it became independent in the 13th century. Of course, like most of its peers, the priory was dissolved in 1537. Happily, the priory church survived and remained in use until 1749 when parts of it collapsed… bringing us back full circle to the build of St Michael and St Wulfad.

Looking down High Street towards a Saturday market. In the foreground on the right-hand side is The Red Lion, yet another former Stone coaching inn.

The oldest church relics are the worn sculptures of a priest and a woman, in the porch, that probably date from the 13th century, while the interior contains some of the previous church's original box pews. Meanwhile, some of the stained glass portrays the martyred sons of King Wulfhere, Rufin and Wulfad, while another depicts the greatest sea victory won by John Jervis, Earl of St Vincent, and Nelson's great leader – this being the prevention of the Spanish fleet joining the French navy in 1797 and thus averting the greatest threat of invasion since the Spanish Armada of 1588. It was also John Jervis who in 1805, commissioned his friend, Sir William Beechey, to paint a picture of St Michael's triumph over Satan, while the earl himself is represented by a fine bust sculptured by Sir Francis Chantrey. John Jervis is also entombed in a mausoleum in the churchyard.

Stone Historic Trivia: From Bronze Age Ditch to Lymestone Brewery

In terms of ancient history, there is a Bronze Age ring ditch at nearby Pirehill, which is located just to the south-west of the town, while Burybank to the north-west of the town is the site of a later Iron Age hillfort. Several hundred years later in 7th century Anglo-Saxon Mercia, it is thought that the aforementioned King Wulfhere had his fortified Royal Mansion where the hillfort at Burybank had stood, and which covered around four acres. Also in Stone is what is known as

Motley Pits – an old entrenchment that may also be Anglo-Saxon.

As already covered in the Burston section, one school of thought believes that the tale of Wulfhere and his sons, Rufin and Wulfad, was made up by 12th century storytellers – and which would therefore negate the theory that Stone was named after the stones that were piled upon the bodies of the princes to form their tomb. Other credible theories, therefore, are that it may have been named in Mercian times after the remains of a Roman bridge or perhaps a milestone on a former Roman road. Or perhaps it is named from an even older megalith that has long-since disappeared, a natural rocky outcrop, or from a quarry where stone was cut – the latter being a fair guess as sandstone has long been quarried on the north side of the town. What seems less open to doubt, though, is that the boys' mother, Ermenilda, founded a priory above their graves in Stone. Another priory was then built for the Augustinian order of monks in the same spot in around 1135. Of this priory, there are a few remains including some walling in Abbey Street, while a house called The Priory in Lichfield Street still possesses the rib-vaulted undercroft or crypt of the medieval priory.

Moving forward to the medieval period, Stone's market charter was granted in 1251 by Henry III. Jumping forward another 500 years to 1745, the Duke of Cumberland built extensive winter fortifications and a

The Trent and Mersey Canal at Stone.

camp at Stone, with the aim of bringing his army down from the unforgiving Staffordshire Moorlands and the Peak District, where they had been deployed to prevent Bonnie Prince Charlie's Jacobite army of around 6,000 men from reaching Derby. Charles was encamped at Leek at this time, but the forces never engaged each other. As Arthur Mee states, "the chance of an encounter and a swift decision between the rival forces... might have averted the horrors of Culloden [a year later]."

In the same century, Stone benefitted from being on the 93.5 mile-long Trent and Mersey Canal which was built between 1766 and 1777. The Stone part of the canal, though, was navigable by 1772 as it was at the end of the initial 48 mile run from the Derwent Mouth in Derbyshire to Stone. The town therefore became the headquarters of the canal company who were based at Westbridge House, although the offices were later moved to Stoke-upon-Trent. Also established in Stone in 1780 was the brewer John Joule & Sons Ltd who built their warehouses right on the Trent and Mersey Canal, perfect for trade with coal coming in and beer going out. The company was then followed by a second brewer, Montgomery & Co., who was located on what is now Mount Industrial Estate. Both breweries were eventually taken over by Bass of Burton upon Trent in the mid-20th century, with Montgomerys subsequently closed in March 1968 and Joules in October 1974 along with the adjacent bottling plant. Conversely, Lymestone Brewery, was opened in Stone in 2008, and apparently, you can still get a pint of both Lymestone and Joules at the Swan Inn.

The arrival of the railways in the mid-19th century eventually ended Stone's era as both a coaching town and a canal town. Stone was on the North Staffordshire Railway's main line which was opened on 3rd April 1848, and ran from Stoke-on-Trent to Norton Bridge, around 3 miles south-west of Stone, while in 1849, a branch line was laid from Stone to Colwich. The introduction of the railways to Stone did mean that other industries flourished, particularly shoe works, and by 1851 there were 16 shoe works in the town. The indus-

In the background, alongside the Trent and Mersey Canal, are the warehouses of John Joule & Sons Ltd, a local brewery who established themselves here in the late 18th century.

try however declined after Australia, the main market for shoes, imposed an import tax on the industry.

Sticking with the 19th century, Stone's Catholic church of the Immaculate Conception and St Dominic, is the final resting place of William Ullathorne, who became the first Roman Catholic bishop of the diocese of Birmingham in 1850, holding the post for thirty-eight years until his death. Before 1850, though, he had been a sailor, a monk and then, still aged only twenty-five he left Britain to become chaplain to New South Wales for five years. On his return, he painted such a scathing picture of the treatment of convicts that this went some way towards the cessation of transportation to Australia.

Stone Quirk Alert:
Lock, Stock and One Smoking Cannon

On completion of the Star Lock at Stone a grand opening was held and which included a cannon that would be fired in celebration! However disaster struck and the firing cannon badly damaged the new lock... which then had to be completely rebuilt! Meanwhile, did you know that the headquarters of the National Association of Chimney Sweeps is also located in Stone?

NAME (STATUS):	**STOWE** (Ward of Lichfield)
POPULATION:	5,051
DISTRICT:	Lichfield
EARLIEST RECORD:	*Stowe*, 1242
MEANING:	Assembly place or holy place.
DERIVATION:	From the Old English word *stōw* (place, assembly place or holy place).

Stowe Geographical Trivia

Yet again, we have another place-name that occurs twice in Staffordshire – although in this case only one of the two places is called simply "Stowe" – this being the ward that covers a large part of northern Lichfield. The ward is home to the large, attractive pool known as Stowe Pool as well as St Chad's church which is located alongside the pool, while nearby are several roads with "Stowe" or "Nether Stowe" in their title. The other Staffordshire "Stowe" is Stowe-by-Chartley a village and civil parish of 418 people which is situated at the eastern edge of the Stafford district on the A518 between Stafford and Uttoxeter. As for the inclusion in the Shire-Ode of the singly-named "Stowe", this was purely for rhyming and scanning purposes; essentially a single-syllabled place-name was required to sit at the centre of the fictitious Trentham Triangle!

Returning to Stowe Pool, it is actually a reservoir, built in 1856 by the South Staffordshire Waterworks Co. for the supply of clean water to the Black Country. Before 1856, Stowe Pool had been a simple mill pond, with Stowe Mill located just to the west of St Chad's church. However, the reservoir hasn't been used for water supply since 1968 and today it is simply a public amenity used for recreation purposes. Stowe Pool is also a designated SSSI site as it is home to the native white-clawed crayfish.

Stowe Church: St Chad's

St Chad's church is named after the 7th century Anglo-Saxon churchman who was initially the abbot of several monasteries. However, he later went on to become first the "Bishop of the Northumbrians", a post which eventually became the Archbishop of York, and then later still, in 669, became the "Bishop of the Mercians and Lindsey People", establishing his see at Lichfield. Appointed to the latter post by King Wulfhere of Mercia, it was Chad (*Ceadda* in Old English) who moved the see to Lichfield from its former home at Repton in Derbyshire. Chad was later canonised as a saint, and his exploits are firmly featured in the works of the Venerable Bede, along with those of his brother, Cedd, with Bede crediting the pair with introducing Christianity to Mercia. Bede also states that his dwelling place was "a shallow watery valley where a stream divided to form a small island". He then founded a small monastery beside a springwater well and, according to Bede, he prayed naked at this well. It was also here that he baptised converts to the Christian

Stowe Pool, with St Chad's church at its northern shore (above and bottom), and a long-distance shot towards Lichfield Cathedral from the pool's southern shore (below).

faith, including the tragic princes Wulfad and Rufin (see Burston and Stone for more on them). Chad also built a church here which he initially dedicated to St Mary but which, after his death, was re-dedicated in his name.

Far left: The 14ᵗʰ century tower of St Chad's church at Stowe. Parts of the church incoporate its Norman predecessor, but none of the Anglo-Saxon church built by Chad (before he became St Chad) remain.

Left: Looking down the nave of St Chad's church towards the chancel.

When St Chad died in 672, he was buried close to his church, but in 700, his bones were removed to the new cathedral in Lichfield which had just been completed, and his shrine became a centre of pilgrimage.

Of St Chad's Anglo-Saxon church, nothing remains, but accounts describe it as a small building built of stone or wood with a thatched roof and small windows. A stone church took its place in the 12ᵗʰ century and parts of this incarnation are included in the current church, such as the rounded Norman window arches on both the inside and outside wall of the south aisle. However, many of the Norman windows were replaced during the 13ᵗʰ century with the pointed arches that are still in place today, while the trefoil-headed south door was also added at this time. It was also during the 13ᵗʰ century that the nave pillars were rebuilt, with the hexagonal pillars on the south side differing considerably from the later octagonal pillars on the north side. The tower was started towards the end of the 13ᵗʰ century and completed in the 14ᵗʰ century while the next two centuries saw alterations to windows with 14ᵗʰ century decorated style and 15ᵗʰ century perpendicular style appearing. The roof then had to be rebuilt following damage caused by cannon and musket during the English Civil War, when Parliamentary troops used St Chad's as a storehouse for their scaling ladders and other equipment. Finally, in 1840, the north aisle was rebuilt while in 1862, the chancel and chancel arch were fully restored, the brick clerestory was removed and a new roof was constructed. The nave roof was then replaced in 1952 with metal used instead of wood as the former roof had been ravaged by death-watch beetles!

Stowe Historic Trivia: St Chad's Well

We have already talked about St Chad in detail above, where it was mentioned that he used to pray naked at his well. After his death, the well therefore became a place of pilgrimage. Much later, in the 19ᵗʰ century, the well was covered by a 10ft-high stone structure with an arched entrance and steps leading down to the water. These were the days when it was believed that springs had healing powers, and people used to bathe there. However, that particular building was demolished in 1949 and replaced by the present structure.

Later still, in 1995, St Chad's saw the revival of the old tradition of well dressing, with the 1995 well commemorating the 50ᵗʰ anniversary of Christian Aid. However, the locals kept the tradition alive thereafter on each second weekend in September, with a beautiful new well dressing depicting scenes from the bible that are created each year from flowers and foliage pressed into a board of soft clay. The children at the local St Chad's Primary School also make their own smaller well dressing which always sits beside the main one. There is also a service of blessing when water from the well is sprinkled on the congregation by the clergy using a yew-tree branch. Then on Palm Sunday, the Palm Sunday Gospel is read at the well, after which the congregation return to the church for the rest of the service.

Stowe Quirk Alert: The Perfect Wife

Thomas Day (1748-1789) of Lichfield lived at the four-storey Stowe House, overlooking Stowe Pool, and was a member of the famous Lunar Society that also included locals Anna Seward and Erasmus Darwin. Day also spent much of his life trying to mould the perfect wife, having "acquired" two orphan girls named Sabrina and Lucretia. He initially took them to France where he subjected them to a life of drudgery and servitude, but on their return to England, he favoured Sabrina and dispatched Lucretia to be a milliner's apprentice. Lucretia was the lucky one. For as well as making Sabrina carry out all of the household tasks, Day also subjected her to a regime of "training" that was designed to develop stamina, strength and courage. The training included man-handling Sabrina into Stowe Pool, despite knowing that she was unable to swim. Day then made her lie in a nearby field until she dried out. Alas, after years of such treatment, this charming man eventually decided that Sabrina wasn't suitable wife material!

NAME (STATUS):	**TALKE** (Village and Ward)
POPULATION:	3,875
DISTRICT:	Newcastle-under-Lyme
EARLIEST RECORD:	*Talc*, 1086 (Domesday Book); *Talk*, 1252; *Talke*, 1276
MEANING:	Either a Celtic name for a ridge, or "bush on top of the hill".
DERIVATION:	Either from the Celtic word *talcen* (forehead, brow, end or front), or from the phrase "Talk o' th' Hill".
FAMOUS RESIDENTS:	Reginald Mitchell (1895-1937), aircraft designer.

Talke Pubs: The Swan Inn and The Old Queen's Head

These two pubs sit at a busy crossroads on the brow of the hill where Crown Bank, Swan Bank, Audley Road and Chester Road all converge – this almost certainly being the same ridge after which Talke was named over a thousand years ago. It is alleged that the terrible gunpowder explosion at Talke in 1781 (see *Talke Historic Trivia* for more), occurred whilst the soldiers who were carrying a cart-load of ammunition stopped off for a drink at The Old Queen's Head. Meanwhile, the Swan Inn's main historic trivia revolves around landlord Walton Hulse, who in 1921 was shot while lying in bed with his wife, after which the pub's takings were stolen.

Talke Historic Trivia: Five Separate Disasters

Talke is a village, ward of Kidsgrove and former civil parish in the former coal-mining district of north-west Staffordshire close to the border with Cheshire. Talke became a civil parish in 1932 when it was transferred from the disbanded Audley Urban District to Kidsgrove Urban District, both of which had been part of the former county borough of Newcastle-under-Lyme which, itself, was disbanded in April 1974.

Much earlier, in 1781, Talke was the scene of a horrific explosion. The incident occurred when a wagon transporting nearly 2 tons of gunpowder down a hill in Talke was suddenly ignited by a spark created

The Swan Inn, Talke.

The busy crossroads at the brow of Crown Bank and Swan Bank sees St Martin's church and the White Swan on opposite sides of Audley Road, with The Queen's Head sandwiched in between the two.

St Martin's church is home to two beautiful oak figures of Paul and John the Baptist, which are thought to have originated from Moreton Old Hall, just over the border in Cheshire.

Just a little further down Crown Bank from St Martin's church is this wonderful old farmhouse known as Church Farm.

Another angle on Church Farm, parts of which are thought to date back to the 15th century.

This stunning house is located a little further down Crown Bank and according to the date imprinted above the door, it dates from 1577.

by wheel friction. The poor wagoner and all of his horses were killed instantly, while neighbouring houses were also reduced to rubble. The heat from the blast was so intense that it reduced the wagoner's fob watch to a solid mass of metal. Remarkably, Talke was also the scene of a devastating fire the following year (1782) which destroyed many of its houses, and then three years later (1785) had to deal with a catastrophic mining disaster in which 42 men and boys lost their lives.

The mining connection in Talke goes back centuries, but increasingly modern pits began to open during the 18th and 19th centuries to the south-west of the village in what became essentially a coal-mining community following the sinking of a number of pits such as the Jamage pit and the Bunkers Hill pits, run by the Talk O' Th' Hill Colliery and the Bunkers Hill Company, respectively. In fact, the whole area is still known as Talke Pits today, although coal mining ceased in the second half of the 20th century, and the area is now dominated by retail and business parks, as well as the beautiful Parrot's Drumble nature reserve. Alas there is still room for two more Talke tragedies, though, for in 1866 another underground gas explosion here claimed the lives of another 91 men and boys from this small community, while in April 1875 a further explosion in

the Bunkers Hill coal pits claimed another 42 men and boys.

Moving into the 20th century and Talke's most famous inhabitant was Reginald Mitchell (1895-1937). Having initially gained an apprenticeship at Kerr Stuart & Co. of Fenton, a locomotive engineering works, he eventually moved into aircraft design. Between 1920 and 1936 he designed many aircraft, including light aircraft, fighters, bombers and flying boats. However, he is most renowned for his work on a series of aircraft, which culminated in the design of the most iconic fighter aircraft in World War II, the Supermarine Spitfire.

Talke Quirk Alert: Nine Counties

The ridge after which Talke is named is a spectacular vantage point, and from certain places it is alleged that nine counties can be viewed. Meanwhile, adjacent to the village is a spring, the water of which is of a blue milky colour, strongly impregnated with sulphur, and was much in demand in the 19th century for cutaneous diseases.

This is what is known as the Stone Cross in Talke, and it stands across the road from the White Swan – so again, at the aforementioned crossroads. Initially erected in 1253 on the site of Talke's market, following the granting of a market charter by Henry III, only the stone steps now date to the 13th century; the cross was erected in the former's place in 1887.

Three's-Up!

	THE STRAITS	WOODMILL	YEW TREE
STATUS:	Residential Area	Village	Housing estate and ward (Great Barr with Yew Tree)
POPULATION:	12,992 (Gornal Ward)	c.40	12,597
DISTRICT:	Dudley, West Midlands	East Staffordshire	Sandwell, West Midlands
EARLIEST RECORD:	*the Straight*, 1672; *The Streights*, 1777	*Woodmill*, 18th century	*Hewtree*, 1601; *Ewe Tree*, c.1630; *Yew Tree*, 1718
MEANING:	See Three's Up Trivia.	Named after a wooden mill.	Place at the yew tree.
DERIVATION:	See Three's Up Trivia.	As above.	From the Old English word *ēow* (yew tree).

Three's Up Trivia

The Straits is an area of Dudley at the westernmost edge of the county of West Midlands and formerly part of Staffordshire. The area also has roads called The Straits and Straits Road, as well as Straits Brook and Straits Primary School. The place was initially recorded as *the Streight* in 1672, with a number of variations on that spelling appearing over successive years. However, it is not thought that the name is referring to a straight road, but that it probably related to a narrow passage, such as the kind of straits that you find at sea (i.e. the Straits of Gibraltar). In which case, the name is probably Middle English which, in turn, derives from the Old French word *estrait*. And as a "strait" in those days was also used to refer to narrow lanes, alleys or passageways, it is a fair assumption that one such narrow passage existed here, a mile or so east of Himley Hall; indeed, Duignan, 1902, describes the origin as "a steep narrow road between Sedgley and Himley".

Meanwhile, **Woodmill** is located in the parish of Yoxall, and is presumably named after a mill located here. There are certainly references to a sawmill at Woodmill in the late 18th century.

Finally, **Yew Tree** is part of the ward of Great Barr with Yew Tree, which straddles three of the seven districts which make up the metropolitan county of

West Midlands – the three being Walsall, Sandwell and Birmingham. Indeed, the residents of Yew Tree have Walsall phone numbers but are actually aligned to Sandwell Council. The Yew Tree area was heavily developed with housing during the 1950s and 1960s, which is when Judas Priest guitarist and bassist K.K. Downing and Ian Hill were growing up before forming one of the world's greatest rock/metal bands. Actor Matthew Marsden was also brought up on the Yew Tree estate. As for those references to Yew Tree above from 1601, 1630 and 1718, I must confess that these relate to another Staffordshire Yew Tree, but which no longer exists – this being Yew Tree Farm which was located around 2.5 miles west of Madeley.

This pond is perhaps the one used by the mill after which Woodmill is named.

This Methodist church at Woodmill was founded in 1878.

NAME (STATUS):	**TIXALL** (Village)
POPULATION:	241
DISTRICT:	Stafford
EARLIEST RECORD:	*Ticheshale*, 1086 (Domesday Book)
MEANING:	Nook of land where young goats are kept.
DERIVATION:	From the Old English words *ticcen* (kid or young goat) and *halh* (nook or corner of land).

Tixall Geographic Trivia

Tixall lies alongside the north-western border of the Shugborough estate with the River Sow forming the natural boundary between the two. In fact, Tixall sits in between the Shugborough estate to the south and Ingestre Hall and Sandon Hall to the north, homes of the Earl of Lichfield, the Earl of Shrewsbury and the Earl of Harrowby, respectively.

Tixall Church: St John the Baptist

The current church of St John the Baptist was built in 1848, by John Chetwynd Talbot, the third son of the 2nd Earl Talbot of Ingestre, and was designed by T.H. Wyatt and David Brandon of London. This church replaced its predecessor, described as "a small stone church" that was built in 1772, while it is thought that the predecessor to the 1772 church was much larger. There has certainly been a church at Tixall since at least the 12th century, though, so it is possible that four incarnations have existed. The 12th century version was a free chapel under the jurisdiction of the Dean of the Collegiate Church of St Mary, Stafford.

The church of St John the Baptist at Tixall was built in 1848.

Tixall Historic Trivia: Tixall Hall

Tixall Hall was a manor house built in the 1550s by Sir Edward Aston, High Sheriff of Staffordshire, with the gatehouse added later in around 1580. The Astons had actually succeeded the Littleton family to the manor of Tixall when, in 1507, the Littleton heiress married Sir John Aston. Later, in 1627, Sir Walter Aston was raised to the peerage as Lord Aston of Forfar, thus adding to the baronetcy of Tixall Hall. The titles lasted until 1751

This obelisk in the centre of Tixall has an inscription dating it to 1776. It is thought to have been placed here by Thomas Clifford who owned the estate at the time.

when the 5th Lord died, although the fate of the baronetcy is unclear, and descendants of the Aston's to this day stake a claim, but which is still disputed and unrecognised. Nevertheless, the manor passed to the Cliffords, as Thomas Clifford had married the last Lord Aston's sister, and it was Thomas Clifford who rebuilt the hall in around 1780, although he retained the Tudor gatehouse. The Cliffords then sold the estate in 1835 to their neighbour, Earl Talbot, of Ingestre Hall, and thereafter the property was let out to tenants. The hall was eventually demolished in 1927, but the Tudor gatehouse survived once again, and does so to this day. Now also Grade I listed, the gatehouse is available to let for self-catering holidays!

Returning to the Astons, they were staunch Catholics and therefore Tixall Hall became a safe haven for persecuted Catholics. The 2nd Lord Aston was accused of recusancy (refusal to attend Anglican services), although these charges were quickly dropped. More significantly, the 3rd Lord Aston was sent to the Tower of London during the Popish Plot years of 1678 to 1681, the plot a fictitious conspiracy theory concocted by Titus Oates, suggesting a Catholic plot to assassinate King Charles II. This meant that for a short time, Tixall Hall was 17th century headline news, with rumours of Jesuits attending, while other visitors like Viscount Stafford and William Howard were intensively questioned regarding their actions while at Tixall; in short, the hall had been deemed to be one of the main meeting places for the alleged plotters. Thankfully, the 3rd Lord Aston was eventually released

Tixal Wide is a part of the Staffordshire and Worcestershire Canal that had to be widened on the demand of Capability Brown, who had landscaped the gardens of Tixall Hall and wanted the part of the canal that passed through the grounds to look more like a lake!

The only remains of the 16th century Tixall Hall are this Grade I listed gatehouse. The rest of the hall was demolished in 1927 with much of the stone used in the build of St John's church in Stafford.

from the Tower without charge – albeit after seven years of false incarceration.

Returning to Tixall Hall in the late 16th century, it was also where Mary, Queen of Scots was imprisoned for two weeks in 1586. The hall had actually been assessed as a more permanent residence which would have meant the turfing out of Sir Walter Aston, his family and his staff, not to mention having to sell his sixty cattle and his plough oxen! However, on 11th August 1586, the infamous Babington Plot was outed, and Mary found herself met by armed soldiers when out riding at nearby Chartley. The soldiers then took Mary to Tixall Hall while they searched her rooms at Chartley. She was then kept at Tixall for two weeks before being moved to her final destination at Fotheringhay Castle in Northamptonshire. It is recorded that as she left Tixall, Mary wept and said to the people gathered at Tixall's gatehouse: "I have nothing for you, I am a beggar as well as you, all is taken from me."

Tixall Quirk Alert: Tixall Wide

Passing to the south-east of Tixall is the Staffordshire and Worcestershire Canal, which includes a widened part of the waterway known as Tixall Wide or Tixal Broad. The latter was created during canal construction in 1771, but on a certain condition stipulated by Capability Brown who had designed the gardens of Tixall Hall through which the canal would pass. Brown basically wanted the canal to be so wide that it looked like a lake! And he got his wish, too.

Another shot of Tixall Wide.

Also rather quirky is this house known as Bottle Lodge, and which sits at the eastern entrance to Tixall.

NAME (STATUS):	**TRENTHAM, TRENTHAM LAKE, TRENTHAM PARK**
	(Suburb, Lake, Park)
POPULATION:	11,836 (ward of Hanford and Trentham)
DISTRICT:	Stoke-on-Trent
EARLIEST RECORD:	*Trenhum*, 1086 (Domesday Book)
MEANING:	Homestead or river-meadow on the River Trent.
DERIVATION:	From the Celtic river-name possibly meaning "the trespasser" – as in liable to flood – and the Old English word *hām* (homestead) or *hamm* (river-meadow).

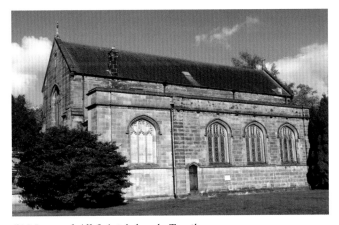

St Mary and All Saints' church, Trentham.

In the background is the northern entrance to St Mary and All Saints' church, while in the foreground are a set of steps that probably date back to Anglo-Saxon times when they would have supported a stone preaching cross.

Trentham Church: St Mary and All Saints

The Grade II-listed St Mary and All Saints' church is located on or close to the site of a 7th century nunnery and a 12th century priory (see *Trentham Historic Trivia* for more on both). Today's church, however, was built in 1844 by Sir Charles Barry for the second Duke of Sutherland – although its nave still retains the Norman pillars initially built for the Norman priory, while the south wall is probably from the Norman church, too.

Trentham Historic Trivia: Nunnery, Priory, Hall, Park, Lake and Gardens

It is thought that there has been a place of worship on or close to the site currently occupied by St Mary and All Saints' church since the 7th century. The first building was thought to be a mid 7th century nunnery built by Werburga, daughter of the Mercian King Wulfhere, and which is now referred to as St Werburga's Nunnery. By the 12th century, the nunnery had been replaced by a Norman priory which became known as Trentham Priory. There is debate as to its origin, with one theory – based on the priory's own records from the late 12th century – suggesting that it was built during the reign of William II (1087-1100), and that its founder was Hugh d'Avranches, 1st Earl of Chester. What is for sure, though, is that the priory belonged to the Augustinian order from around 1150, and was located on the Trentham estate which was owned by

the Earl of Chester. However, on his death, the estate passed to Henry II, who also took over patronage of the priory. Henry then granted additional charters before Pope Alexander III confirmed its religious charters in 1162.

By the 13th century, Trentham Priory was considered one of the wealthiest religious houses in Staffordshire, although the first half of the 14th century saw a dispute over its ownership between the Crown and the Earls of Lancaster. As well as assuming patronage courtesy of their role as lords of the manor of Newcastle-under-Lyme, the house of Lancaster also asserted that Henry III had granted patronage of the priory, in his will, to his son, Edmund Crouchback, Earl of Lancaster. A court case of 1327 ratified this, although the Crown didn't give up their pursuit, and eventually secured control of Trentham Priory in 1344. The priory then continued to acquire land throughout the 14th and early 15th century, mainly used for cultivation and pasture, so by the time of Henry VIIIs *Valor Ecclesiasticus* of 1535, the survey found Trentham Priory to be one of the wealthiest Augustinian priories in the land. Inevitably, the priory was dissolved in 1537, and sold by the Crown to Charles Brandon, 1st Duke of Suffolk. He then sold it to Sir Thomas Pope who, in turn, sold it in 1540 to James Leveson, a wool merchant from Wolverhampton.

Thus began the dynasty at Trentham of the Levesons, the Dukes of Sutherland. The family initially occupied Trentham Priory before Sir Richard Leveson built the first Trentham Hall on the site of the priory between 1630 and 1638. However, Sir Richard didn't have any children, and so his elder brother's daughter, Frances, became the heiress. Frances then married Sir Thomas Gower, 2nd Baronet of Sittenham, and hence the surname Leveson Gower first appeared. Under the Leveson Gowers Trentham Hall was re-built at least twice more, with the final incarnation built between 1833 and 1842. This was under the stewardship of George Granville Leveson Gower, who hired Charles Barry to design the house at the same time that he was working on the rebuilding of Westminster Palace. Barry also designed Trentham's now-famous Italianate gardens

A century earlier, **Trentham Park** had been designed by Lancelot (Capability) Brown. His English 300 acre landscape park included large areas of woodland, while the gardens were designed as a serpentine park, all of which are today collectively known as Trentham Gardens. Brown's most stunning feature, though, is perhaps **Trentham Lake** which is a mile long, and was formed by siphoning off water from the nearby River Trent.

As for Trentham Hall, sadly most of it was demolished between 1912 and 1913 by the 4th Duke of Sutherland, with only the sculpture gallery, clock tower, parish church, the grand entrance and the orangery surviving. Also surviving were the gardens and the ornamental park with its lake and the estate woodlands. All of these survivors were acquired in 1996 by St Modwen Properties, by which stage the buildings were derelict and vandalised and the gardens overgrown and untended. The company then set about restoring Trentham Gardens in 2003 at a cost of around £120 million. The result was stunning, and the former Italianate gardens were re-opened to the public in 2004. Today, there are over 80,000 perennials planted in the Italian Garden, of over 400 different varieties, in 70 flower beds. In 2012, the Trentham Estate was also selected as the site of a Royal Diamond Jubilee wood, containing new woodland of 200,000 native oak trees. Trentham Gardens now attract over three million visitors a year.

As for Trentham Hall, St Modwen originally intended to restore that, too, at a cost of around £35 million. However, plans for a five star hotel have yet to come to fruition, largely owing to the economic recession years. What has been created, though, is the Trentham Monkey Forest, the first wildlife park of its kind in England. The 60-acre forest was opened in July 2005, and contains around 150 Barbary macaques who wander freely and happily co-exist with the visitors. Intriguingly, all of the macaques are individually identified by a tattoo on their inner thigh, while one of the aims of the organisation is to create and preserve a gene pool of this endangered species and to re-introduce groups of macaques into the wild.

In terms of other Trentham history, the Staffordshire

Yeomanry used Trentham as a summer military training camp between 1909 and 1914. However, the place was then bombed by a Zeppelin during World War I, while World War II saw the Trentham Ballroom – which had been opened in 1931 – used as a clearing house by the Bank of England. The grounds were also used to accommodate thousands of French troops, who had escaped the clutches of the Germans, with their ranks including 1,619 men of the 13th Demi-Brigade of the Foreign Legion. This military regroupment camp also later included some Poles and a few German prisoners of war. However, the French camp soon split into pro- and anti-Vichy supporters. Of these, 600 Foreign Legion soldiers left to join the Vichy Legion in North Africa, while another 900 left to join the Free French. Most of them remained at Trentham, though, and did little to improve Anglo-French relations, allegedly killing all of the local deer and fraternising with local girls. Later, Trentham Ballroom was the venue for many dance, rock and pop bands, particularly in the 1960s and 1970s, including mega-bands like The Beatles, Pink Floyd, The Who, and Led Zeppelin. Trentham Ballroom was closed in 2002.

All that remains of the once grandiose Trentham Hall, built between 1833 and 1842, are the ruins of the Grand Entrance and the Orangery (shown above). The rest of the house was demolished between 1912 and 1913.

Trentham Quirk Alert: Divided and Conquered

Most of Trentham has belonged to the city of Stoke-on-Trent since 1922. However, the portion west of the River Trent is actually aligned to the parish of Swynnerton, and thus to the district of Stafford, with this portion containing the parish church, Trentham Gardens and the surviving buildings of the Trentham Hall estate. Meanwhile, we mentioned earlier that the grounds of Trentham Hall were used to accommodate thousands of French troops during World War II. However, on their arrival in June 1940, many of these soldiers were marched from the train station and through the streets of Stoke-on-Trent, a march which was mistaken by many locals to be a German invasion!

BEAUTIFUL TRENTHAM GARDENS

View across Trentham Lake towards Trentham Gardens.

The floral labyrinth with the clock tower visible, a survivor of Trentham Hall.

View across the Italian Gardens towards Trentham Lake.

Reverse view towards the church and the remains of the Grand Entrance.

Looking towards the loggia, the only one of four originals to survive.

A statue of Perseus holding up the Medusa's head, and which stands in front of the lake created by Capability Brown in the 1750s.

Another view of the orangery and clock tower from the Floral Labyrinth.

View from the Italian Gardens towards Perseus.

NAME (STATUS):	**WALL** (Village)
POPULATION:	433
DISTRICT:	Lichfield
EARLIEST RECORD:	*Walla*, 1167
MEANING:	Place at the wall.
DERIVATION:	From the Old English name *weall* (wall or rampart). This refers to the Roman town of *Letocetum* that once occupied this site.

The Trooper at Wall.

St John the Baptist church at Wall.

Wall Pub and Church:
The Trooper and St John the Baptist

The parish church of St John the Baptist was built in 1837, and was designed by the architects Moffatt and Scott, the latter the rather more famous and prolific Sir Gilbert Scott, an English Gothic Revival architect who designed or altered over 800 British buildings. Meanwhile, The Trooper probably dates from around the same time as the church, as it was certainly referenced in 1851.

Wall Historic Trivia: Letocetum

Wall's extraordinary Roman heritage probably owed much to the fact that the settlement was located close to where Watling Street and Ryknield Street crossed – particularly its location on Watling Street which was the main route from London (*Londinium*) to Wroxeter

(*Viroconium*). It was on the higher ground beyond the current church, that the Roman Fourteenth Legion (Legio XIV Gemina) built a fortress in around A.D. 50. The fortress was initially a forward base as part of Publius Ostorius Scapula, the second Roman governor's advancement towards Wales; the portion of Watling Street that ran past the fort was probably constructed around A.D. 70. A series of smaller forts followed the original, but these were abandoned by A.D. 130, with the locals suitably quelled and the frontier of the Roman Empire having been moved significantly further north and west. However, in the military establishment's place was the now-expanding town of *Letocetum*, which had been initially sited on Watling Street, below the forts in the late 1st century (the name *Letocetum* was a corrupted Latinised form of the Celtic name for the place meaning "grey wood"). By the end of the 2nd century, *Letocetum* was a flourishing small town, and had state of the art bath-houses, while a Roman *mansio* was built slightly further up the hill.

The bath-houses were at the centre of *Letocetum* culture, a place for exercise, relaxation, meeting friends or even conducting business. Today's remains still clearly demonstrate that the baths included a *frigidarium* (cold baths), *tepidarium* (warm baths) and a *caldarium* (hot baths). The latter two were also heated by a sophisticated heating system known as a *hypocaust* – with the floors raised on columns of tiles (*pilae*) which allowed the hot air from the furnace to circulate beneath and up through flues in the walls; the stoking yards and furnaces were located at both ends of the suite of heated rooms. The common practise in terms of bath usage was to enter the *frigidarium* from the exercise hall next door. From there, they then moved onto the *tepidarium* and eventually the *caldarium* – although bathers also had the alternative of the *laconium* (a hot dry room). They then came back in reverse order, culminating in a cold bath. Meanwhile, above the baths is the exercise hall, typically an open courtyard back in Rome, but almost certainly covered in inclement Britannia. It was here that people engaged in ball games, wrestling and weight training, building up a healthy sweat before bathing – although this itinerary wasn't mandatory; you could simply go straight into the *apodyterium* (the changing rooms) if you wished!

Further up the hill from the exercise hall are the remains of the 2nd century *mansio*, and which was probably a two-storey building. It provided lodgings for

THE AMAZING LETOCETUM

The remains of the Roman town of Letocetum. In the foreground are the foundations for the Roman baths while further up the hill are the remains of a Roman mansio.

View from the Mansio at the opposite corner looking down towards the Roman baths.

officials travelling on government business as well as accommodation for important visitors, plus it probably housed the administrators of *Letocetum's* local government, too. It would have had an open courtyard known as an *atrium*, an informal meeting place or somewhere to do business. The *mansio* was also equipped with, stables, a kitchen, a formal garden and a gallery on the first floor. The space in between the bath-houses and the *mansio* was occupied by a street which then connected with Watling Street – and indeed, some of the cobbles of that street still survive outside the entrance to the bath-house.

Also appearing by the 2nd century was a burial area beyond the western edge of the settlement, while the late 3rd and early 4th centuries saw around 6 acres of land at the eastern end of the settlement enclosed with a stone wall which was surrounded by an earth rampart

and ditches. However, by the 4th century, it would appear that *Letocetum* had fallen into decline, and the focus in the area had shifted to Lichfield – although civilians continued to live inside *Letocetum's* walls and on its outskirts until the late 4th century.

Wall Quirk Alert: Horns Down

Excavations at Wall have revealed evidence of a first century pagan Celtic shrine, with a number of carved stones, some with horned human heads – thus suggesting a religious sanctuary of the Celtic *Cornovii* tribe, as their name possibly means "worshippers of the Horned One". However, some of those stones had been inserted upside-down in a wall, suggesting that the Romans may have destroyed the shrine, but preserved some of the stones lest the hostility of the deity be bestowed upon them.

Left: *View up Watling Street, Wall.* Right: *This Romanesque milestone was erected by the people of Wall in 2012 to commemorate the Diamond Jubilee of Queen Elizabeth II.*

The Best of the Rest

BROMLEY	Status:	Population:	District:	Earliest Record:
	Suburb	12,630	Dudley, West Midlands	*Bromle*, 1300
		(Kingswinford South)		
Meaning:	Woodland clearing where broom grows.			
Derivation:	From the Old English words *brōm* (broom) and *lēah* (woodland clearing).			

MILES GREEN	Status:	Population:	District:	Earliest Record:
	Village	8,437	Newcastle-under-Lyme	*Miles Grene*, 1539
		(Audley rural parish)		
Meaning:	Possibly relates to the Mee family, courtesy of a reference to *Mees Green* in 1733.			

OAK HILL	Status:	Population:	District:	Earliest Record:
	Built-up area	5,744 (Boothen &	Stoke-on-Trent	*Ochull*, 1346
		Oak Hill ward)		
Meaning:	Hill on which oak-trees stand.			
Derivation:	From the Old English words *āc* (oak) and *hyll* (hill).			
Historic Trivia:	In the early 19th century, the settlement clustered around Oak Hill Hall, while by 1892, the growing settlement was linked by a branch line to Stoke's steam tramway. These were replaced by motorbuses in the early 20th century which is also when the place expanded into a significant housing estate.			

OVERLEY	Status:	Population:	District:	Earliest Record:
	Hamlet	c.25	Lichfield	Unknown
Meaning:	Woodland clearing on a ridge.			
Derivation:	From the Old English words *ofer* (flat-topped ridge) and *lēah* (woodland clearing).			

RED BULL	Status:	Population:	District:	Earliest Record:
	Hamlet	c.50	Newcastle-under-Lyme	*Red Bull*, 1733
Meaning:	Named after an 18th century pub which stood where the A53 and B5415 cross today.			

ROBIN HILL	Status:	Population:	District:	Earliest Record:
	Road	c.100	Staffordshire Moorlands	*Robinstone*, 1685
Meaning:	Unknown. Robin Hill is a road and area to the south of Biddulph Moor, off New Street.			
Historic Trivia:	Charles William Brown was born at Robin Hill on 5th March 1882. After a life in mining, where he had			
	risen to Deputy Mine Manager by the age of twenty-nine, Brown retired and began to paint, mainly			
scenes from	the industrial landscape of the Potteries. These paintings can now be found in the Potteries Museum			
	and Art Gallery.			

Left to right: Bromley is very much a residential area on the outskirts of Dudley, but it is also home to three gravel pits, including Middle Pool, shown here; entrance to Miles Green from the west, along Station Road; the hamlet of Overley, immediately west of Alrewas, only consists of five houses, all on Overley Lane.

ROSEVILLE	Status:	Population:	District:	Earliest Record:
	Res. area	1,387	Dudley, West Midlands	Unknown
Meaning:	"Village where roses grow" – before the place was absorbed by the West Midlands metropolis.			

SILVER END	Status:	Population:	District:	Earliest Record:
	Res. area	13,935 (Brierley Hill ward)	Dudley, West Midlands	*Unknown*
Meaning:	Unknown			
Trivia:	Located 3 miles south-west of Dudley town centre, the place was home to a pottery and a Methodist church in the 19ᵗʰ century, both on Silver Street.			

TRIANGLE	Status:	Population:	District:	Earliest Record:
	N/A	N/A	Lichfield	20ᵗʰ century
Meaning:	Triangle is a three-sided grassy area with trees formed by three roads just south of Burntwood. However, there was once *another* place called Triangle in Staffordshire, around a mile south of Ellenhall in the Stafford district, and which was recorded as *Trygle* in 1365. The assumption is that this place, which no longer exists, was probably formed by the shape of the land in conjunction with medieval roads, tracks or footpaths. Finally, the AA Close-Up Britain Road Atlas also reveals a *third* place called Triangle, this one in the Staffordshire Moorlands, a mile north-east of Thorncliffe. Once again, this looks to be a triangle of roads whose routes are dictated by the hilly terrain there – although the two long sides of this isosceles stretch for around a mile each!			

WAIN LEE	Status:	Population:	District:	Earliest Record:
	Hamlet	c.30	Staffordshire Moorlands	Unknown
Meaning/ Derivation:	Likely to have something to do with a woodland clearing, deriving from the Old English name *lēah* (wood, woodland clearing or glade).			

Left to right: *The Wickenstones lie close to Robin Hill on Biddulph Moor – allegedly these gritstone outcrops are the southernmost point of the Pennines; deceptive from this angle, but this is the three-sided triangle at Triangle, Burntwood, looking down towards its south-eastern point; the road known as The Dale in Ashley Dale.*

Finally, here are the places that are shown on the AA Close-Up Britain Road Atlas, but for which there is little or no information about place-name origin:

Place-Name	Location
ASHLEY DALE	Adjoins village of Ashley to the south, and is named after the road called The Dale.
ASHLEY HEATH	Adjoins both Ashley and Ashley Dale to the south-west.
THE HEATH	Area at the north-western edge of Uttoxeter.
THE WOODS	Residential area on the south side of the M6 between Walsall and West Bromwich, close to the other featured residential areas of Yew Tree and Stone Cross.
WOOD END	Area at the southern end of Hanbury, 5 miles west of Burton upon Trent.

Bibliography

Books

Arthur Mee, *The King's England: Staffordshire* (The King's England Press, 1994)
M.W. Greenslade and D.G. Stuart, *A History of Staffordshire* (Phillimore & Co. Ltd`, 1984)
A.D. Mills, *Oxford Dictionary of British Place Names* (Oxford University Press, 1991)

Information Panels and booklets at:

Abbots Bromley Parish Council
Alstonefield: St Peter's church
Bentley Cairn
Brewood: St Mary and St Chad's church
Burston
Burton upon Trent: Andressey Island
Castle Ring, Cannock Chase
Churnet Valley Railway
Croxden Abbey
Dudley Priory
Fauld
Ilam: Church of the Holy Cross
Kinver: Holy Austin Rock
Lichfield: St Chad's church
Maer: St Peter's church
Onecote: St Luke's church
Stafford Castle
Tamworth Castle
Trentham Gardens
Wall

Websites

http://blackcountryhistory.org
http://en.wikipedia.org/wiki
http://greatbarrhall.com
http://hauntonvillage.co.uk
http://keeleparish.org
http://lichfieldlore.co.uk
http://northstaffsminers.btck.co.uk
http://nsmg.apedale.co.uk
http://thejournalofantiquities.com
http://alittlebitofstone.com
http://www.abbotsbromley.com
http://www.alstonefield.org
http://www.bbc.co.uk
http://www.birminghammail.co.uk
http://www.blackcountrybugle.co.uk
http://www.brewoodandcovenparish.org.uk

http://www.british-history.ac.uk/vch/staffs
http://www.britishlistedbuildings.co.uk
http://www.broughtonchurch.com
http://www.burton-on-trent.org.uk
http://www.chasefarmshop.co.uk
http://www.churnet.co.uk
http://www.churnet-valley-railway.co.uk
http://www.dailymail.co.uk
http://www.domesdaybook.co.uk
http://www.dormandiesels.com
http://www.haberdashersarms.com
http://www.halesclub.co.uk
http://www.hauntedrooms.co.uk
http://www.heatonhousefarm.co.uk
http://www.heritagepubs.org.uk
http://www.hints-village.com
http://www.hollybushinn.co.uk
http://www.joulesbrewery.co.uk
http://www.leek-news.co.uk
http://www.madeleyvillage.co.uk
http://www.megalithic.co.uk
http://www.meir-heath-windmill.co.uk
http://www.midlandsheritage.co.uk
http://www.ourladyandstwerburgh.co.uk
http://www.ourvillagechurch.org.uk
http://www.parksandgardens.org
http://www.peakdistrictinformation.com
http://www.peakdistrictonline.co.uk
http://www.ranton.info
http://www.roman-britain.org
http://www.rushallparish.org
http://www.staffordshirehoard.org.uk
http://www.staffsmoorlands.gov.uk
http://www.staffspasttrack.org.uk
http://www.stjamesdudley.org.uk
http://www.stmargaretsgreatbarr.org.uk
http://www.stokesentinel.co.uk
http://www.stonnall-history-group.org.uk
http://www.telegraph.co.uk
http://www.thebluemugge.co.uk
http://www.thepotteries.org
http://www.thestaffordshireknot.co.uk
http://www.thetimes.co.uk
http://www.tixall-ingestre-andrews.me.uk
http://www.towerbrewery.co.uk
http://www.traditionalflower.co.uk
http://www.trentham.co.uk
http://www.tutburycastle.com
http://www.walsalladvertiser.co.uk
http://www.visionofbritain.org.uk
http://www.visitinghistoryinstaffordshire.com